NONPROFIT ESSENTIALS

Effective Donor Relations

Janet L. Hedrick, CFRE

WILEY

John Wiley & Sons. Inc.

Library of Congress Cataloging-in-Publication Data:

Hedrick, Janet.
  Effective donor relations / Janet Hedrick.
    p.   cm. – (The AFP fund development series)
  Includes bibliographical references and index.
  ISBN 978-0-470-04036-2 (pbk.)
  1. Fund raising. 2. Endowments. 3. Nonprofit organizations–Management. I. Title.
  HV41.2.H43 2009
  658.15'224–dc22

                                                                2008042939

Printed in the United States of America
10 9 8 7 6 5 4 3 2 1

The AFP Fund Development Series

T he AFP Fund Development Series is intended to provide fund development professionals and volunteers, including board members (and others interested in the nonprofit sector), with top-quality publications that help advance philanthropy as voluntary action for the public good. Our goal is to provide practical, timely guidance and information on fundraising, charitable giving, and related subjects. The Association of Fundraising Professionals (AFP) and Wiley each bring to this innovative collaboration unique and important resources that result in a whole greater than the sum of its parts. For information on other books in the series, please visit: http://www.afpnet.org

The Association of Fundraising Professionals

The Association of Fundraising Professionals (AFP) represents over 30,000 members in more than 197 chapters throughout the United States, Canada,

Mexico, and China, working to advance philanthropy through advocacy, research, education, and certification programs.

The association fosters development and growth of fundraising professionals and promotes high ethical standards in the fundraising profession. For more information or to join the world's largest association of fundraising professionals, visit www.afpnet.org.

2008–2009 AFP Publishing Advisory Committee

CHAIR: Nina P. Berkheiser, CFRE
Principal Consultant, Your Nonprofit Advisor

Linda L. Chew, CFRE
Development Consultant

D. C. Dreger, ACFRE
Senior Campaign Director, Custom Development Solutions, Inc. (CDS)

Patricia L. Eldred, CFRE
Director of Development, Independent Living Inc.

Samuel N. Gough, CFRE
Principal, The AFRAM Group

Audrey P. Kintzi , ACFRE
Director of Development, Courage Center

Steven Miller, CFRE
Director of Development and Membership, Bread for the World

Robert J. Mueller, CFRE
Vice President, Hospice Foundation of Louisville

Maria Elena Noriega
Director, Noriega Malo & Associates

Michele Pearce
Director of Development, Consumer Credit Counseling
Service of Greater Atlanta

Leslie E. Weir, MA, ACFRE

Director of Family Philanthropy, The Winnipeg Foundation

Sharon R. Will, CFRE

Director of Development, South Wind Hospice

John Wiley & Sons, Inc.:

Susan McDermott

Senior Editor (Professional/Trade Division)

AFP Staff:

Jan Alfieri

Manager, New Product Development

Rhonda Starr

Vice President, Education and Training

Gratitude is not only the greatest of virtues, but the parent of all the others.

Cicero

The deepest craving of human nature is the need to be appreciated.

William James

Feeling gratitude and not expressing it is like wrapping a present and not giving it.

William Arthur Ward

Contents

Foreword   ix

Acknowledgments   xiii

About the Author   xv

1 Donor Relations: What?   1

2 Donor Relations: Why?   19

3 Acknowledgment   43

4 Recognition: Part 1   79

5 Recognition: Part 2   127

6 Stewardship   177

7 Donor Relations: Other Topics   191

Final Thoughts on Donor Relations   223

Appendixes   227

Foreword

Everywhere we travel, we hear two stories. The first is one of great not-for-profit organizations celebrating record-setting fundraising successes and announcing extraordinary gifts. The rise of the superdonor and the importance of the top 1% of the gifts is changing the face of philanthropy.

Unfortunately, too often we also hear stories from donors who have made philanthropy an important part of their life but whose experiences in making those charitable gifts has been disappointing. The acknowledgments are late or nonexistent. Reports on the project never happened. Staff members did not answer simple questions.

That is why this work by Janet Hedrick is so important. For too long, we have thought of donor relations and stewardship as getting receipts out in a timely manner and making sure the names were spelled correctly in the annual report. While both of those actions remain important, the list is far from complete. Today's programs must meet the needs of donors, program officers, and the future of the development program.

Part of the shift in the importance of donor relations is because of changes in the world. The Greatest Generation may be the *last* generation with a high degree of confidence in organizations. Baby Boomers and Gen Xers grew up with mistrust of "the Establishment" and the Millennials are emerging as a networked generation that finds many traditional structures and organizations irrelevant.

Some of the changes are a result of advances in technology. More than half of individuals pumping gas at the local station no longer ask for a receipt from the automated credit card machine built into the gas pump; they believe the system will work seamlessly. Anyone of us can go online right now and check the value of our mutual funds or stock statements—in real time. It is hard for donors today to understand why we cannot report once a year on their gifts or pledges. Many new fundraising ventures, like DonorsChoose.org, have been created that use the new technologies to promote good stewardship.

Some of the changes result from the entrepreneurial economy, where donors of means are used to reshaping the world and seek to use their philanthropy to shape organizations and their programs. Back in the days when most fundraising was either an annual appeal, or a once in a lifetime capital campaign or a once-a-generation call to raise dollars for a new swimming pool at the Y, or steeple for the church, or chemistry building at alma mater, the donors could rally around a project and understand how their gifts mattered. Today, most gifts are focused on specific programs, and the outcome of the dollars is not immediately obvious. Donors, therefore, want more accountability.

Some of the changes come from the shift in fundraising itself. As development staff turnover has increased and campaigns have become longer, the natural informal relationships between institution and donor have been lost, making formal stewardship efforts more important. As AT&T used to state, *the system is the solution*. The personal dimension is critical, but must be supplemented with organizational support.

A decade ago, *donor relations* was barely on the radar screen of development professionals. Today, there are professionals focusing their careers in the area; professional groups are emerging and conferences are now frequently organized to improve the efforts and share best practices.

In this book, Janet Hedrick does more than outline the challenges; she shares insights into the strategies for success. It is obviously a must-read for donor relations professionals; but more important, it should be carefully studied by chief development officers because they are in the position to make the changes—large and small—necessary to maintain the important linkages between organization and philanthropist.

This work is extraordinarily important, because the subject is so important. As we conduct feasibility study interviews for major colleges, universities, and health-care organizations, we hear over and over again of bad stewardship and donor relations. If philanthropic support is going to sustain the culture over the next generation, then donors must feel connected to important causes and the dynamic institutions that are carrying out important work.

Bruce Flessner
Founding Principal
Bentz Whaley Flessner
Bill Tippie
Principal
Bentz Whaley Flessner

Bruce Flessner

Founding Principal

Bentz Whaley Flessner

Bill Tippie

Principal

Bentz Whaley Flessner

Acknowledgments

When one writes a book that covers "acknowledgments," the task of saying a heartfelt "thank you" to all those who have contributed to the effort is exceedingly difficult.

Over the more than thirty years that I have been a development professional, I have met a vast array of persons who have taught me so much. The development professionals and the other colleagues at the organizations that I have served through the years have provided valuable insights and inspiration. Also along my journey I have been fortunate to meet so many wonderful individuals who embody the philanthropic spirit and give so generously to make the world a better place. They also have added to my rich learning experience.

I must thank all of those who have attended the presentations that I have given over the last fifteen years. Their questions and ideas are the fabric of this book. From my first presentation on this topic entitled "New Ways to Say Thank You: Creative Approaches to Acknowledgment and Recognition" to my upcoming presentation called "Leave Them Wanting to Give More: The Power of the Donor Experience," the process of preparing the presentation is just one small part of my learning experience. With each and every presentation, I hear stories of the strategies that have made our relationships stronger with those who believe in and support our organizations' missions. The creativity and enthusiasm with which these professionals bring value to the donor experience is extraordinary!

My colleagues at Bentz Whaley Flessner have been supportive and encouraging as I have developed this manuscript. I want to thank each of them. I want to express special gratitude to the principals at the firm, Bruce Flessner, Bill Tippie, Bruce Dreon, and Joshua Birkholz, for their belief in and support of me.

A special thanks to Bill Tippie, the principal with whom I work most closely at the firm. When we discussed my joining Bentz Whaley Flessner in 2004, he indicated that members of the firm are encouraged to make presentations and to write articles and books. My comment was, "Does that mean I get to write my book?" After I told him about the plans for this book, he told me that he would support me in every way possible and would not let me forget about my plans. He has honored that commitment and has been supportive every step of the way.

My heartfelt thanks to Josh Birkholz for taking my lead and getting his book finished first. Seeing his book in print has motivated me to keep focused and to complete this book.

I also want to thank Jan Alfieri at the Association of Fundraising Professionals (AFP), who asked me to conduct an audio conference on this topic and who later suggested that I should write a book on the topic. I also want to thank Susan McDermott and Brandon Dust, my editorial team at John Wiley & Sons, Inc. for their patience and helpfulness.

Last, but not least, is my gratitude for the members of my family who have believed in me. My brother Russell and his wife Susan, who let me call their house my home during the holidays, and their children Emily, John Michael, Allison, and Sam are my constant cheerleaders. Likewise I am truly grateful for the Worshams and the Gleims, who are my "other" family, for their love and support. I also know that my parents would be proud. For the joy that they found in my accomplishments, I will always be thankful.

About the Author

Janet L. Hedrick, CFRE, is a senior associate in the Washington, D.C. office of Bentz Whaley Flessner. Her areas of expertise include planning, implementation and evaluation of annual, capital, and planned giving programs; assessment and enhancement of donor relations and stewardship programs; and training and motivating campaign volunteers and development staff.

The clients she has served include Children's Hospital of Wisconsin; Miami Children's Hospital Foundation; Arkansas Children's Hospital; Connecticut Children's Medical Center; Children's Mercy Hospitals and Clinics in Kansas City, Missouri; Riverside HealthCare Foundation in Kankakee, Illinois; Sacred Heart Hospital in Eau Claire, Wisconsin; Evangelical Community Hospital in Lewisburg, Pennsylvania; Northern Michigan Regional Hospital Foundation in Petoskey, Michigan; Group Health Community Foundation in Seattle, Washington; and Inova Health System Foundation in Falls Church, Virginia.

Ms. Hedrick has also provided counsel to twelve public broadcasting stations, located in Nevada, Utah, Illinois, West Virginia, North Carolina, Pennsylvania, Ohio, Indiana, and Florida, as part of the Major Giving Initiative (MGI) for public television sponsored by the Corporation for Public Broadcasting.

Prior to joining the firm in 2004, Ms. Hedrick served as director of clinical campaigns and planned giving for the UMass Memorial Foundation, the philanthropic arm for both the University of Massachusetts Medical School and the UMass Memorial Health System, in Worcester, Massachusetts. Other positions have included vice president of fund development for the Sisters of

Providence Health System in Springfield, Massachusetts, executive director of the Millard Fillmore Health, Education, and Research Foundation and vice president for development at the Millard Fillmore Health System in Buffalo, New York, chief development officer at St. Christopher's Hospital for Children in Philadelphia and director of development at Johns Hopkins Children's Center — the Department of Pediatrics at Johns Hopkins Hospital in Baltimore.

Ms. Hedrick began her career in development in 1977 as Director of Annual Giving at Longwood College (now Longwood University) in Farmville, Virginia, after having taught mathematics and physics at Parry McCluer High School in Buena Vista, Virginia. She also served as Director of Development at Hood College in Frederick, Maryland, prior to taking her position at Johns Hopkins in 1983.

Ms. Hedrick holds a Master of Education degree from the University of Virginia and a Bachelor of Science in Mathematics from Mary Washington College (now University of Mary Washington) in Fredericksburg, Virginia. She is a member of Phi Beta Kappa and an active member of the Association of Fundraising Professionals (AFP), Association for Healthcare Philanthropy (AHP), Association of Donor Relations Professionals (ADRP), and National Committee on Planned Giving (NCPG), and is a Certified Fund Raising Executive (CFRE).

She served as president of the Greater Philadelphia Chapter of AFP, served on the boards of the Western New York and Western Massachusetts Chapters of AFP, and was the founding president of the Central Massachusetts Chapter of AFP. She has served on the AFP National Nominating and Diversity Committees. She also served on the Committee for Revision of the AFP Survey Course and developed the section on individual giving in the Annual Giving Module of the course.

She has taught classes on fundraising, including "Fundamentals of Fund Raising" at Villanova University in Philadelphia; "Developing the Board Partnership" at University of Pennsylvania in Philadelphia; and "Advanced Fund Raising" at the University of Massachusetts in Amherst, Massachusetts. Ms. Hedrick developed a continuing education program on fundraising for Canisius College in Buffalo, New York and taught the initial class of the course.

Ms. Hedrick is a frequent presenter at local, regional, and international conferences throughout the United States and Canada. In addition to speaking for AHP Regional and International Conferences, AFP Chapter meetings and workshops and International Conferences, and ADRP Annual Conferences, she has given presentations for PBS National Development Conferences, Association for Care of Children's Health (ACCH) National Conferences, Delaware Valley Association of Directors of Volunteer Services, Nonprofit Management Center in Buffalo, NY, Center for Nonprofit Management, Nashville, TN, Women in Development of Western Massachusetts, Women in Development of Central Massachusetts, LDS (Latter Day Saints) Hospitals and the Deseret Foundation in Salt Lake City, Utah, and Donor II (Campus Management Corporation) in Charlotte, North Carolina and Orlando, Florida.

Ms. Hedrick contributed a chapter, entitled "Obtaining Funding for Video Projects," in *Television and the Hospital Child: Issues and Creative Approaches* (1988), a publication of the Association for the Care of Children's Health (ACCH), has written articles for fundraising newsletters, and has been quoted in publications, including articles in *Advancing Philanthropy*, the publication for members of the Association for Fundraising Professionals (AFP).

Ms. Hedrick was a member of a fundraising executives' delegation to the Republic of South Africa in 2001, sponsored by People to People Ambassador Programs. As a member of the Rotary Club in Worcester, Massachusetts, she served on the District Committee for GEMINI (Global Emergency Medicine Initiatives). She assisted in securing funds for a group of emergency physicians to travel to the Dominican Republic in 2003 to train caregivers in that country. Ms Hedrick also accompanied the group on the trip to the Dominican Republic.

Ms. Hedrick currently serves on the board of directors of the Challenger Center for Space Science Education (CCSSE), an international, not-for-profit organization that was founded by the families of the astronauts lost during the last flight of the Challenger Space Shuttle in 1986. Ms. Hedrick serves as the chair of the development committee of the organization that has created close to fifty Challenger Learning Centers in the United States, Canada and the UK. Each educational center includes an interactive computerized simulator with a Mission

Control room patterned after the NASA Johnson Space Center and an orbiting Space Station where students become astronauts and engineers, solving real-world problems as they share the thrill of discovery on missions through the Solar System.

Ms. Hedrick and her Quaker Parrot, Peridot, live in Alexandria, Virginia.

CHAPTER 1

Donor Relations: What?

After reading this chapter, you will be able to:

- Define the terms associated with donor relations.
- Explain the difference between *stewardship* and *donor relations*.
- Describe the three components of donor relations.
- Define *gratitude*.
- Explain what *donor centered* means.
- Understand the principles of the Donor Bill of Rights.

Defining *Donor Relations*

In the 1980s, the term *donor relations* was not frequently used in the field of development. In the latter years of the 1990s, the term began to be heard more frequently, and in the first decade of the twenty-first century it became the name used to describe a group of activities central to the overall development process. Organizations began adding *donor relations* to their development or advancement functions and a new emphasis was put on this aspect of fundraising.

The new level of interest and attention for donor relations paralleled a change in attitude about those activities that would come to be known as *donor*

1

relations. Prior to the 1980s, most organizations viewed these activities as necessary but seldom approached them as basic elements of the overall development program.

In 1991, James M. Greenfield, in *Fund-Raising: Evaluating and Managing the Fund Development Process* (John Wiley & Sons, Inc.), noted:

> In their quest to acquire an increased number of new contributors each year, charitable organizations might overlook their current donors, who are supporting them faithfully. Donors are the best prospects for repeat gifts as well as for new gifts, larger gifts, and estate gifts. Donor relations is perhaps the greatest sin of omission within fund development programs.

As organizations began to recognize the true value of maintaining and upgrading a donor's support, the roles of acknowledgment, recognition, and stewardship shifted from being rote activities to being strategic actions. The field of donor relations became the responsibility of the professional staff and the principles of donor relations were integrated into the many aspects of the development and institutional advancement programs at charitable organizations.

RULES OF THE ROAD

Location is to real estate as relationship is to philanthropy.

The scope of *donor relations* and the level of sophistication are different for every organization. For some organizations, the term means sending thank-you letters for contributions. For others, donor relations includes recognizing donors with a list of names on a wall or in a report, and some organizations include sending stewardship reports in their donor relations program. For many, donor relations involves events to express appreciation to those who have supported the organization.

In simple terms, donor relations is everything that happens between asking for contributions. The many activities previously mentioned, including thank-you letters, recognition lists on a wall or in a report, sending stewardship reports, and special events, are included in donor relations. In fact, all of the activities, or the personal touches, that are involved in building a relationship with an individual, corporation, foundation, association, or any other source of funding can be described as *donor relations*. While donor relations can be defined as activities in a process, a donor relations program is most successful when it is the expression of an organization's overall commitment to a donor-centered approach to fundraising.

The Power of Words

The *AFP Fundraising Dictionary* does not define *donor relations*. However, the dictionary definition of *stewardship* is broad and could be a definition of *donor relations*.

The *AFP Fundraising Dictionary* defines *stewardship* as:

> **stewardship**, *noun* **1** a process whereby an organization seeks to be worthy of continued philanthropic support, including the acknowledgment of gifts, donor recognition, the honoring of donor intent, prudent investment of gifts, and the effective and efficient use of funds to further the mission of the organization. **2** the position or work of a steward.[1]

Many people use the terms *stewardship* and *donor relations* interchangeably. However, donor relations can be viewed as having three components, with stewardship being one of the three. The term *donor relations* has come to mean the acknowledgment, recognition, and stewardship provided to the person, organization, corporation, or foundation that makes a charitable gift.

RULES OF THE ROAD

Donor relations: Everything that happens between "asks."

Donor relations, as the name implies, is a set of strategies that helps an organization build its relationship with the persons who contribute to that organization. All three aspects of donor relations are important in renewing a donor's support, upgrading a donor's support, and building a donor's confidence in an organization. Acknowledgment, recognition, and stewardship are important in cultivating a donor's interest in an organization and in moving the donor to a deeper sense of commitment and greater financial investment in the organization.

Each aspect of donor relations has specific characteristics, and by examining each component of the process, the importance of each aspect becomes clearer.

Acknowledgment is the process of saying "thank you" for the gift. The acknowledgment of a gift may include a receipt, a letter, a phone call, a handwritten note, an email message, or a combination of these communications. Acknowledgment is one or more private communications between the organization receiving the contribution and the person, organization, corporation, or foundation that made the gift.

Recognition is the process of expressing gratitude for a charitable contribution in a public way. The organization may recognize the donor by listing the donor's name in a publication, in a display of names in a program or on a wall, in a press release, or in special presentations. Providing a gift that acknowledges the donor's support that the donor may display in the home or office is also a way to recognize a donor.

Stewardship is the process of using the gift as the donor intended and communicating with the donor about the use of the gift. The organization is being accountable and is letting the donor know that the organization used the gift as the donor desired. Included in stewardship of some gifts, especially those for endowment, is reporting on the investment of those gifts. *Stewardship* also conveys the impact of the gift in fulfilling the mission of the organization. The definition of *stewardship* in the *AFP Fundraising Dictionary* includes "the honoring of donor intent, prudent investment of gifts, and the effective and efficient use of funds to further the mission of the organization," but does not mention reporting back to the donor, which is critical to meaningful stewardship.

EXHIBIT 1.1

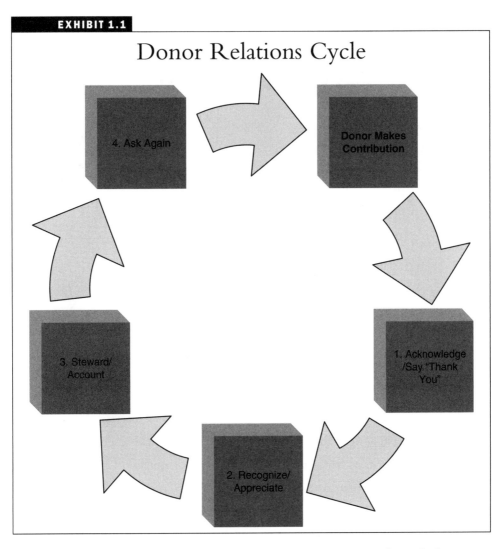

Donor Relations Cycle

Another approach to the donor relations program is a cycle with four *active* parts, or the four *A*'s:

1. Acknowledge

2. Appreciate

3. Account

4. Ask again

The four-part cycle (see Exhibit 1.1) parallels the approach of the three components. "Acknowledge" is the step of thanking the donor for making the gift. "Appreciate" is the recognition component and "account" is the

EXHIBIT 1.2

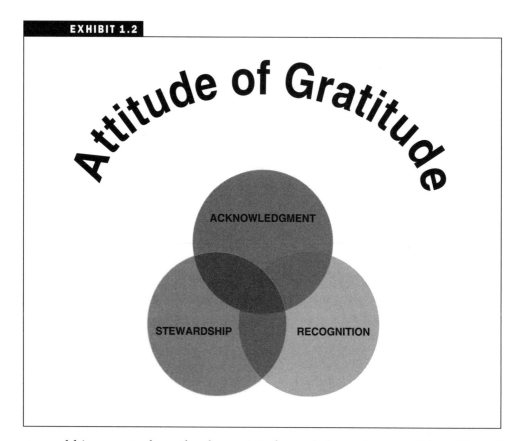

stewardship aspect where the donor is informed about the use of the gifts and the results or outcomes from the gift. "Ask again" is not included in the earlier description of donor relations, but is the next step in both processes that moves the process back to the solicitation of the donor.

In either scenario, the components of donor relations are not independent and separate from one another. They are interconnected and should flow from one to another. All three components are expressions of gratitude (see Exhibit 1.2). Donor relations is more than the sum of its parts. Acknowledgment, recognition, and stewardship should complement one another and together should create a meaningful and unified strategy for a donor.

Two central activities are critical to effective donor relations. The first is communications and the second is involvement or engagement. Communication, whether by mail, phone, Internet, or face-to-face, contributes to building the relationship with the donor. Meaningful communication is two-way and provides the donor with opportunities to provide input, ask questions, make recommendations, and express concerns. As the relationship grows, communication becomes more frequent and is more likely face-to-face.

The second activity central to donor relations parallels communicating with donors. The strategies in a donor relations program are designed to bring the donor closer to the organization. Building a relationship requires involvement in the life of the organization, getting to know the people that lead the organization, including staff and key volunteers, and feeling like a member of the family. The donor who has a close relationship will talk about the organization using the term *we* rather than *you*.

An effective donor relations program will seek to communicate with donors and will focus on strategies that involve and engage the donor in the life of the organization.

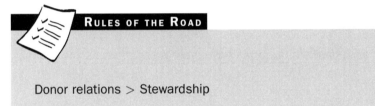

RULES OF THE ROAD

Donor relations > Stewardship

The Meaning of Gratitude

Gratitude is a *positive* emotion or attitude that an organization needs to convey to the people who choose to support that organization and its mission. Acknowledgment, recognition, and stewardship are the actions that an organization uses to express the feeling of gratitude. The way that organizations communicate and involve donors in the life of the nonprofit is the means by which an organization lets a donor experience the feeling of being appreciated by the organization. Sincere gratitude expressed in various ways over time is the key to building the relationships that result in commitment and in investment for an organization.

The donor relations program goes beyond acknowledgment, recognition, and stewardship in that these actions alone will not build the relationship. The feeling or attitude of gratitude behind those actions and the meaningful, thoughtful, and individualized nature of the actions will make the difference in creating the bond that is desired between the organization and the donor.

IN THE REAL WORLD

A highly important aspect of business today is customer relations. Businesses recognize that their best customers are past customers. Many organizations ask customers to sign up for mailing lists or email lists. Direct-mail flyers, catalogs, sales brochures, and other information pieces are sent primarily to those who have done business with them in the past.

Businesses have customer loyalty programs, from Talbots, which sells clothing for women, men, and children, to Hallmark Gold Crown stores, to grocery stores, pharmacies, and, of course, airlines' frequent-flyer programs. Some of the customer loyalty programs are called *memberships* and one must pay an annual fee. Barnes & Noble bookstores would be in that category. The key chains carried by consumers today often have more member cards for these businesses on them than they have keys. In addition, our wallets are filled with various cards from hotels and car rental companies. Each business offers incentives for frequent use. These may be discounts or certificates for future purchases. Each is intended to motivate the customer to buy more from the specific business. The programs are successful and, thus, more businesses add these programs to get customers to come back.

When one takes a flight, the pilot says over the public address system, "We recognize that you have a choice among airlines, and we thank you for choosing XYZ airline. We hope that when you need to make travel plans in the future, you will choose XYZ again."

The dentist sends the new patient a letter thanking the person for selecting this practice over the others from which one can choose. After shopping in a clothing store, a woman receives a handwritten note from the salesperson with whom she did business. The local car dealership calls a customer within two or three days to ask about the quality of service the customer received when his car was serviced. A handwritten note with a bottle of water and a snack are in the hotel room to welcome back a guest who frequently stays at that specific group of hotels.

Donors have choices, also. Recognizing their gifts as often as possible and in as many ways as possible ensures that they will continue to choose your cause when making their charitable decisions.

Donor–Centered Fundraising

The term *donor-centered fundraising* is used frequently in development and is a principle that development departments endorse. One often sees the "Donor Bill of Rights" hanging on the wall in the development or institutional relations office, on the website, and in the donor relations manual. Making the Donor Bill of Rights a living document takes commitment and work. The concept behind the Donor Bill of Rights is critical to understanding what *donor centered* means. The responsibility for fundraising includes respect for those who make philanthropic gifts, honesty in dealing with those who support the causes in which they believe, and fulfilling the donor's desire to make a difference and to feel good about giving. In simple terms, the donor and the donor's interests are the key elements of fundraising and the relationships that the development staff forges between donors and others in the organization are the essence of fundraising.

Those in development need to remember that their jobs are about the donor. "The donor comes first" and "The donor is always right" are two adages that seem appropriate for every development office or department. When questions arise and decisions are made, the donor's interest should be the most important consideration.

TIPS AND TECHNIQUES

Share the Donor Bill of Rights

When an organization endorses the Donor Bill of Rights, it takes a giant step in building a culture of philanthropy among its internal and external constituencies. Having the board of the organization as well as the board of the organization's foundation, if one exists, review and endorse the Donor Bill of Rights makes the leadership aware of the principles behind the Donor Bill of Rights and sends a message to staff, volunteers, and donors of the intent of the organization to operate in a donor-centered fashion.

After the board of an organization endorses the Donor Bill of Rights, the document needs to be shared among the organization's constituencies. The following are ways to share the Donor Bill of Rights.

- Hang a framed copy of the Donor Bill of Rights in key locations in the organization, such as near a recognition display, in administrative offices, and in the development, foundation, or institutional advancement offices.
- Post the Donor Bill of Rights on the organization's website.
- Include the Donor Bill of Rights in annual reports or other publications.
- Include the Donor Bill of Rights in board orientation materials and review the document with new board members.
- Include a copy of the Donor Bill of Rights in a new-donor or new-member packet.
- Include in the Donor Bill of Rights in the donor relations manual for the organization.
- Review the Donor Bill of Rights with all new employees of the organization as part of orientation along with other information about the role that philanthropy plays at the organization.

Periodically, in surveys on donor satisfaction, donors should be asked whether they are familiar with the Donor Bill of Rights to determine whether efforts to share the document have been successful.

If a donor wants to make a gift to support a specific program that is not available at the organization that the donor approaches, donor–centered thinking can help guide the organization. If the program is included in the organization's strategic plan and the timing of the gift will fit with other funding to make the program happen, the organization may decide to accept the gift and will explain how the gift can be helpful. However, if the donor wants to support a specific program that the organization does not have and has no plans to introduce, the response should be different. For example, a donor wants to make a gift to a children's hospital for research in SIDS (Sudden Infant Death Syndrome), or alumni want to support their college's equestrian program. If the children's hospital does not currently have research in SIDS and the college has discontinued its equestrian program, those organizations should not accept the gifts.

Being donor centered means being honest with donors in explaining that the organization cannot fulfill their expectations and assisting the donors in finding an organization that can meet their wishes. The children's hospital identifies where research in SIDS is occurring, and the college finds out where equestrian programs are offered and assists the donors in making gifts to support the programs in which they have interest. If an organization cannot fulfill the intent of the gift, the donor is not pleased when an organization accepts the gift and uses it in another way.

The story is told that a salesperson in Nordstrom's, which is known for extraordinary customer service, helped a customer by gift wrapping an item that the customer bought at Macy's. The same principle applies here. Helping donors or customers accomplish their goals is the way to put the donor or the customer first.

Another example of donor-centered fundraising is the year-end appeal. Organizations that have a fiscal year that ends on June 30 often send letters to donors in May asking for support by the "end of the year" so the organization can meet its annual goal. While that strategy may work because donors care about organizations meeting their goals, a more donor-centered approach is to ask donors to consider making gifts in the autumn months before the end of the donor's year.

The donor-centered organization will craft its message in a way that appeals to the donor and potential donor. Letters about the "end of the year" should be scheduled and worded to reflect that the end of the year is December 31 for individuals. The timing of the request should be based on the donor and the donor's frame of reference rather than the organization and the organization's frame of reference.

A survey conducted by the Direct Mail Association indicates that an organization has the best chance of getting its publication read if it is received in February through May or September. January, August, October, and November are mediocre months and, not surprisingly, June and July, when many people are busy with vacations and outings, are the worst months for direct mail.

Letters in February through May should be more focused on the beginning months of the year, and letters in September, October, and November should be directed to end-of-year giving. If organizations are donor centered, they recognize that many major donors tend to make gifts late in the calendar year, often between Christmas Day and December 31, and those organizations prepare for that pattern of giving.

Donor centered implies that the actions that are used to say "thank you" express appreciation, and that reports back to the donor are not focused on the gift, but are focused on the person who chose to make the gift. If an organization keeps the person's choice to contribute to this specific organization at the center of its thinking, its messages will be more thoughtful and meaningful.

Donor centered also means being flexible and recognizing that every donor is unique with different interests, values, goals, and expectations. The donor-centered organization listens to its donors and is willing to assist them to the fullest extent possible. Some donors like to receive flowers on special occasions while others see flowers as a waste of resources.

One way for members of the staff of an organization to get a sense of why donor relations is important is for them to think of their personal experiences outside the realm of fundraising, such as when the staff member gave another person a gift, perhaps for a birthday or another special occasion. The staff member should think about the feeling involved in making the gift and the expectations that accompanied that gift. Perhaps the staff member did not expect a thank-you note but received one. Or the staff member may have expected to receive a thank-you note and did not receive one. Talking about what a thank-you message may have meant and what was included or not included in the message may be helpful in creating a sense of why saying "thank you" is so important.

Another aspect of giving is seeing or knowing that the recipient used or enjoyed the gift. Gift cards have become popular for special occasions and remove the guesswork of choosing a gift. However, knowing how the recipient used the gift card can be meaningful to the donor. Asking staff to put on their donor hats and to think like donors can be challenging for some but can be helpful in creating a better understanding of the importance of interactions and communication with donors.

A donor-centered program is one where staff members in departments other than development include donors in their thinking and assist donors in a prompt and appropriate fashion. When the finance office cannot provide information needed by a donor to make a gift because other matters are more important and questions are raised by members of the finance department or others as to whether these gifts are really worth the trouble, donor-centered fundraising is absent. However, when a staff member is planning an event for the president's office and approaches development to select a donor who will be attending to serve as the president's assistant for a magic trick that is planned for entertainment, the organization is donor centered. When a staff member in another department is considering an outreach and public relations effort in the community and immediately approaches the development staff to ask how major donors and major donor prospects might be involved, the organization is donor centered.

When a multitude of gifts arrive in response to specific volunteer activity or at the end of the year, the staff at the donor-centered organization is excited by the positive response. When the development staff complain about the amount of work they have to do to handle the larger-than-normal number of gifts, donor-centered thinking is not occurring.

DONOR TOUCHPOINT MANAGEMENT

Donor TouchPoint Management (DTM) is a strategy for effective donor relations. The term *touchpoint*, which originates with marketing, is defined as "all of the communication, human and physical interactions customers [donors] experience during their relationship lifecycle with the organization."[2]

In 2004, Hank Brigham described a fast-growing movement among those organizations with an interest in improving their customer-centricity through a better understanding of customer interactions, or touchpoints. He called this movement *Customer Touchpoint Management* (CTM).

In the corporate context, touchpoints include advertising, websites, and interactions over the phone or in a store. Mr. Brigham notes, "Touchpoints are important because customers form perceptions of your organization and brand based on their cumulative experiences." He also points out that "CTM-oriented organizations know they can best enhance relationships with customers by improving touchpoints across the entire enterprise."[3]

Relationships with customers are not exclusively the responsibility of the sales and customer service staff. If invoices are not accurate, if the phones are not answered professionally, if the place of business or office is not clean, the relationship can be damaged regardless of how effective the sales and customer service strategies are.

Likewise, in nonprofit organizations, donor satisfaction depends on far more than the interactions that donors have with the development officers with whom they work or those events and activities that the donor relations staff orchestrates. The donor experience is the result of all of the interactions that a donor has with the organization. A name misspelled, a rude or abrupt response to a question, or a complacent attitude about the person's prior giving can have an impact on the relationship a donor has with an organization.

Thinking of donor relations as "Donor TouchPoint Management" gives us a broader view of the process that improves donor loyalty, donor interest, and donor commitment. The "donor experience" does not end with a gift acknowledgment. The experience merely *begins* with the letter or the phone call that expresses gratitude.

The Thanksgiving card, the phone call from a board member to thank the donor for a recent gift, the invitation to a seminar on a topic of interest to the donor, the small group gathering with the president or chair of the

Donor Bill of Rights

In the Donor Bill of Rights (see Exhibit 1.3), one of the ten rights specifically addresses acknowledgment and recognition, but all of the rights speak to the donor's place in the development program. The Donor Bill of Rights calls for organizations to inform donors, to assure donors, and to give donors access to information. The document addresses what a donor should expect and clearly

EXHIBIT 1.3

Donor Bill of Rights

Philanthropy is based on voluntary action for the common good. It is a tradition of giving and sharing that is primary to the quality of life. To ensure that philanthropy merits the respect and trust of the general public, and that donors and prospective donors can have full confidence in the non-profit organizations and causes they are asked to support, we declare that all donors have these rights.

I. To be informed of the organization's mission, of the way the organization intends to use donated resources, and of its capacity to use donations effectively for their intended purposes.

II. To be informed of the identity of those serving on the organization's governing board, and to expect the board to exercise prudent judgment in its stewardship responsibilities.

III. To have access to the organization's most recent financial statements.

IV. To be assured their gifts will be used for the purposes for which they were given.

V. To receive appropriate acknowledgement and recognition.

VI. To be assured that information about their donation is handled with respect and with confidentiality to the extent provided by law.

VII. To expect that all relationships with individuals representing organizations of interest to the donor will be professional in nature.

VIII. To be informed whether those seeking donations are volunteers, employees of the organization or hired solicitors.

IX. To have the opportunity for their names to be deleted from mailing lists that an organization may intend to share.

X. To feel free to ask questions when making a donation and to receive prompt, truthful and forthright answers.

The Donor Bill of Rights was created by the American Association of Fund Raising Counsel (AAFRC), Association of Healthcare Philanthropy (AHP), the Association of Fundraising Professionals (AFP), and the Council for the Advancement and Support of Education (CASE). It has been endorsed by numerous organizations.

articulates the need to be honest and forthright with donors. Donor relations echoes the principles embodied in the Donor Bill of Rights and gives organizations a framework within which to acknowledge those who give, to show appreciation for giving, and to report on the impact of the donor's philanthropic commitment.

Summary

While the term *donor relations* is relatively new in the vernacular for fundraising, the concept is central to building the relationships with donors that are critical to strong development programs. Donor relations includes everything that happens between the solicitations of a donor. *Donor relations* is often used interchangeably with *stewardship*. However, if donor relations is described as having three basic components, stewardship is only one part of donor relations. Donor relations can be described as acknowledgment, recognition, and stewardship, or as *acknowledge, appreciate,* and *account,* followed by *ask again.* Acknowledgment, recognition, and stewardship are the actions that convey the feeling or attitude of gratitude of an organization. Organizations that communicate with donors and provide opportunities for donors to get involved are effectively using gratitude to build their relationships with donors. Donor relations needs to be donor centered and focus on the donor's interest and expectations. The Donor Bill of Rights provides standard principles for a donor relations program.

Notes

1. Online at www.afpnet.org, Barbara R. Levy, Editor, R. L. Cherry, Lexicography Editor. Copyright 1996–2003. *AFP Fundraising Dictionary,* Association of Fundraising Professionals (AFP) formerly NSFRE, all rights reserved.
2. "Defining Customer Touchpoints" by Hank Brigman. www.imediaconnection.com. Published: November 02, 2004. Article:
3. Ibid.

CHAPTER 2

Donor Relations: Why?

After reading this chapter, you will be able to:

- Explain why donor relations became important at the end of the twentieth century.
- Describe the purpose of donor relations.
- Understand how donor relations fits in the development program.
- Conduct an inventory of a donor relations program.

The Emergence of Donor Relations

The three components of donor relations are not new to development. Saying "thank you," recognizing donors on walls and in lists, and telling donors how gifts have been used have been part of the development process for years. However, with the introduction of the term *donor relations*, these activities have been given an increased level of importance in fundraising.

The question may be asked as to why the term *donor relations* was introduced and why more attention was given to the activities of acknowledgment, recognition, and stewardship at the end of the twentieth century. An examination of what was happening in the field of fundraising offers some clues.

Fundraising and the fund development profession were changing quickly in the 1980s and the 1990s, as were technology, business, and other fields.

Educational institutions that had been raising money for many years were launching campaigns with far greater goals than ever before. Campaigns to raise millions of dollars were becoming campaigns to raise billions of dollars. Campaigns were becoming perpetual and subsequent campaigns were planned long before the current campaigns were scheduled to end.

More individuals were making eight- and nine-figure mega-gifts to a multitude of causes and these gifts were being publicized more prominently than ever before.

Leaders of organizations were looking to philanthropic support to fill the gap as other sources of revenue were shrinking and needs for capital and endowment dollars were rising. Expectations for private support for hospitals and health-care organizations, environmental causes, cultural and arts organizations, social-service agencies, and community grassroots organizations were escalating. Organizations were expanding their professional fundraising staffs and the demand for experienced development professionals was increasing. The field of development was becoming both more strategic and more scientific. Targeted marketing, demographic study, wealth screening, and statistical analysis were being used more extensively to improve results.

At the same time, scrutiny of fundraising was greater than in the past. As a result of scandal and controversy, donors and potential donors were demanding more accountability from nonprofit organizations. The cost to raise a dollar was examined more closely and organizations were asked to increase net revenue from fundraising and to reduce the associated costs.

The consequence of these changes was a closer look at every aspect of development with an eye to where programs could be made more efficient and more effective.

One of the many facts that emerged from this analysis was the decrease that had occurred in the continuity of giving. A donor was less likely to continue giving to an organization than ever before and that trend was proving costly to the success of development programs.

To shift that trend would require building greater loyalty and satisfaction with donors, and *donor relations* emerged in response to that need. Donor relations would play an increasingly important role in development for three reasons:

1. Competition for the philanthropic dollar

    Each year the number of charitable organizations increases and donors are asked to support more organizations than ever before. For an organization to distinguish itself from others, it needs to make the donor feel appreciated and needs to let the donor know the contribution is being used wisely. While many donors support multiple organizations in their lifetimes, donors usually choose a selected few for major and planned gifts. Those few are most likely those with which the donor has been involved, those that the donor has supported over an extended period of time, and those with which the donor has the closest relationships. Effective donor relations helps an organization differentiate itself from others and build a stronger relationship with its donors, creating a loyalty that will result in continued support at more generous levels.

2. Cost to acquire a new donor

    Given the cost to acquire a new donor, organizations are realizing that the value of a new donor is in renewed and increased gifts over the lifetime of the donor. Acquisition of new donors through direct mail is recommended as a long-term strategy that seldom generates income with the initial solicitation. The income is a result of the renewals of those new donors. One way to secure continued giving is through expressing appreciation for contributions through acknowledgment and recognition and letting donors know how the first gift and subsequent gifts make an impact.

RULES OF THE ROAD

Asking for a major gift on the first visit is like proposing marriage on the first date.

    Organizations are more sophisticated than ever in analyzing the results of their various programs. Close attention is given to the cost to raise a dollar or the return on investment in development. Presidents, executive directors, and board members are anxious to have their development staffs find ways to decrease the cost or to increase the return on investment. Considering the high cost of donor acquisition, which may approach $1.25 to $1.50 to raise $1.00 using direct mail and/or phone programs, the investment in acquiring donors can be justified only if the organization is successful in keeping those donors, and the donor's potential lifetime value, based on renewal and upgrade analysis, is adequate.

To maximize their investments in acquiring donors, organizations need to express gratitude, offer recognition, and demonstrate good stewardship. In these ways, organizations can convert new donors into repeat donors and can build relationships that will result in larger gift commitments over time. These strategies contribute to increasing the lifetime value of the new donor and increasing the return on the investment made in donor acquisition.

3. Emphasis on major and planned gifts

With closer analysis, organizations recognized that major and planned giving were the most cost-effective methods of fundraising. To increase the effectiveness of overall programs, a shift was made to focus on major and planned giving. The role of direct mail, phone solicitation, television, radio, and Internet fundraising was redefined in terms of bringing in new donors from which future major donors would come. Organizations became less dependent on special events as the high cost in dollars, as well as in staff and volunteer time, became clear.

As organizations enhanced their development programs to focus on cultivating major and planned gifts, the role of donor relations became critical. Expressing gratitude and showing the impact of a gift would be used to cultivate a donor's interest and to set the stage for future gifts of greater magnitude. As organizations developed strategies for cultivating relationships with donors and potential donors, donor relations was recognized as a key to building the trust and commitment of donors who have the capacity to make significant and transformative gifts. A donor may have an interest in an organization when the first or second gift is made, but a relationship developed over time is critical to the donor making the major gift or planned gift that is desirable.

The Purpose of Donor Relations

Two questions need to be asked when considering the purpose of donor relations. First is the question of why gifts are acknowledged. Answers include that acknowledging a gift is the right thing to do, the donor needs a receipt or letter for tax purposes, the donor needs to know that the contribution was received, and the donor expects to receive a letter acknowledging the gift. While these responses are correct, the most important reason goes beyond doing the right thing and doing what is expected.

The second question is why donors are thanked for making gifts. The two questions at first glance may seem to be the same, but the first question is about the gift and the second is about the donor. Understanding the purpose of donor relations requires that the process center on the donor and on building the relationship that will lead to future gifts.

From the development process perspective, the most important reason for thanking a donor for making a gift is that saying "thank you" is the first step in getting the next gift. If this step is missed or done poorly, the relationship with the donor may be irreparably harmed. Likewise, recognition and stewardship are important to getting subsequent gifts.

When looking for persons, organizations, corporations, and foundations to support a charitable organization, the best place to begin is with those who have already made gifts. Just as businesses know their best clients are past clients, organizations know that their best donors are past donors. However, in both cases, the prior experience needs to be positive for loyalty to develop. Giving for a donor is positive when the donor feels the gift is appreciated and makes a difference. Donor relations, similar to client relations in a business, is designed to give the donor that positive experience.

 **RULES OF THE ROAD**

While many principles from marketing may apply in development, marketing and development are not the same:

Philanthropy is not a purchase!

A *donor* is not a consumer!

A *contribution* is not a purchase!

Major and planned gifts are seldom a donor's first gift to an organization. Reports of multi-million-dollar commitments are usually accompanied by stories about the donor's long-term relationship with the organization. Many have served as board members or in other leadership capacities and have made numerous gifts.

Several important factors are necessary for an individual, corporation, foundation, or organization to make a significant commitment to an organization. Among them are trust and confidence in the organization's ability to make a difference. The best way for an organization to gain the trust and confidence of a potential major gift donor is to demonstrate that ability through donor relations. Acknowledging, recognizing, and most importantly, reporting back to a donor on the use of a gift are the keys to establishing the credibility of the organization.

On occasion, the process for building a relationship that leads to a major gift commitment is described as being similar to the process of courtship and marriage. In both cases, the end result is a major commitment. In most cases, when marriage is proposed, the person being asked is not surprised by the question and the person asking is almost sure of the answer. In major gift fundraising, the ultimate question is seldom a surprise to the donor and the person asking on behalf of the organization is almost sure of the answer. In getting to know one another, courtship on one hand and cultivation on the other hand, the actions along the way are important in building the relationship. In courtship, the activities are designed to bring the two people closer together and to build trust and confidence in one another. In cultivation, the activities along the way, including acknowledgment, recognition, and stewardship, are designed to bring the organization and the donor closer together and to build trust and confidence.

TIPS AND TECHNIQUES

Donor Relations: An Inventory

This inventory is designed for you to evaluate your current donor relations program:

1 Have you written a personal thank-you note to a donor in the past week?

_____YES (1) _____ NO (0)

2 Have you called a donor in the past week to say "thank you"?

_____YES (1) _____ NO (0)

3 Has your CEO/executive director called a donor in the past week to say "thank you"?

_____YES (1) _____ NO (0)

4 Has your board chairperson called a donor in the past week to say "thank you"?

_____YES (1) _____ NO (0)

5 Has anyone other than members of the development staff, the CEO, or the board chair signed a thank-you letter from your organization in the past week?

_____YES (1) _____ NO (0)

6 When your CEO/executive director signs thank-you letters, how often are personal notes added to the letters?

_____ALWAYS (2) _____ SOMETIMES (1)

_____ SELDOM/NEVER (0)

7 How long after receiving a contribution is the respective thank-you letter usually mailed?

_____24 HOURS (4) _____ 48 HOURS (3)

_____72 HOURS (2) _____ 1 week (1)

_____ More than a week (0)

TIPS AND TECHNIQUES (CONTINUED)

8 In thank-you letters, do you indicate whether the contribution qualifies the donor as a member of one of your recognition groups?

_____YES (1) _____ NO (0)

9 Do you have a written acknowledgment plan for your program that indicates what donor gets what type of letter, note, phone call, and/or newsletter, when, and from whom?

_____YES (1) _____ NO (0)

10 Do you follow the written acknowledgment plan?

_____YES (1) _____ NO (0)

11 Do you use special types of letters for gifts of certain magnitudes?

_____YES (1) _____ NO (0)

12 Do you have a special type of letter for first-time donors?

_____YES (1) _____ NO (0)

13 Do you have a special type of letter for reactivated lapsed donors?

_____YES (1) _____ NO (0)

14 Do you have a special type of letter for those who have increased their gifts?

_____YES (1) _____ NO (0)

15 Do you have a special type of letter for second or third gifts in the same year?

_____YES (1) _____ NO (0)

16 Does your thank-you letter include acknowledgment of receiving a matching gift form?

_____YES (1) _____ NO (0)

17 When you receive a matching gift from a company or corporate foundation, do you let the donor know the match has been received?

_____YES (1) _____ NO (0)

18 Do you thank donors more than once for a gift?

_____YES (1) _____ NO (0)

19 Have you revised your standard acknowledgment/thank-you letters in the past 30 days?

_____YES (1) _____ NO (0)

TIPS AND TECHNIQUES (CONTINUED)

20 How often do you usually revise your standard acknowledgment/thank-you letters?

_____MONTHLY OR MORE FREQUENTLY (3)

_____QUARTERLY (2)

_____ANNUALLY (1)

_____LESS FREQUENTLY THAN ANNUALLY (0)

21 Do you have written guidelines on recognition?

_____YES (1) _____ NO (0)

22 Do your guidelines include the following?

○ Whether matching gifts are included in determining gift club levels

_____YES (1) _____ NO (0)

○ Whether support for a special event is included in determining gift club levels

_____YES (1) _____ NO (0)

○ Which donor constituencies (individuals, corporations, foundations) are included in gift club recognition

_____YES (1) _____ NO (0)

○ Whether donors are recognized when the pledge is made and/or when the pledge is paid

_____YES (1) _____ NO (0)

○ When the year begins and ends for gift club purposes

_____YES (1) _____ NO (0)

23 Do you provide recognition for cumulative/lifetime giving?

_____YES (1) _____ NO (0)

24 Do you provide recognition for bequest intents?

_____YES (1) _____ NO (0)

25 Do you provide recognition for other planned gifts?

_____YES (1) _____ NO (0)

26 Do you know how much you can spend on ''benefits'' in your gift clubs without decreasing the tax deduction of the donor?

_____YES (1) _____ NO (0)

㉗ Do you know what is required in the acknowledgment if the gift is more than $250?

_____YES (1) _____ NO (0)

㉘ Do you develop stewardship plans for donors that indicate when a report on the impact of the gift will be given to the donor?

_____YES (1) _____ NO (0)

㉙ Are stewardship visits included in cultivation plans for major donors?

_____YES (1) _____ NO (0)

㉚ Do your board members participate in your acknowledgment, recognition, and/or stewardship activities?

_____YES (1) _____ NO (0)

㉛ If you have a planning session or a planning retreat for development staff, is donor relations (acknowledgment, recognition, and stewardship) included in your planning?

_____YES (1) _____ NO (0)

TOTAL SCORE: _____

☐ 36–40 EXCELLENT   ☐ 15–21 FAIR

☐ 29–35 VERY GOOD   ☐ 8–14 NEEDS IMPROVEMENT

☐ 20–28 GOOD   ☐ 0–7 NEEDS MORE IMPROVEMENT

Where Donor Relations Fits

Effective development programs are often described as comprehensive and integrated programs. If each part of a program is seen as separate and distinct, sometimes referred to as *silos,* the overall program will not reach its full potential. Annual giving and membership programs, major giving and planned giving, special events, and capital campaigns are interrelated and support one another in the comprehensive, integrated program. Donor relations needs to be included in a similar way.

To fully incorporate donor relations into a development program, every development staff member needs to understand the importance of donor

EXHIBIT 2.1

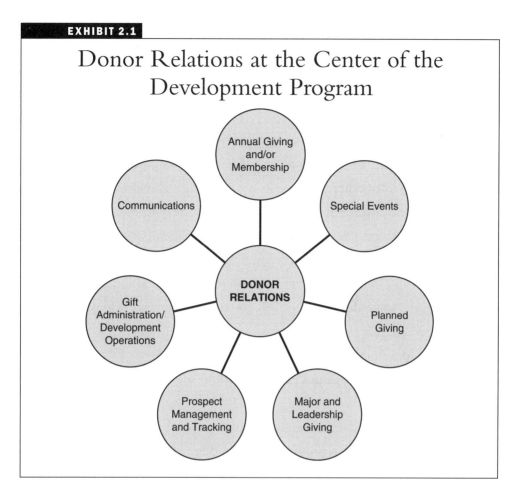

Donor Relations at the Center of the Development Program

relations and must take responsibility for its implementation. Effective donor relations needs to be woven into the development program and donor-centered thinking must be a guiding principle for the program. Donor relations must be at the core of the development program and must play a role in every aspect of fundraising (see Exhibit 2.1).

Saying that donor relations is the responsibility of every member of the staff is easy. But in reality, organizations that have recognized the value of donor relations have assigned donor relations to existing staff or have added one or more persons to their staffs to make sure that donor relations is addressed in their development programs.

Organizations place the persons responsible for donor relations in a variety of different places in the structure of the development office; some have decided that the donor relations function belongs in the communications department rather than in the development department. Finding the right place for the donor relations staff is a challenge because donor relations is central to all fundraising.

At first glance, donor relations is seen as happening after the gift and as not producing revenue. Like other functions that occur subsequent to the gift that do not generate dollars directly, such as processing gifts, maintaining data, and generating reports, donor relations is assigned to development services. For similar reasons, prospect research and prospect management often are considered part of development services, although many will argue that they fit better with major giving. While many view donor relations as the function of development services, some define donor relations as part of major and planned giving and others assign it to those responsible for special events. As is the case for all aspects of a development program, communications is vital to effective donor relations, but donor relations probably should not be considered a communications function.

But donor relations does not fit neatly into any of these areas of responsibility. Having a donor relations program involves three functions.

1. *Planning the program.* The planning, which needs to be strategic, involves the analysis of the current program, getting input and cooperation of key persons and groups, planning the changes or additions to the program, and determining how and when the program will be evaluated and revised. The planning phase of the program involves six steps (see Exhibit 2.2).

2. *Implementation and management of the program.* In this phase, letters, postcards, notes, scripts for calls and messages, text for websites, newsletters and publications, and agendas for chairpersons and hosts of events are written; events are planned; photographs are taken; videos are produced; information is gathered from various sources; stewardship reports are prepared; recognition displays are designed, fabricated, installed, and updated; and visits with donors are scheduled. The implementation and management phase of donor relationships requires the cooperation and support of many

EXHIBIT 2.2

The Steps in Planning a Donor Relations Program

1. Analysis of the current program

   ○ Qualitative and quantitative information

2. Establishing goals and objectives

   ○ Measurable outcomes for the program

3. Developing tactics and strategies to achieve goals and objectives

   ○ Timeline

   ○ Specific actions

   ○ Responsible persons

4. Outlining the involvement of others

   ○ Development staff

     ■ Professional staff

     ■ Support staff

   ○ Senior leaders of the organization

     ■ President or executive director

     ■ Chief financial officer

     ■ Head of Marketing or Communications

   ○ Others at the organization

     ■ Department heads

       ● Deans at colleges and universities

     ■ Staff in president's office

     ■ Staff in finance office

     ■ Other staff

     ■ Constituents or clients

       ● Students

       ● Alumni

       ● Patients

       ● Members

   ○ Board members and other volunteers

5. Identifying the resources needed to support the program
   - Staff
   - Budget
6. Defining when and how the program will be evaluated
   - Qualitative information
     - Surveys
     - Interviews
     - Focus groups
     - Anecdotal information
   - Quantitative information
     - Achievement of measurable goals and objectives
     - Correlation of specific strategies to specific donor behaviors
       - Rate of retention of donors
       - Increases in giving

persons and logistics of many kinds. Implementation and management means making sure that actions happen smoothly and on schedule.

3. *Day-to-day process for recording and reporting these activities.* Measuring the effectiveness of a donor relations program requires that actions be documented and recorded. Reports of various types are also necessary. The development services staff usually take care of this piece and participate in the implementation of a number of strategies, especially those related to gift entry and the gift acknowledgment process.

Initially, as organizations added donor relations to their development programs, some of these aspects of donor relations were overlooked. The question remains as to where donor relations fits in the program from a practical and staffing perspective to make sure all aspects of donor relations are handled.

The answer to this question differs from organization to organization. Some may assign various aspects of the donor relations program to existing staff, or they may hire one or more designated donor relations staff members. Larger and more complex organizations may hire a number of staff members. Another factor influencing staffing will be whether the donor relations function is centralized or not.

For example, in a large university, a complex health-care system, or a national organization with many affiliates or chapters, the donor relations program may be handled by a central office, or the program or some aspects of the program may be the responsibility of individual colleges, units, facilities, or chapters.

One way to clearly define the roles and responsibilities for donor relations and to provide guidance and direction for staff is the development of a Donor Relations Manual (see Exhibit 2.3). The manual should be updated annually and should include policies and procedures, definitions for the roles of staff and volunteers, and a current plan and schedule. Other items in the manual may be a mission statement for donor relations (see Exhibit 2.4), the Donor Bill of Rights, sample reports, job descriptions, assessment tools, and workflow charts. For large organizations, the manual may detail the central functions and/or describe the responsibilities of each division.

EXHIBIT 2.3

Donor Relations Manual

CONTENTS

Mission Statement

Goal of Program

Acknowledgment

- ◆ General Guidelines
- ◆ Acknowledgment Plan
- ◆ Receipts and Letters
- ◆ First-time Donors
- ◆ Tribute Gifts

Recognition

- ◆ Recognition Societies
  - ○ Annual Giving
  - ○ Lifetime Giving
  - ○ Planned Giving

- ◆ Naming/Renaming Opportunities
- ◆ Special Events
    - ○ Recognition Event: Annual Giving
    - ○ Recognition Event: Planned Giving
    - ○ Dedications
- ◆ Annual Report

Stewardship

- ◆ Stewardship Reports
- ◆ Website: Impact of Giving
- ◆ Personal Visits

Program Assessment

- ◆ Donor Satisfaction Survey
- ◆ Other Assessment Tools

Appendixes

A. Donor Bill of Rights

B. Sample Reports

C. Job Descriptions

D. Organization Chart

E. Office Procedures

F. Sample Naming Agreement

EXHIBIT 2.4

Sample Mission Statement

Mission Statement

ABC Organization seeks to express gratitude to donors, to recognize donors for their support, and to report back to donors on the impact of their gifts. Through meaningful and consistent contacts with donors, ABC strives to foster positive feelings about giving by helping donors recognize the importance of their giving and to develop and strengthen lifelong relationships between the donor and ABC.

The Donor Relations Program at ABC Organization is focused on keeping donors informed and involving them in the life of ABC, as well as instilling in them the confidence that their gifts are an investment in the continued success of ABC.

Goal

The goal of the Donor Relations Program at ABC Organization is to enhance the fundraising efforts of ABC. Ideally, donors will give repeatedly and at increasingly higher levels because of their sense of feeling connected with ABC and their positive feelings about giving.

IN THE REAL WORLD

An article by B. Joseph Pine II and James H. Gilmore, entitled "Why Experience Marketing Pays," appeared in *strategy + business* in fall 2004. In the article, the authors pointed out that in 1954, Peter Drucker, in *The Practice of Management*, said, "The aim of marketing is to make selling superfluous." Pine and Gilmore added, "The aim of experiences is to make other forms of marketing superfluous."

Companies cited in the article as understanding "the principle that the experience *is* the marketing" include American Girl, Inc. and Recreational Equipment Inc. (REI).

The American Girl phenomenon, which began in 1986, is based on dolls from various historical periods, including Felicity from colonial-period Williamsburg; Samantha, who lives in New York during the Great Depression; Addie, whose family escapes from slavery via the Underground Railroad; the latest doll, Julie, whose parents are divorced in the 1970s; and several others. Each doll has a set of stories that give young girls the opportunity to feel connected to the doll's experiences. Being old enough to have an American Girl doll has become a rite of passage for many young girls.

To add to the experience, the company has built a physical marketing experience for its customers with its American Girl Place, first in Chicago and now in New York and Los Angeles. Mothers, fathers, aunts, and grandparents with their daughters, nieces, and granddaughters are the primary customers for the myriad activities at the American Girl Place. Activities include a live production performed by a cast of young girls in the American Girl Theater, afternoon tea that includes dolls in highchairs in the American Girl Cafe, photo sessions to place the girl and her doll's image on the cover of the *American Girl* magazine, and hair styling for the dolls in the hair salon. In addition to paying scores of dollars for these experiences, visitors spend hours shopping for books and accessories and clothing both for the dolls and for the girls.

The outdoor equipment retailer REI, a pioneer of in-store experiences, created a flagship location in its hometown of Seattle, complete with a rock-climbing wall, a bicycle track, walking trails, and other amenities that enable customers to experience the gear before they buy it. After the success in Seattle, the company built a Minneapolis store with a cross-country ski trail and one in Denver with a kayaking experience.

Whether the experience is in a physical or virtual place, these examples point out the importance of experiences to successful marketing. Highly imaginative advertisements have become the norm for marketing in recent years. Commercials that feature young people dancing to promote clothing from the Gap Inc. and the "basketball-passing, sneaker-squeaking, breath-exhaling commercials" for Nike are but two examples.

When a person thinks of Mazda, thoughts go to "*Zoom, zoom, zoom.*" The focus of advertising Mazda is not the car, but the experience of driving the car.

A woman called in to *Car Talk*, a weekly program on National Public Radio, to tell the two brothers who host the program that she was in love with a car and wanted some advice. She and her two young sons had gone to a car show and were attracted to a vehicle that this woman knew was not practical. She explained that her interest, which she described as an obsession, was not rational but emotional. The car had been portrayed in commercials as being a vehicle that was fun to drive. She related that when she drove it, she would envision the advertisement and the idea that driving the vehicle was a fun experience. The hosts of the program suggested she drive the vehicle for about a week before deciding whether to buy it, but expressed the opinion that she was going to buy this vehicle.

Just as marketing is about the "experience," successful donor relations is about the experience—the donor experience. Creating physical places for experiences for consumers can be compared to getting donors to the physical locations of the organizations they support to give them the experience of seeing firsthand what their contributions have accomplished.

Pine and Gilmore described marketing "experiences" as designed *"to attract new customers and rekindle the interest of existing customers."* And they noted that through these experiences, the *"companies generate additional demand for core offerings"* and the experiences *"become the entrée for a relationship and host of potential transactions."*

Likewise, donor relations programs are *designed to attract new donors and rekindle the interest of existing donors.* Through positive donor experiences, organizations are generating additional commitment and the experiences *"become the entrée for a relationship and host of potential contributions."*

Element of Surprise

In their book, *Made to Stick*, Dan Heath and Chip Heath reported that they "pored over hundreds of sticky ideas" and observed "the same six principles at work." They determined that those that "stick" have the six common principles shown in Exhibit 2.5. All of the principles that are described have relevance in thinking about and planning for donor relations. However, the one principle that stands out as most important is "unexpectedness." In their book, Dan and Chip explain:

> How do we get our audience to pay attention to our ideas. . . . We need to violate people's expectations. We need to be counterintuitive. We can use surprise—an emotion whose function is to increase alertness and cause focus—to grab people's attention.[1]

Adding an element of surprise to acknowledgment, recognition, and stewardship makes an organization stand out from the others and gets the donor's attention. Developing new and creative strategies for showing gratitude to donors in unexpected ways can make a difference in building a relationship.

For example, receiving a Thanksgiving card from an organization probably qualifies as unexpected, although as more and more organizations are sending greetings around the Thanksgiving holiday, that strategy may be losing its element of surprise. After an organization sends a Thanksgiving card three years in a row, the donor may continue to find the greeting meaningful but is probably

EXHIBIT 2.5

Six Common Principles of Sticky Ideas

1. *Simplicity*. Simplicity means finding the essential core of ideas. Proverbs are the ideal in simplicity. Ideas need to be both simple and profound.

2. *Unexpectedness*. Unexpectedness is the way to get an audience to pay attention to ideas. Surprise—an emotion whose function is to increase alertness and cause focus—can be used to grab people's attention.

3. *Concreteness*. Ideas must be explained in terms of human actions, in terms of sensory information. Mission statements, synergies, strategies, and visions are often ambiguous to the point of being meaningless. Ideas that stick are full of concrete images.

4. *Credibility*. "When the former surgeon general C. Everett Koop talks about a public-health issue, most people accept his ideas without skepticism." But in most day-to-day situations, authority is not inherent. Ideas that stick have to carry their own credentials. Ways to help people test ideas for themselves are required.

5. *Emotions*. Getting people to care about ideas means making them feel something. A statistic doesn't elicit any emotions. People are wired to feel things for people, not for abstractions.

6. *Stories*. Telling stories is a way to get people to act on ideas. Stories help connect people to ideas.

A clever mnemonic for this checklist of the six principles for creating a successful idea is: Simple Unexpected Concrete Credentialed Emotional Stories (SUCCESs).

Source: www.madetostick.com.

not surprised to receive the card. To keep the donor's attention, the organization may need to change the format or style of the Thanksgiving greeting on a regular basis. For example, rather than sending a card every year, the organization may choose to use a photo, one or more quotes from those expressing thanks for the services provided by the organization, or a handwritten note from a staff member.

Keeping the element of surprise in the donor relations program requires creative thinking and new ideas on a continuing basis. Keeping the program fresh with new strategies is essential to interacting in meaningful ways and to building relationships with donors over time.

The Donor Experience

The trend in marketing is to sell the *experience* of using a product rather than the product itself. For example, advertisements about cars focus on the experience of driving the car, the promotion of baby products centers on the happy family, and the marketing of cards highlights the experience of the person opening the card.

Children learn early in life that if behaving in a particular way has positive consequences, repeating the experience is likely to produce positive outcomes. They also learn that if an experience is not pleasant, repeating the behavior is not a wise choice. Teaching children desirable actions by using positive reinforcement is a basic tenet of education.

The patient experience is referenced in the health-care organization, the student experience is the focus in educational settings, and the hospitality industry is aware that the experience of the person who stays at a resort is the added value that is expected for higher prices.

RULES OF THE ROAD

Out of every 100 individuals who stop giving to your organization, *only 4 move away or die.*

- Fifteen have decided to make their gifts to other organizations.
- Fifteen are unhappy with your organization.
- Sixty-six think you do not care about them.

Source: Judith Nichols, *Pinpointing Affluence in the 21st Century.*[2]

In many ways, donor relations is about the donor experience. The success of donor relations can be evaluated by examining the donor experience, determining whether the experience was pleasant and enjoyable and met the donor's expectations, and observing the behavior of the donor after the donor experience. Meeting the donor's needs, whatever they may be, is essential to making the donor feel that the contribution made a difference and was a worthwhile investment. The experience will have an impact on the donor's desire to repeat the experience.

If a person makes a gift to an organization and any step or interaction prior to the next gift is not done thoughtfully, the donor's experience will be less than desirable. The following can certainly influence the donor's experience and can have an impact on the donor's continued support of the organization:

- There is a delay in receiving an acknowledgment letter.
- There is an omission or misspelling of the donor's name in a publication.
- The gift is not used within a reasonable amount of time.
- The request for the next gift is inappropriate with regard to amount, project, or timing.

The following scenario is an illustration of how *one element* of the donor relations process can influence the donor's overall experience. An individual makes a generous gift to a hospital for the recruitment of a doctor in a specific specialty. The donor receives appropriate acknowledgment in a timely fashion and is recognized for the contribution in a meaningful way. However, following the gift, the donor did not receive any information about the impact of the gift. After two years, the donor asks about the recruitment of the physician and learns the hospital has not been successful in recruiting the physician. Several factors, including the national shortage of doctors in a number of specialties may have contributed to the difficulty in recruiting the doctor. Nevertheless, the donor's expectations were not met. While acknowledgment and recognition were acceptable, the stewardship of this gift was not pleasing. The donor is likely to be disappointed and may question future support of the hospital. When gifts for specific purposes are made, communication is essential. Reasonable expectations

A hospital in Texas created a program for donors and potential donors called "Experience the Mission." A group of donors and potential donors were invited to spend a day at the hospital to see and experience the work that happened at the hospital each day. The select group of donors arrived in the morning, received white coats with their names embroidered on the pocket just like the white coats that physicians wear, had coffee and tea, and were given a brief overview of what the day would include. Each person would accompany a physician throughout the day. Activities might include watching surgery, visiting radiology, consulting other physicians, nurses, and technicians, as well as meeting patients and families of patients. At the end of the day, the group would gather to talk about their experiences. Comments from participants were positive, such as "I had no idea that you did these things."

The outcomes of the Experience the Mission program included increased giving from participants and an increased interest in involvement. While tours of organizations can be meaningful, the opportunity to observe what happens each day in an organization adds value to the donor experience.

Experience the Mission can be adapted for other organizations. For a public television station, the donor may sit in when a tape is being edited, watch a program being taped, or attend an outreach program in the community for children and their families. For cultural organizations, the donor may get to watch a rehearsal from backstage. In educational organizations, donors may participate in classes or attend presentations by students. Giving donors the opportunity to have meaningful experiences at the organizations they support can be incorporated into the donor relations program and can contribute to the donor experience.

need to be established at the time the gift is made. In this case, the donor should have been advised at the time of the gift of how long it might take to get the new physician and should have received periodic updates on the recruitment process.

In this case, the development officer that is assigned to this donor may feel that the use of the gift is not within the control of the development staff. On some occasions, that may be true. However, the development officer needs to make sure that the wishes of the donor are likely to be realized before accepting a gift and, if the organization embraces the philosophy of donor relations, that the importance of using the contribution in a timely fashion will become a priority for those who are involved in meeting donor expectations.

The donor experience involves every action, interaction, and communication from the moment donors make a gift to the time they make their next gift.

Summary

The field of development was rapidly changing in the last two decades of the twentieth century. The efficiency and effectiveness of fundraising programs was under scrutiny and an emphasis was placed on efforts to increase philanthropic support and decrease the cost of fundraising. The lack of continuity regarding donors was addressed by implementing plans to acknowledge and recognize donors and to report back to them on the uses of their gifts. The overall strategy is designed to build long-term relationships that will result in increased giving and greater commitment to organizations. Placing donor relations into the development program of an organization requires an integrated and comprehensive approach that addresses the many aspects of donor relations. One element of the effective donor relations program is *unexpectedness*, which means creating an element of surprise. Using surprise to get the donor's attention requires creativity in continuously keeping the program fresh with new strategies. In many ways, donor relations is about making the donor experience positive so that the donor wants to repeat the experience in the future.

Notes

1. *Made to Stick: Why Some Ideas Survive and Others Die,* Random House, New York, 2007.
2. *Pinpointing Affluence in the Twenty-First Century: Increasing Your Share of Major Donor Dollars*, Judith E. Nichols, Ph.D, CFRE Bonus Books, Inc., April 2001.

Acknowledgment

After reading this chapter, you will be able to:

- Explain the importance of thank-you letters.
- Describe the methods of acknowledgment.
- Define the critical factors for the acknowledgment.
- Describe the key elements of a thank-you letter.
- Develop an acknowledgment plan.
- Explain what it means to say "thank you" seven times.
- Prepare special acknowledgment letters.

The Importance of the Thank-You Letter

One of the first phrases that young children learn is "thank you," and as children grow older, many learn how to write *thank-you notes*. The South Dakota Department of Education includes in its writing standards for the third grade that students can apply the writing process to compose text for a friendly letter, thank-you notes, and invitations. In Arkansas, writing thank-you notes is included in the curriculum for first-graders.

With the many forms of rapid communication today, including text messaging from cell phones, the practice of writing thank-you notes is not as prevalent as in the past. Receiving a handwritten note that expresses a person's gratitude has become a pleasant surprise for many individuals. Thank-you cards have become popular and even receiving a thank-you card can be a surprise.

Saying "thank you" is important in many situations. In fact, sending a thank-you letter is cited as one of the most overlooked components in a successful job search. When a person is conducting a job search, one objective is to *stand out* from the other candidates. Sending a thank-you letter is recommended as one of most effective ways for an interviewee to become notable among the crowd.

RULES OF THE ROAD

Saying "thank you" is the first step in getting the next gift.

Two key components of the thank-you letter following a job interview are being prompt (the letter is sent within 24 to 48 hours after the interview), and being specific. The more specific the letter, the more likely the interviewer will remember the interviewee.

The same principles apply to the thank-you letter that an organization sends out after receiving a contribution. The letter has the potential of making the organization *stand out* from the others for the donor. The thank-you letter from an organization should be prompt and should be specific. These are important aspects to making the letter serve its intended purpose.

Another recommendation regarding thank-you letters after job interviews is that the interviewee should not rely on a thank-you by email. While standards may be changing and some employers have indicated that they appreciate receiving thank-you notes by email, it is recommended that interviewees send hardcopy thank-you letters through the mail. A hardcopy letter provides permanence and formality.

Likewise, while an organization may choose to send an email message to thank a donor for a gift, that message should not be a substitute for a thank-you

IN THE REAL WORLD

A generous donor was making a gift of $1,000 each month to an aquarium. She indicated that acknowledging each gift was not necessary. But the development officer wanted to find an appropriate way to express gratitude to the donor. The development officer asked a group of student interns to work on a way to thank this special donor. The students developed a series of thank-you notes from the various fish and other creatures in the aquarium. Each thank-you note featured a picture of the fish or creature and was written from that creature in first person. The respective fish or animal told the donor about its species and its interesting habits and included a "thank you" for the donor's support. The donor was pleasantly surprised and enjoyed this new way of being acknowledged for her giving.

letter in the mail. An email thank-you message is appropriate if the organization knows that the donor uses email, and certainly an email message provides a way to express gratitude immediately. However, a thank-you letter should follow promptly and should be specific to the donor and to the gift the donor made.

An article in the *New York Times* on October 9, 2007, entitled "Thank-You Note Enters College Admission Game," suggests that writing thank-you notes after visiting a college is "a testament to how carefully students court college admissions offices these days" and describes thank-you notes as the new frontier in college admissions.

The article indicates that guidance counselors and parents are suggesting that students write thank-you notes after visits to campus. Colleges are receiving more thank-you notes than ever before; once again, the purpose for the thank-you note or letter is to *stand out* from the others.

In the article, a counselor from a high school in Rockville, Maryland, reported that a student approached her for a sample thank-you note. The advisor noted, "In this competitive atmosphere, people are looking for anything they think will help them stand out." The 16-year-old student indicated "she had been writing thank-you notes since she was young. She even recalled birthday presents being taken away until the notes were written."

The dean of admission at Princeton said, "Is it necessary to write a thank-you note? No. But I'm still in favor of them. Expressing gratitude is a lovely quality." The article recommends that counselors and teachers, especially those who write recommendations for students, should receive thank-you notes.

While saying "thank you" may not be required for students who visit colleges, it is required for organizations receiving gifts from individuals, corporations and businesses, foundations, organizations, and others.

An acknowledgment or thank-you letter, note, card, message, or call is the expression of gratitude that the donor deserves for choosing to make a philanthropic gift to an organization. The communication that occurs after a commitment is made, whether the commitment is a pledge to make a gift or a contribution, begins the process described as *donor relations*. The thank-you establishes two-way communication and is critical to the relationship that an organization wants to build with a donor. Saying "thank you" to a donor is the first step in getting the next gift.

TIPS AND TECHNIQUES

Other Times to Say "Thank You"

Throughout the year, donors appreciate being remembered on special occasions. Each of the following days could be an opportunity to say "thank you" for the donor's interest and commitment to an organization:

- Thanksgiving
- National Philanthropy Day
- New Year's Day
- Valentine's Day
- Fourth of July
- Mother's Day or Father's Day
- Founder's Day or other significant date for organization
- Donor's birthday

Tips and Techniques (continued)

- Religious holidays, as appropriate
- Anniversary of donor's gift
- Birthday and/or anniversary of the death of the person in whose memory the gift was made
- Birthday of person for which an organization is named:
  - Johns Hopkins (May 19): Johns Hopkins University/Hospital
  - John F. Kennedy (May 29): The John F. Kennedy Center for the Performing Arts
  - Elizabeth Glaser (November 11): Elizabeth Glaser Pediatric AIDS Foundation
  - John Joseph Cardinal Glennon (June 14): Cardinal Glennon Children's Medical Center
- Birthday of significant person associated with the organization:
  - Clara Barton (December 25): American Red Cross
  - Albert Einstein (March 14): The National Academies
  - Benjamin Franklin (January 17): University of Pennsylvania/Pennsylvania Hospital
  - Thomas Jefferson (April 13): University of Virginia

Methods of Acknowledgment

In some development offices, the word *acknowledgment* has become synonymous with the thank-you letter. While *acknowledgment* is less prevalent in referring to a thank-you letter than in the past, frequently questions are asked or comments are made about the acknowledgment being mailed or going out. Unfortunately, the use of the word in this way has led to many thinking of acknowledgment as just a letter.

Acknowledgment is expressing gratitude, verifying receipt of a gift, and assuring the donor that the gift will be used wisely. Organizations have many methods available for acknowledging gifts. While all gifts should be acknowledged in writing, acknowledgments can also be made through a phone call, an email message, or a handwritten note. Acknowledgment can be made in a video format and provided to the donor on a DVD. A broad-based acknowledgment may be expressed on the home page of an organization's website or in an email blast.

EXHIBIT 3.1

Choosing the Person to Say "Thank You" to Donors

In most instances, the thank-you letter from an organization comes from the president, chief executive officer, executive director, vice president or director of development, or another member of the development staff. Occasionally, a thank-you letter or note will be signed by a board member or committee chairperson.

Another option is to have those providing or those who are receiving or have received the services of an organization say "thank you." Their experience and connection to the organization brings a special element to their expression of appreciation to a donor. "Thank you" from other persons associated with an organization can be meaningful and will stand out for the donor receiving the letter:

Adoption agency	Adult who was adopted as a child; parents of an adopted child; birth mother of a child
Animal shelter	Person who has adopted an animal; local veterinarian; child whose pet came from the shelter
Art museum	Curator; docent; artist; student
Educational organization	Teacher; student; parent of a student
Hospice	Patient; family member of a patient; volunteer
Hospital	Doctors; nurses; past patients; volunteers
Social service organization	Staff who work with clients; current or past clients
Symphony	Musician; conductor; child who attended a concert or special program
Youth organization	Child; parent; adult who had an experience with the organization as a child

---

In addition to the various methods of acknowledgment, the person making the acknowledgment may vary. The person who says "thank you" is often the chief development officer or the president, CEO, or executive director of the organization. Others who may acknowledge gifts include the chairperson of the board, another member of the board, a volunteer, or a person who has been served by the organization. Organizations may have others specific to the organization who would be willing to say "thank you" through letters, phone calls, or notes (see Exhibit 3.1). In organizations where those who are served are unknown, such as with a rape crisis hotline, the people who answer the phones and provide counsel to callers may be the best ones to sign thank-you letters. The content of the letter may include the reasons why a person chooses to provide this important assistance in time of crisis.

Organizations that serve children or have children involved have a wonderful and meaningful way to express gratitude. Children can say "thank you" through drawings and notes and letters. A thank-you card signed by a number of different children (perhaps with just first names and ages when confidentiality is required) can convey a powerful message of thanks. A child can make a drawing that illustrates his experience and can tell the story that accompanies that drawing. If the child is very young, an adult can write the story as the child tells it. Sharing the drawing and the story with a donor can be a meaningful expression of gratitude.

In colleges and universities with named scholarship funds, the thank-you received by the donor from the student who receives that scholarship is very meaningful. Colleges and universities will often develop a folder about the student to share with the donor. In that folder is information about the student, such as age, hometown, extracurricular activities in high school, and academic awards received.

Organizations receive notes of appreciation from time to time for the services provided and, unfortunately, too often the development office never sees them. However, such a note can be shared, with the permission of the person writing it, with donors as a way of expressing gratitude. For example, a director of a hospice program reported sending a thank-you note that simply said, "No

The *Made to Stick* principle of concreteness can be used to enhance the acknowledgment process.

> When you give to Mercy Corps, they follow up with an email that gives you a concrete vision of how you've helped. For instance: "Your support of $40 provides a Zimbabwean family with clean drinking water for two years."
>
> Lots of charities have figured out that, in soliciting donations, they need to anchor abstract amounts of money in real-world descriptions (e.g., "Adopt a goat for $60," "$200 pays for the translation expenses in a human-rights field visit," etc.).
>
> . . . Mercy Corps uses the same principle after the fact. You get the initial satisfaction of giving, and then Mercy Corps follows up and says, effectively, "Thanks for your gift—and, by the way, a Zimbabwean family thanks you, too."

Source: Dan Heath, *Made to Stick* blog, December 20, 2007.

words of gratitude could be more meaningful than those received each day from those served by the hospice." Enclosed with the note were quotes from the thank-you notes that the organization had received.

TIPS AND TECHNIQUES

Saying "Thank You" at Thanksgiving

Thanksgiving has become a popular time of year to express gratitude to donors. The reasons for an organization to consider a letter or card at Thanksgiving include:

- Expressing gratitude at Thanksgiving is appropriate, given the meaning of the holiday.
- Thanksgiving greetings are not lost in the multitude of greetings that are received during the Christmas holidays.

TIPS AND TECHNIQUES (CONTINUED)

- Thanksgiving is not a religious holiday, which is important if donors include persons of multiple faiths.
- A Thanksgiving greeting is sent about the time of National Philanthropy Day (November 15), a time for celebrating philanthropic support.
- The donor has more time from Thanksgiving to the end of the year to make a year-end gift than from Christmas to the end of the year.

Possible messages for a Thanksgiving greeting include:

- *In this season of change, we give thanks for your support. May the glorious colors of the season brighten your Thanksgiving.*
- *Thanksgiving is an ideal time to express our gratitude. Your generosity has an impact on thousands of lives within the XYZ community and beyond. May that knowledge illuminate your holiday season.*
- *Thanksgiving to us means a special occasion when we can express our sincere thanks to those whose friendship and support we cherish. May you and your family have a bountiful day of joy and gratitude.*
- *In this season of gratitude, we give special thanks for your friendship and support. Best wishes for a joyous Thanksgiving.*
- *At Thanksgiving more than ever, our thoughts turn gratefully to those who have made our achievements possible. And in this spirit we say, simply but sincerely, thank you and best wishes for a happy Thanksgiving.*
- *May the good things of life be yours in abundance at Thanksgiving and throughout the coming year.*
- *There is no time more fitting to say "thank you."*

Note: If an organization has donors from both Canada and the United States, Thanksgiving is celebrated at different times in the two countries.

Critical Factors for the Acknowledgment

The donor needs to feel that the thank-you from an organization is authentic. An acknowledgment, whether a letter, phone call, or personal note, needs to go beyond saying "thank you for the contribution." The acknowledgment needs to convey "thank you" to the person or persons who chose to make the gift. Remembering the person or persons behind the gift is helpful in making the messages personal and meaningful.

TIPS AND TECHNIQUES

Strategy for First–Time Donors

The rate of retention for first-time donors is much lower than the rate of retention for those who have made multiple gifts. Recognizing the high loss of these new donors, organizations are paying more attention to first-time donors and are developing specific strategies for acknowledging the first gift that a donor makes. Some organizations are developing "Welcome" packets for first-time donors. These packets are usually sent to all first-time donors regardless of the size of the gift. Three to five items are recommended for the packet.

Contents of the Welcome packets may include:

- Personalized "Welcome" letter from president, CEO, or executive director of the organization
- Handwritten note of thanks
- Most recent annual report and/or newsletter
- Brochure, if already available, on mission of organization
- Video or DVD on organization
- Brochure on recognition program
- Copy of Donor Bill of Rights
- Magnets and/or bookmarks
- Invitation or "save the date" notice for upcoming event
- Calendar of events
- New donor survey

The four critical factors for an effective and authentic acknowledgment are:

1. Promptness

An acknowledgment should be provided to a donor as quickly as possible. A phone call or an email message can occur as soon as the gift is received. The written acknowledgment should also be sent promptly. A standard should be established by the development office for the timeframe in which an acknowledgment letter or note will be in the mail.

The maximum timeframe from receiving a gift to mailing a written acknowledgment should not be greater than 48 hours. If the process takes longer than 48 hours, the process should be reviewed to find out how responses can be made in a more timely fashion.

For many organizations, the standard has become 48 hours after the receipt of the gift. For some, the timeframe has been shortened to 24 hours. Yet, many organizations have not achieved the 48-hours standard and are getting acknowledgments out in as much as a week to a month after a gift is received.

One of the challenges for the development services or gift processing staff is achieving the balance that is required between speed, accuracy, and volume (see Exhibit 3.2). For donors to receive meaningful thank-you letters promptly, the three aspects need to be weighed. If days are spent on multiple reviews to assure accuracy, the system is out of balance. Likewise, if letters are not accurate, names are misspelled, or amounts or designations of gifts are incorrect, the system needs improvement. If certain times of the year, such as late December or after a major event or mailing, produce a volume of gifts that cannot be handled

EXHIBIT 3.2

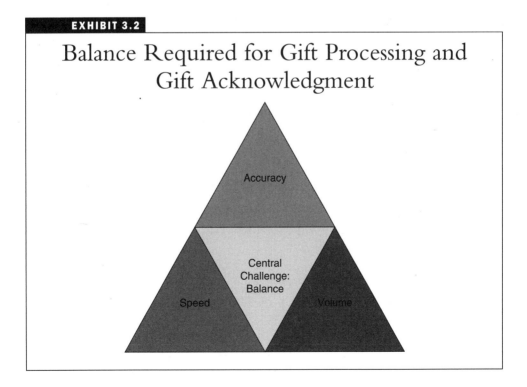

Balance Required for Gift Processing and Gift Acknowledgment

in a timely and accurate manner, the need for additional assistance during those times needs to be addressed.

2. Personal

An impersonal acknowledgment does not convey sincere gratitude. A donor can usually recognize a letter that is generic enough to fit any contribution. With available technology, a letter can be personalized effectively and easily. An acknowledgment letter should not be a "Dear Friend" letter, unless the name of the donor is not known, which occurs rarely. (This may be the case if a gift is made by a third party and the donor wishes to remain anonymous.) Being personal includes using the appropriate name in the salutation. If the executive director of the organization calls a couple by first names, the letter should be written to "Mary and John" rather than to "Mr. and Mrs. Smith." Even if the executive director crosses out the formal name and handwrites "Mary and John," the letter is not as personal as where the correct salutation was used initially. The crossing out of a name clearly indicates that somebody else prepared the letter and the executive director is just signing it. Most development database management systems have a way for the organization to capture the salutations that are used by key individuals, such as the chief executive officer/executive director, board chairperson, volunteer solicitor, and chief development officer.

Other opportunities to make an acknowledgment letter or note personal is to include a piece of information that indicates the donor is known by the person signing the letter. The information may be in reference to a specific interest or relationship the donor has with the organization. Handwritten personal notes at the bottom of letters can also make a letter more personal.

Some organizations refrain from handwritten notes, feeling that it indicates that the person signing the letter may not have written the letter. However, most organizations have found the opposite to be true and that donors see the handwritten note as being more personal.

3. Appropriate

The acknowledgment should be appropriate for the specific donor and for the specific gift. Referring to a gift of $10 as "generous" is probably not appropriate. Reference to "loyal" support when the contribution is the first made by the donor is not appropriate, either. If a gift is made for a specific purpose, the acknowledgment should reflect the special purpose of the gift. An acknowledgment can reflect that the gift is the first gift from the donor, the first gift in several years, or a gift far greater than those in the past. Likewise, noting that the donor is "loyal" and has been giving for 20 years or more is appropriate when saying "thank you." Just inserting in a generic letter that the gift is designated for a specific purpose may not be adequate to make the letter truly appropriate for the donor.

4. Informative

An acknowledgment letter or a phone call, email message, or handwritten note provides an organization with an opportunity to share information about itself and its mission. The information should be factual, such as how many people have been served by the organization in the past year or about a new program that has been introduced at the organization. Information may highlight recent or current activities, accomplishments, and results or outcomes, or convey a story about a person or persons served by the organization. The thank-you is an opportunity to give donors a closer look at the organization.

Elements of the Thank-You Letter

A thank-you letter can have a number of elements (see Exhibit 3.3). As with any letter, the opening should grab the donor's attention. Penelope Burk, author of *Donor-Centered Fundraising* and president of Cygnus Applied Research Inc., cites as an example the first line of an Alzheimer's Association letter: "You remembered for those who can't."

The Acknowledgment Plan

An organization needs to develop a written acknowledgment plan (see Exhibit 3.4) that describes the methods that will be used to express gratitude to donors from various constituencies and for gifts of various sizes. The plan should

EXHIBIT 3.3

Elements in the Thank–You Letter

Following are the suggested elements of the thank-you letter for a contribution to an organization:

1. If possible, begin with a sentence that will grab the donor's attention:

    The parents of the child whose heart was repaired today thank you for giving their child the chance to live, to run and play and experience the wonder of childhood and the promise of dreams for tomorrow.

2. Provide a direct thank-you for the specific gift, noting any specific restrictions on the gift:

    Thank you for your contribution of $5,000 for ABC Children's Hospital to support the Children's Heart Center.

3. Include how the gift will have an impact on the organization:

    Your generous gift will assist us in continuing to provide quality care to the children from throughout the region and beyond who suffer from severe heart problems. As you know, these anomalies threaten not only the quality of life for these children but also frequently rob them of life itself.

4. Add information and/or data about the organization that builds the donor's knowledge about the mission:

    Over the past six months, we have provided health care to more than 4,000 children in the hospital's pediatric emergency department, including approximately 100 youngsters with life-threatening illnesses or injuries and 40 children that have needed heart surgery. These children received the special patient care that was required from the specially trained doctors and nurses in the hospital's pediatric intensive care unit. The pediatric intensive care unit, which has 24 beds, was fully occupied for several weeks in the fall. As you may know, the pediatric intensive care unit at ABC Children's Hospital is the only unit of its kind within 250 miles of XYZ City.

5. Include a newspaper article or other evidence of the organization's mission being fulfilled (optional):

    Enclosed is an article that describes the outstanding report that ABC Children's Hospital received from DEF Consortium on the outcomes that the hospital has for young patients with heart anomalies. We are proud of the report. It confirms that our pediatric cardiology program is one of the best in the nation and that ABC Children's Hospital with your help is saving the lives of children.

6. Say "thank you" again:

We are thankful to you for your continued support of and commitment to ABC Children's Hospital.

7. Close with a statement that suggests continued interest and support:

We look forward to your continued support.

8. Whenever possible, have the person signing the letter add a handwritten personal note.

EXHIBIT 3.4

Acknowledgment Plan for Annual Giving Individual gifts

Annual contribution $1–$49	• Computer-generated receipt/thank-you within 48 hours
	• Enclosure of Annual Giving Gift Clubs information sheet
Annual contribution $50–$99 "Friends"	• Acknowledgment letter signed by chief development officer within 48 hours
	• Enclosure of Annual Giving Gift Clubs information sheet
	• Special listing in the annual report
Annual contribution $100–$499 "Century Circle"	• Acknowledgment letter signed by chief development officer within 48 hours
	• Enclosure of Annual Giving Gift Clubs information sheet
	• Special listing in the annual report
	• Follow-up thank-you call by Annual Giving Committee member
	• Thanksgiving card

Annual contribution $500–$999

"Circle of Gold"

- Acknowledgment letter signed by chief development officer within 48 hours
- Enclosure of Annual Giving Gift Clubs information sheet
- Special listing in the annual report
- Follow-up thank-you call by Annual Giving Committee member
- Invitations to special events
- Leather bookmark with letter signed by CEO (2 months after gift)
- Thanksgiving card

Annual contribution $1,000–$4,999

"Council of 1,000"

- Acknowledgment letter signed by CEO within 48 hours
- Special listing in the annual report
- Invitation to special events
- Follow-up thank-you call by board member
- Leather bookmark with letter signed by CDO (2 months after gift)
- Certificate of membership
- Invitation to annual meeting
- Special ribbon on nametag at events
- Name on recognition plaque
- Birthday card
- Thanksgiving card

Annual giving $5,000 and above

"President's Circle"

- Acknowledgment letter signed by CEO within 48 hours
- Special listing in the annual report
- Invitation to special events
- Follow-up thank-you call by chairperson of the board
- Leather bookmark with letter signed by CDO (2 months after gift)
- Certificate of membership

- Invitation to annual meeting
- Special ribbon on nametag at events
- Name on recognition plaque
- Invitation to participate in small discussion groups with others in President's Circle and leaders of the organization
- Invitation to breakfast or lunch with CEO and/or board chairperson
- Birthday card
- Thanksgiving card

| Annual gifts from members of the board | • All gifts by board members will receive a personal thank-you letter from the CEO within 48 hours of the receipt of the gift and will be acknowledged as above according to the size of the gift. |

CEO: chief executive officer/president/executive director.
CDO: chief development officer.

be developed with input from various members of the development staff and should be reviewed and updated at least quarterly. While the plan is called an *acknowledgment plan*, it includes recognition opportunities as well. In this context, recognition is viewed as saying "thank you" and acknowledging gifts also.

To begin the development of an acknowledgment plan, first decide how the donors will be segmented for the purpose of saying "thank you." The groups may include types of donors, such as trustees, employees, or corporations; levels of giving, such as less than $100, $100 to $499, $500 to $999, and so on; or types of gifts, such as restricted gifts for a specific program or campaign, or for a memorial or tribute.

The second step is to determine the types and methods of acknowledgment (and recognition) that donors may receive. Reviewing what other organizations have provided for their donors may be a resource for ideas. However, giving donors tangible items should be approached with care. In some cases, special tangible items with significant meaning to the donor may be appropriate, but in general what donors seek and what the organization desires are involvement and engagement with the organization. An organization should identify those activities that already take place at or for the organization to which donors at various levels might be invited. Rather than creating events solely for donors, existing events provide opportunities to bring donors closer to the organization and may be more interesting for donors with specific interests. The work involved for the development staff is also less demanding, which is critical when the staff may be limited. This approach also gives donors the opportunity to meet a broader base of persons involved in the life of the organization.

TIPS AND TECHNIQUES

Tangible Thank-You Gifts

Many organizations, such as public television and radio stations, have been successful in securing support through offering premiums to donors at various levels. Other organizations have used various types of address labels to encourage direct-mail giving.

These organizations have discovered that many of the persons who make these contributions approach their giving as purchasing or as "transactions" rather than as philanthropic giving. Analysis has demonstrated that getting these donors to increase giving is a function of what the donor receives in return for the contribution.

To change the transaction mode of giving, many public broadcasting stations have started to refer to premiums as *thank-you gifts*. On websites, when the donor makes a gift, a checkbox labeled "Select your Thank-You Gift" is available. The default or first choice in the list is "No gift please—put all my money toward great WXYZ programs." The message is also being communicated during on-air pledge drives.

In contrast, for those organizations where those who contribute are more philanthropic than transactional, most donors are not eager to receive tangible items in return for their support. Many are concerned that the nonprofit is spending their gifts to buy things that they do not want or need. A thoughtful gift that has meaning for the specific donor, such as a framed photo of the donor with the student who received a scholarship as a result of the donor's gift, is much better received than the paperweight that everyone at that gift level received.

TIPS AND TECHNIQUES (CONTINUED)

Another challenge that comes with giving tangible items to donors is delivering the items. The item can be distributed at a recognition event and mailed to those who did not attend the event. However, mailing some items can be costly and time-consuming. Public television and radio stations often need outside vendors to send out premiums because of the time and cost involved.

Many development offices have stacks of items that were going to be hand-delivered after a recognition event that was held last year or the year before. The development staff needs to be realistic about hand-delivering items to large numbers of persons who may not be top prospects for future gifts. Whether the donors even want these items is also a consideration.

Specially designed gifts that have a meaning that relates to the organization and its mission are meaningful for donors at upper gift levels and the cost of such items can be justified when the donor has made significant gifts over time. At lower gift levels, where tangible gifts are less expensive and often more generic, the donor may perceive what is being provided as another gift club *tchotchke* or bauble.

However, small gifts that can be enclosed with a thank-you letter provide a way to send a second or third acknowledgment to follow the initial thank you by 6 to 12 weeks. This letter might come from a person different from the person from whom the initial letter and phone call came. Donors usually appreciate the small gifts that are enclosed with a letter as thoughtful gestures. A token gift should be a nice, simple, inexpensive item that can be tucked into a letter without increasing postage, such as a decal, magnet, or bookmark that is designed specifically for the organization. Bookmarks are popular as they serve as "private" reminders to the donor and are perceived to be useful. These small gifts may be included in a welcome packet for a new donor, may be distributed at an event, may be included with a thank-you letter, or may be used on an ad-hoc basis.

The third step is to determine which groups of donors should receive which types of acknowledgment and recognition. In most cases, the types of acknowledgment and recognition increase with the size of the gift and the existing relationship of the donor. An organization may want to approach the process differently and use more strategies at the lower levels as a means of increasing retention and upgrades in giving.

The third step needs to identify what activities or communications will happen when and who will be responsible for making those things happen.

Thought needs to be given to tracking the activities in the plan so that reports can be created to determine the impact of the various strategies. Realistic goals are important for the initial plans. Implementing several strategies effectively and in a consistent manner is more valuable than trying to put myriad activities and communications in place and failing to achieve the plan. Initial plans may need to be modified and some strategies reserved for a later date. The keys to developing and implementing an effective plan are to engage everyone in the development office in the creation of the plan and to develop the systems and processes required for the successful implementation of the plan in advance of putting it into action.

The acknowledgment plan needs to define what donor is acknowledged in what ways, when, and by whom. The plan includes the activities at the time of receiving the gift as well as those that are used throughout the year to say "thank you."

TIPS AND TECHNIQUES

A Picture Is Worth a Thousand Words

Eight pumpkins, each with a letter from the words THANK YOU boldly printed on its side, were carried by a group of eight students to various places on campus for photos. The photos, which depicted the campus in its full autumn colors, were used on the cover of the note cards that were signed by the students and were sent to donors around the time of Thanksgiving.

Other colleges have used students sitting in a space that was renovated with contributions of alumni to the annual fund, holding the letters that spell THANK YOU, for a postcard to express gratitude to donors. Another educational organization used a similar plan with students holding the letters for THANK YOU, but in this case, the students were donning New Year's Eve hats, carrying noisemakers, and throwing confetti. This card was mailed shortly after the beginning of the year.

In each of these cases, students were featured. For educational organizations, the students are the ones who benefit from the donors' contributions and are among the best people to say "thank you."

Saying "Thank You" Seven Times

Saying "thank you" when a gift is received has been the basic practice for non-profit organizations for years. The donor relations approach goes beyond a single thank-you at the time of the gift and involves saying "thank you" multiple times in a variety of ways between the time one gift is made and the time the next gift is requested. In fact, organizations are encouraged to say "thank you" seven times for a contribution.

Referred to as an old Chinese custom, a golden rule of sorts, an adage, a rule of thumb, a standard, or best practice in effective fundraising, "saying 'thank you' seven times" is commonly mentioned as important in showing appreciation for a gift.

The practice of saying "thank you" seven times is reported in stories from other countries and other cultures. In stories from Nigeria, the words *Na gode*, meaning "Thank you," are repeated seven times. *Hodja* stories from Turkey include characters saying "Thank you seven times below the earth" or "Thank you seven times above the heavens." The phrases "Thank you seven times" or "Thank you seven times over" are also used to express gratitude much as one would say "Thanks a lot." In many cultures, one is not considered truly grateful unless one has said "thank you" seven times for a gift.

TIPS AND TECHNIQUES

Host a Thank-a-thon

A *thank-a-thon* is an effective way to express gratitude to a number of people at one time and uses volunteers rather than staff to make the contacts. The thank-a-thon brings volunteers together to say ''thank you'' to donors by phone or by handwritten note. The persons contacted may be first-time donors, donors from a specific constituency, or donors of a specific size of gift.

To conduct a telephone thank-a-thon, a room equipped with a number of phones is the ideal setting. If the organization has a *phone-a-thon*, the thank-a-thon could be conducted the day before the solicitation calls begin or after the solicitation calls are completed. The thank-you calls on the day before the phone-a-thon would be made to those who have already made their annual gifts while the calls after the phone-a-thon may include both those making contributions prior to and during the phone-a-thon.

Another thank-a-thon could be conducted that prepares handwritten notes for a select group of donors. The first step would be defining the group of donors that would be contacted. For the purposes of measuring the impact of handwritten notes, the selected donors should be randomly divided into two groups. One of the groups would receive the handwritten notes and the other group would not. The second step would be recruiting the volunteers. If the organization has an auxiliary or another group of volunteers who have regular meetings or social gatherings, the group could be approached to assist the organization with its thank-a-thon.

Preparation for the thank-a-thon would include the logistics of when and where and would involve getting all of the materials together for the event.

Suggested Plan

11:45 A.M.	Group of 6 to 12 volunteers gather; welcome is extended and appreciation for the group's willingness to help is expressed by an appropriate person from the organization.
12 NOON	Lunch for the volunteers and a couple of persons from the organization.
12:30 P.M.	Group gathers in another location to write thank-you notes. Instructions are reviewed with the group. Group begins writing notes.
1:30 P.M.	Fifteen-minute break for coffee and cookies or other refreshments.
2:30 P.M.	Conclude the day.

Volunteers are provided with the following:

- Note cards and envelopes
- Names and addresses of donors
- Ink pens
- Postage stamps
- Sample scripts and/or a list of key phrases

TIPS AND TECHNIQUES (CONTINUED)

Volunteers address the envelopes, write the notes, and seal and stamp the envelopes. Before the notes are mailed, the personal handwritten notes from the volunteers are recorded on the accounts of those donors as *actions* or *contacts*.

A member of the development staff should be on hand from the time the volunteers arrive until they leave to answer any questions. The following day the staff member should thank, by handwritten note if possible, all of the volunteers for their assistance.

At a defined point in the future, following the next solicitation of those donors who received the handwritten notes, a report should be generated that shows the impact of the notes. The responses to the solicitation should be compared for the two groups that were created at the beginning of the process, those receiving the handwritten notes and those not receiving the notes. The volunteers who participated in the thank-a-thon should be given a report on the program's results.

Not only are donors receiving handwritten notes from volunteers whose names they may recognize, but the volunteers are involved and engaged in the fundraising process in a meaningful way.

Much has been written about the number *seven* and why it is preferred over other numbers. References are made to the seven days of Creation, seven deadly sins, seven virtues, and so forth. The number "seven" in the Bible is symbolic of completeness and perfection. "Seven" is used in the Bible over 300 times. In the Book of Revelation, the number "seven" is used 54 times. There are seven churches, seven angels, seven spirits, seven stars, seven seals, seven trumpets, seven vials, seven personages, seven dooms, and seven new things. The word "finished" is also connected to the number "seven" in the Bible. The seven-branch menorah is one of the oldest symbols of the Jewish faith and is often seen in temples and synagogues. Seven is said by some to be magical and lucky. It is reported that when the number seven appears in the title of the book, the book will sell better.

When some development professionals hear that they should say "thank you" seven times, the reaction can be disbelief. One might envision sending seven thank-you letters at the same time or over a limited time. That practice seems irrational and many are concerned that donors will feel that their money has been wasted.

Saying "thank you" seven times does not mean sending seven thank-you letters when the gift is received. It means being aware of the need to say "thank you" in a multitude of ways and the need to adequately express gratitude before asking for the next gift. It means thinking about different ways to say "thank you" to a donor.

For example:

1. The day the gift is received, the president of the organization calls the donor to say the gift has been received and that the organization appreciates the donor's support.

2. A letter from the chairman of the board is sent to the donor, officially acknowledging the receipt of the gift.

3. Six weeks later, the chief development officer sends the donor a leather bookmark that bears the organization's name and logo with a thank-you note.

4. The donor is invited to a special event, such as the organization's annual meeting.

5. The donor receives a copy of the organization's annual report with a note from the president that expresses appreciation for the donor's support and that encourages the donor to read the report to see the impact that the gift has made in the life of the organization.

6. The donor receives a Thanksgiving card from the organization.

7. The donor receives a newsletter or publication that features news on the organization.

8. The next request for a contribution, whether by mail, phone, or in person, begins with a thank-you for the donor's past support.

Saying "thank you" seven times means looking for opportunities to say "thank you" and creating those opportunities whenever possible.

RULES OF THE ROAD

The maximum time from receiving a contribution to mailing a written acknowledgment to a donor should not be greater than 48 business hours.

In the previous example, saying "thank you" includes acknowledgment, recognition, and stewardship. Recognition of a donor in a list in a publication or on a wall is a way to say "thank you." Providing a stewardship report that gives the donor an account of the gift's impact is, in itself, a means of expressing gratitude to the donor. In addition, a letter may accompany the stewardship report and may begin with a thank-you to the donor. As stated in Chapter 1, the three components of donor relations overlap, and one single action can be a form of acknowledgment or saying "thank you," a way of recognizing the donor and expressing appreciation, and a chance to report on the use of the gift. Saying "thank you" seven times is about expressing gratitude and appreciation multiple times through acknowledgment, recognition, and stewardship.

IN THE REAL WORLD

Mark J. Marshall, a colleague at Bentz Whaley Flessner, shares his experience on making gifts and getting thanked by the organizations.

The day was Monday, December 31. He decided to make a series of online contributions, all of which were relatively small. He made five gifts, one to an environmental organization and four to various colleges. He was a first-time donor to all of the organizations.

He reported that the procedure was significantly different for each organization, particularly as it related to the process and the gift processing vendor.

IN THE REAL WORLD (CONTINUED)

One college to which he had intended to make a gift had a note on its web page indicating that gifts made after 2:30 P.M. would not be processed in that calendar year. So he did not make a gift to that one.

Mark received instant emails acknowledging each gift. Some of the email messages came from the gift-processing vendor and some from the organizations.

The responses from each organization after that varied:

January 2—A personal email from one of the colleges, thanking him and acknowledging him as a donor. A standard thank-you letter followed later.

Around January 10—A standard thank-you letter from college number 2 with a personalized note on the bottom.

Around January 10—A standard, but "very nice," thank-you letter from the environmental organization.

Around January 14—A standard thank-you letter with no personalization from college number 3.

College number 4 never acknowledged the gift.

How would your organization's response compare with those of the organizations that Mark supported?

The number of times that an organization says "thank you" may not be seven. An organization may say "thank you" five, six, eight, or ten times before the next gift is requested. The number of times that an organization says "thank you" depends on the donor, the gift, and the relationship with the donor.

The adage that an organization should say "thank you" seven times keeps the organization focused on the importance of expressing gratitude and the role of donor relations in the development process.

Special Acknowledgments

Every thank-you or acknowledgment letter, note, card, or message should be special. It should reflect the gift and the donor making the gift appropriately.

In some cases, the thank-you or acknowledgment needs another element that reflects the special nature or type of gift made.

Special acknowledgments include those for:

- *First-time donor.* A communication with a person, business, corporation, foundation, or organization making an initial gift to the organization should *welcome* the donor as a supporter of the organization. Some organizations provide a new-donor or new-member packet of information to the new donor. The new-donor or -member packet or folder may be included with the initial gift acknowledgment or may be sent to the donor as the second thank-you following the initial acknowledgment by several days or a week or two.

- *Reactivated donor.* If a donor makes a gift after several years of not giving, the acknowledgment should *welcome* the donor back. Indicating that the donor's support was missed and thanking the donor for returning as a supporter can make the gift more personal and meaningful. The letter may highlight several of the organization's recent accomplishments and point out that the donor's support will help the organization continue to achieve its mission.

- *Multiple-gift donor.* When a donor has made multiple gifts within the year, the thank-you for second, third, and subsequent gifts should acknowledge the *additional* gift(s) to the organization. If the total giving for the year puts the donor at a threshold for a recognition society, the qualification for membership in that recognition program should be included in the letter.

- *Matching-gift donor.* When a donor uses an employer's program that matches the gifts of its employees, the donor should be thanked for taking advantage of the opportunity to *double* or *triple* the size of the gift. In most cases, the donor will include a matching-gift form with the contribution. It is appropriate to note in the letter that the form was received and has been forwarded to the appropriate person or department.

  - If the company's matching gift is included in qualification of the donor for a recognition program and the two gifts combined will put the donor into a recognition category, the organization should make the donor aware of the qualification and membership in the recognition program.

- If a donor has included a matching-gift form in prior years but has not included a form with the gift being acknowledged, mentioning the donor's past matching gift and encouraging the donor to use the matching-gift option if still eligible is also appropriate.

- When the gift is received from the company that matches the donor's gift, the organization should send a thank-you to the company. In addition, the organization should send a letter to the donor to indicate the matching gift has been received, that the matching gift will be used for the same purpose as the donor's gift, and that the organization appreciates the donor's efforts to secure the corporate matching gift. (Note: The matching-gift company will usually stipulate that the corporate gift be used for the same purpose as the donor's gift. If not, the organization may use the gift for any purpose. However, most organizations designate the matching gift for the same purpose as that of the donor's gift. Donor-centered thinking would lead an organization to consider where the donor would want the gift used. In most cases, the donor would want the matching gift to supplement the original gift and serve the same purpose.)

- *Special-constituency donor.* If the donor of a gift is a member of a special constituency, such as a board member; an active volunteer; an employee; a former student, patient or client; or a vendor, the thank-you letter should make note of the affiliation and express gratitude in the context of what it means to have donors from that group support the organization.

- *Memorial or tribute donor.* Gifts that are made in memory of a deceased person or in honor of a person or a special event need to be acknowledged both to the donor and to the family of the person being remembered, the person being honored, or the persons related to the event being celebrated.

- In the acknowledgment to the donor, thanking the donor for the "thoughtful" or "meaningful" remembrance or tribute is the key message. However, it is also important to let the donor know that the family of the person being remembered or the person(s) in whose honor the gift is being made will receive notification of the gift. It should be noted in the letter to the donor that the amount of the gift will not be included in the notification letter.

- In the notification letter to the family of the person in whose memory the gift is made or to the person in whose honor the gift is being made, the name and address of the person making the gift should be included. The amount of the gift should not be included. If multiple gifts are made, the total of all gifts may be indicated.

- For memorial gifts, as soon as the development office is aware of the person's death and knows that the family has requested that memorial gifts be made to the organization, a letter of condolence should be sent to the family. The letter should express appreciation for the family's thoughtfulness in requesting that gifts be made to the organization, should indicate that notifications will be sent to the family on a regular basis, perhaps weekly, with the names and the addresses of those who have made memorial gifts, and note that the total of all gifts will be reported to the family but that individual gift amounts will not be reported, as the size of an individual gift is confidential information. If appropriate, the organization may send gift envelopes with the organization's return address preprinted on them for the family to share with those who wish to make gifts. Some organizations will provide these envelopes to the funeral home designated by the family.

 TIPS AND TECHNIQUES

Reports on Memorial Gifts

Development staff members frequently look for ways to build relationships with the donors who make memorial or tribute gifts to their organizations.

TIPS AND TECHNIQUES (CONTINUED)

In most cases, the person who has made the gift did so because the family requested that gifts in memory of the loved one be made to the specific organization. Likewise, if somebody asks that in lieu of gifts for a special occasion gifts be made to a designated nonprofit, the motivation is not based on the interest in the organization but rather on the honoree's request.

Organizations that have attempted to get memorial and tribute donors to make subsequent gifts have usually been disappointed by the response rate. Many nonprofits that conduct direct-mail campaigns exclude onetime memorial and tribute donors from their mailing lists since the response rate is much lower than for any other group of donors.

Organizations need to shift their focus from the donors of those gifts to the people who ask that those gifts be made. The families of the persons in whose memory gifts are made and those who ask that contributions be made to the organization in lieu of gifts to the honorees are the people who have relationships with the organization.

One strategy for acknowledging the thoughtfulness of the family in requesting memorial gifts be made to the specific organization that can build the relationship with the family is putting together a record of those who gave as a keepsake for the family.

When the receipt of gifts in memory of a person has ended, usually when no gifts have been received for a couple of weeks, the organization can thank the family again by putting together a simple record of the persons who made gifts. On the first page is the name of the person in whose memory the gifts were made along with the dates of birth and death and possibly an appropriate quote. The other pages would include the names and addresses of all those who made gifts in memory of that person, usually in alphabetical order. At the end of the report the total amount contributed and any specific purpose for the gifts would be noted. The pages can be placed in a report holder or organized in another simple way. If possible, the report should be delivered to the family by a member of the development staff. If the family member resides in another city and travel would not be appropriate, mailing the report with a follow-up phone call would be recommended. Families find this report thoughtful and value it as a meaningful keepsake.

- *In-kind gift donor.* A gift-in-kind is a non-cash contribution and is usually a tangible item—something that a person can physically touch, carry, or place in an attic or garage, as opposed to cash, stocks, or real estate. An acknowledgment for a gift-in-kind needs to be carefully worded since the regulations that govern the tax deductibility of gifts-in-kind differ significantly from those for other assets, such as cash, securities, and real estate. The thank-you letter should include a physical description of the gift-in-kind, whether the item will be used for the exempt purpose of the organization, and whether the item will be used or sold. The letter should not give any dollar value for the item and should indicate that the valuation of the gift is the responsibility of the donor (see Exhibit 3.5). Even if the donor provides a copy of an appraisal, the acknowledgment letters should not refer to the value of the gift.

- Gifts-in-kind include tangible items such as personal collections, equipment, books, food and beverages, works of art, software, furniture, jewelry, and stamps.

- The most important information for a donor to know is whether the organization can use the gift to further its mission or purpose:

  - An art museum may use donated artwork, including paintings, sculptures, photographs, and prints, to expand its collection. Likewise, a library may take books and other printed materials to enrich its collection. In both cases, the items are being used to support the organization's mission.

  - If the charitable organization will use the asset for a purpose related to its core mission—and not sell the asset—then the donor is allowed to deduct, within limits related to the donor's income, the entire value of the asset. If the asset does not have a "related use," a purpose related to the mission of the organization, the donor is permitted to deduct the lower of the fair market value or the cost basis of the asset.

  - Organizations that accept tangible gifts cannot appraise those gifts for tax purposes. The organization may provide a list of appraisers, but

EXHIBIT 3.5

Sample Thank-You Letter for a Gift-in-Kind

Dear _____:

Thank you for your thoughtful gift of a rug to XYZ organization. The rug, which is primarily brown, red, and gold, is 12 feet by 20 feet in size. [*The donor may have indicated that the rug was an oriental rug. However, it will probably not be obvious whether the rug is an oriental or not. Describing the physical characteristics of the rug is recommended. Likewise, what a donor may describe as a ruby ring would be described as "a ring with a red stone" in the thank-you letter.*] The rug will be sold by XYZ organization with the proceeds from the sale being used to fulfill the mission of the organization. [*Whether an organization uses an in-kind gift in fulfilling its mission will have an impact on the donor's tax deduction. An art museum accepting a painting that will become part of the museum's collection differs from a hospital accepting the same painting. The organization's plans for the gift are important and should be stated.*]

The Internal Revenue Service stipulates that the donor of such a gift needs to provide valuation of the gift for tax purposes. More information on taxes and gifts-in-kind is available from the Internal Revenue Service. We recommend that you consult with a tax advisor.

Your gift will assist us in [*specific information about goals and objectives of the organization*].

We appreciate your continued support of XYZ organization.

Sincerely,

Jane Doe

President, XYZ Organization

legally the organization is prohibited from doing an appraisal or paying for one. If the value of the gift is over $5,000, and the donor plans to take a tax deduction, the donor must file an appraisal along with IRS Form 8283.

- While a contribution of services is considered a gift-in-kind, donated services are not tax-deductible. The donor may deduct any out-of-pocket expenses incurred in the course of performing services for the organization. Included would be meals, lodging, and travel expenses, when performing services requires travel, as long as no significant element of personal pleasure, recreation, or vacation is included in the travel. This provision on the value of donated services applies to an artist who can deduct only the out-of-pocket expenses involved in creating a painting, sculpture, photograph, or other artwork that is donated. The work involved is considered personal services and is not tax-deductible. For example, an artist can deduct only the cost of the canvas and the cost of the paints when giving a painting to a nonprofit.

- Acknowledgments for donated services should clearly state what the services were and that they are appreciated. The letter may state that a person who donates services may deduct out-of-pocket expenses incurred in providing those services. Suggesting that the donor consult with the Internal Revenue Service and a tax advisor is also recommended. As in the letter for tangible gifts-in-kind, the text of the letter may include: "More information on taxes and gifts-in-kind is available from the Internal Revenue Service. We recommend that you consult with a tax advisor."

IN THE REAL WORLD

Wikipedia, the free online encyclopedia, cites a study that demonstrates how gratitude may serve to reinforce behavior. Carey and colleagues found that customers of a jewelry store who were called and thanked showed a subsequent 70% increase in purchases. In comparison, customers who were thanked and told about a sale showed only a 30% increase in purchases, and customers who were not called at all did not show an increase.[1] Rind and Bordia found that restaurant patrons gave bigger tips when their servers wrote "thank you" on their checks.[2]

Is the same true for nonprofit organizations? Are those donors who are called and thanked for their gifts more likely to renew their support and to make gifts

Summary

The acknowledgment of a gift, whether by letter, card, note, phone, or email, sets the stage for the donor relations process and is the first step in getting the next gift. If the thank-you or acknowledgment phase of donor relations is not properly conducted, the relationship with the donor may be harmed.

"Thank you" may be expressed in many ways and by a variety of people. An effective thank-you must be prompt, personal, appropriate, and informative. The process for preparing acknowledgments requires a balance in speed, accuracy, and volume. The initial thank-you needs to be a written communication that is mailed within 48 hours of receiving the contribution. Names need to be spelled correctly and information in the letter must be correct. A thank-you letter should begin with a strong opening that gets the donor's attention.

An organization should develop a written acknowledgment plan and should review and revise the plan on a regular basis. The acknowledgment plan is segmented by constituency type and by gift size and details the *what*, *when*, and *who* for every communication with donors.

The rule of thumb is that an organization should say "thank you" seven times before asking for a next gift. This does not mean sending seven thank-you letters, notes, or cards at the same time. The adage that an organization should say "thank you" seven times is a reminder that it needs to take every possible opportunity to express gratitude for the support of its donors.

While every acknowledgment should be appropriate for the specific donor, several situations call for special letters. Special acknowledgments are needed for first-time donors, those who make multiple gifts, those who use corporate matching-gift programs, those who make in-kind gifts, and those who make memorial and tribute gifts, to name a few.

Notes

1. Carey, J. R., Clicque, S. H., Leighton, B. A., & Milton, F. (1976). "A Test of Positive Reinforcement of Customers," *Journal of Marketing, 40*, 98–100.
2. Rind, B., & Bordia, P. (1995). "Effect of Server's 'Thank You' and Personalization on Restaurant Tipping," *Journal of Applied Social Psychology, 25*, 745–751.

CHAPTER 4

Recognition: Part 1

After reading this chapter, you will be able to:

- Explain the importance of recognition.
- Describe ways to recognize donors.
- Determine whether and how to use an annual donor report.
- Plan, create, and manage donor recognition displays.
- Develop a list of named-gift opportunities.
- Plan and manage recognition events.

The Importance of Recognition

Recognition goes beyond acknowledgment and makes the organization's gratitude for a donor known to others. While acknowledgment is just between the organization and the donor, recognition involves making others aware of a donor's contribution.

Recognition can take a variety of forms, including lists of donors' names in newsletters, reports, and other publications; lists of donors' names on a temporary or permanent wall display; lists of donors' names on a website; area recognition plaques for those who have chosen specific gift opportunities; naming of buildings, rooms, programs, and specific funds; press releases and media coverage; and celebrations and events.

Recognition may be developed for a group of donors who have similar characteristics, such as size of gift or donor constituency, or recognition may be specific for a particular donor. Recognition for a specific donor may include a news release about that donor's gift or may include a profile of the donor on a website or in a publication. In publicizing a specific donor's gift, key components in the recognition include what the gift will make possible, the donor's relationship to the organization, and the donor's motivation for making the gift.

Donors have responded positively to the practice of listing names on wall displays and in publications for many years. However, if donors are asked whether they want recognition for their giving, most will say that recognition is not important to them. Few will admit that getting their names listed is a motivation for giving, yet organizations have seen time and again that offering recognition for giving generates more gifts at higher levels.

According to Maslow's hierarchy of needs, proposed by Abraham Maslow in his 1943 paper, *A Theory of Human Motivation* (see Exhibit 4.1), after physiological and safety needs are fulfilled, the third layer of human needs is social. Humans need to feel a sense of belonging and acceptance, whether it comes

EXHIBIT 4.1

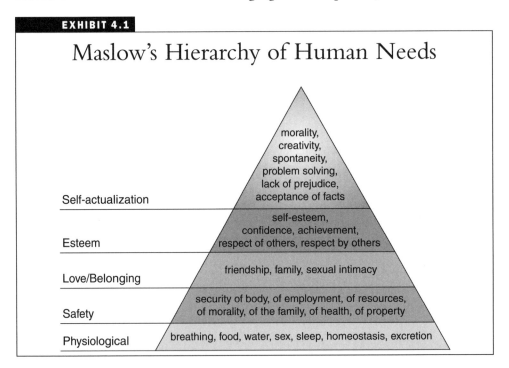

Maslow's Hierarchy of Human Needs

Self-actualization — morality, creativity, spontaneity, problem solving, lack of prejudice, acceptance of facts

Esteem — self-esteem, confidence, achievement, respect of others, respect by others

Love/Belonging — friendship, family, sexual intimacy

Safety — security of body, of employment, of resources, of morality, of the family, of health, of property

Physiological — breathing, food, water, sex, sleep, homeostasis, excretion from a large social group (such as clubs, religious groups, professional organizations, sports teams) or small social connections (family members, mentors, close colleagues, confidants).

The fourth level of human needs is esteem. All humans have a need to be respected, to have self-esteem and self-respect, and to respect others. People need to engage themselves to gain recognition and have activities that give them a sense of contribution and to feel accepted and self-valued.

Seeking recognition for supporting a nonprofit organization is consistent with the basic human need of belonging and acceptance and with the need to have the respect of others, which contributes to self-esteem.

Recognition Preferences

In *Developing Major Gifts: Turning Small Donors into Big Contributors*, Laura Fredricks identifies and describes the five most common preferences for recognition:

1. *The Expectants.* As much publicity and recognition as the organization can offer.

2. *The Moderates.* Some publicity, but not too much.

3. *The Frugal.* Some publicity, but do not spend any money.

4. *The Secretive.* Privately recognized, yes; publicly, no.

5. *The Anonymous.* No one can know about the gift.

The desire and the expectation for recognition vary from donor to donor along a continuum from very public to very private (see Exhibit 4.2). However, a few basic principles are universal for all donors:

- Giving recognition a personal touch based on the interests of the donors is what distinguishes one organization from the next in the mind of the donor.

- Recognition does not need to be expensive, but should be creative and thoughtful.

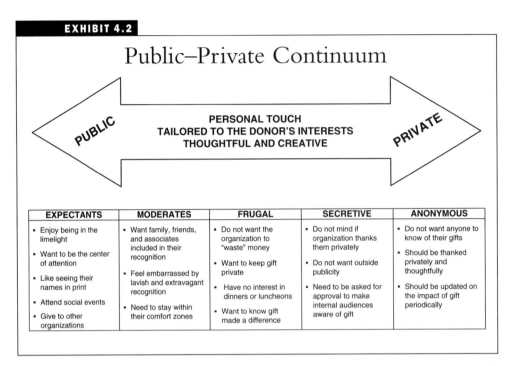

EXHIBIT 4.2

Public–Private Continuum

PUBLIC

PERSONAL TOUCH
TAILORED TO THE DONOR'S INTERESTS
THOUGHTFUL AND CREATIVE

PRIVATE

EXPECTANTS	MODERATES	FRUGAL	SECRETIVE	ANONYMOUS
• Enjoy being in the limelight • Want to be the center of attention • Like seeing their names in print • Attend social events • Give to other organizations	• Want family, friends, and associates included in their recognition • Feel embarrassed by lavish and extravagant recognition • Need to stay within their comfort zones	• Do not want the organization to "waste" money • Want to keep gift private • Have no interest in dinners or luncheons • Want to know gift made a difference	• Do not mind if organization thanks them privately • Do not want outside publicity • Need to be asked for approval to make internal audiences aware of gift	• Do not want anyone to know of their gifts • Should be thanked privately and thoughtfully • Should be updated on the impact of gift periodically

- What the organization, especially the relationship manager on the development staff, has learned about the donor during cultivation, which usually occurs over an extended period of time, should guide the plans for recognition.

The Anonymous Donor

The definition of *anonymous* is "having no known name, or identity, or source." A gift made anonymously would be one where nobody knows where it originated. That level of anonymity happens on occasion, but more often than not, the donor is asking that a limited number of persons know about the gift and that public recognition be avoided. The donor does not want to be listed in an honor roll of donors or in any publication that is distributed to others. The reasons why donors ask for anonymity are varied. Some fear that other organizations will be approaching them for contributions; or perhaps they do not want friends or family to know of their giving. Others feel that recognition is not necessary and just do not want it.

When a person asks that a gift be made anonymously, the meaning of that statement can be interpreted in various ways. The donor may mean something totally different from what the organization receiving the gift *thinks* the donor means. Understanding what an anonymous donor desires is not always easy and can be an area for potential mistakes unless handled carefully.

Some organizations interpret a donor's request to be anonymous as meaning the donor wants no contact with the organization. The organization will not enter the donor's name and address in the database and will not acknowledge the gift. The organization will simply create a record for "Anonymous." The organization will certainly find it difficult to build a relationship with a donor whose name and address are not recorded.

As a general rule, an anonymous donor does not want public recognition but should receive acknowledgment and stewardship. The anonymous gift should be acknowledged by one of the select persons who know about the gift and the donor's desire to be anonymous should be stated in the acknowledgment, whether by letter, phone, or personal visit. The anonymous donor should be thanked appropriately in the weeks and months after the gift. The anonymous donor should also receive a stewardship report. While the person may not want recognition, communication that the gift was used wisely and had an impact on those served by the organization is important to the relationship with the donor.

Asking an anonymous donor to clarify the meaning of *anonymous* can be a good idea. Organizations have found that the anonymous donor may change the definition of *anonymous* when a donor wall is erected after a major fundraising effort or when named-gift opportunities are available during a capital campaign. While the donor may not want to be listed in a report that is being sent out to others, he might want to be included on the donor wall or might want to choose a named-gift opportunity. The anonymous donor might want the person in whose memory or honor the gift was made to be recognized through a named-gift opportunity. The name of that person could appear in a specific place and the anonymity of the donor would remain intact.

When putting up a recognition wall or area recognition plaques, contacting the anonymous donors to make sure that the desire to be anonymous includes *not* being listed on the wall or in a special area is a good idea and can prevent hurt feelings after the wall is erected or area plaques are installed.

How anonymous donors should be handled has been debated over the years. One school of thought is that the development officer should convince the donor that the organization will benefit from the donor's identity being known and that she should allow the organization to recognize the gift. From this point of view, the donor is being told that pride should be associated with supporting the organization and that she should proudly give the organization permission to list her name.

On the other side of the coin is the opinion that the donor's request to be anonymous should be honored and any discussion to the contrary would not be in keeping with a donor-centered approach to fundraising.

Taking the middle ground is probably the best course of action. First and foremost, the donor's desire to be anonymous should be honored. However, making sure what the donor means by being anonymous is critical to effective donor relations. Whether the donor wants no recognition or limited recognition is an important piece of information.

Telling people who are reluctant to be recognized for a gift that by being recognized they are helping the organization by encouraging others to give may be appropriate. When donors feel that recognition of their gifts will motivate others to give, some will see their gifts as having added importance and will want to help the organization achieve increased giving. However, any conversation on the topic should be handled as sharing information, not as pressuring a donor. Making a donor feel uncomfortable will not set the stage for future gifts.

Recognition does not always need to be public. Recognition might involve a small gathering of family and friends to celebrate the donor's generosity and more importantly to celebrate the impact the gift will have for the organization.

Recognition Gift Clubs

Creating recognition gift clubs is a way that many organizations provide recognition to their donors. A gift club is a recognition program for a group of donors with similar characteristics. The common thread may be the level of giving, the type of giving, the frequency of giving, the constituency type, or a specific interest or affinity. Recognition gift clubs are designed to encourage donors to make contributions and to increase their contributions from year to year. The three main types of recognition gift clubs are the ones for annual giving, for lifetime giving, and for planned giving. Recognition gift clubs provide opportunities to engage donors in the life of the organization through its membership "benefits" and "privileges."

The topic of recognition gift clubs is discussed in detail in Chapter 5.

Annual Reports

A corporate annual report is the document that a company presents at its annual general meeting for approval by its shareholders. It consists of various reports and financial statements, which may include the following:

- Chairperson's report
- CEO's report
- Auditor's report on the financial statements
- Balance sheet
- Statement of retained earnings
- Income statement
- Cash flow statement
- Notes to the financial statements

The annual report for a nonprofit organization is similar in that it includes various reports and financial information. The annual report for many charitable organizations has evolved to include a list of names of donors to the organization.

Kivi Leroux Miller, President of EcoScribe Communications, describes on the website www.NonprofitAnnualReports.net how an annual report can be helpful to a nonprofit organization. An annual report can:

- Communicate not just an organization's activities, but its accomplishments during the past year.
- Convince existing supporters that their funds are being well spent.

- Attract new donors.

- Educate community leaders and influential decision makers about the work of the organization on important issues.

- Recognize special people, including donors and volunteers.

- Serve as a historical record of the organization's progress.

In the past, for many nonprofits, the annual report and the list of donors were separate documents. The list of names of donors was printed in a separate document called the "Honor Roll." Educational organizations have included the Honor Roll in their alumni publications and some organizations have listed the names of donors in monthly or quarterly newsletters or other publications rather than in a comprehensive report once each year.

Organizations that have quarterly or bimonthly magazines or newsletters often use one of the issues as their annual report. The publication may remain the same but include the list of donors for that year as a section, usually at the back or in the center, of the magazine or newsletter. Some put the list of donors on a different color or different texture paper to make it stand out. Some organizations dedicate the entire issue to the annual report and may title it a special edition. The cover may look similar to those during the rest of the year while the format of the publication may change totally for the report on giving.

One strategy for smaller organizations has been to develop a list that begins in January and grows over the course of the year. Each monthly or quarterly newsletter would contain the names of those who have given from January 1 up until the time the newsletter is published. The process may begin on July 1 and proceed through June 30 as well. This plan might be called the *progressive annual report*. The advantages include:

- Donors who contribute early in the year receive recognition in each issue of the newsletter.

- Mistakes made in listing names can be corrected before the final copy for the year is produced.

- The listing becomes a frequent reminder to those who have not given.

The challenges with this type of listing include keeping the growing list of names interesting and justifying the additional cost both in printing and possibly postage for the additional pages in the newsletter.

For some, the printed documents that list donors have remained separate documents over the years. For other organizations, the annual report and the list of donors have been combined and the resulting document has been called an *annual report*, the *honor roll*, a *report on giving*, or a *report on philanthropy*. This report, regardless of its name, has been considered an important component of donor recognition.

For many organizations, the annual report that includes a list of donors by gift club or by size of gift has been a strategy for recognizing those who have given. Getting one's name listed in the annual report is cited as a benefit of giving at certain levels. For example, in the letters that requested gifts from potential donors, the fact that donors of $50 or more are listed in the annual report might be cited as a benefit of giving at that level. In inviting donors to increase their giving to the $1,000 level, the recognition of those who give at that level in the annual report was included as one of the benefits of being a member of the XYZ Circle, the recognition group for annual gifts of $1,000 or more.

In addition to the lists by amount, educational organizations have included listings by class and have created comparisons of classes by percentage participation. As organizations continued to develop and refine the reports, they began to use the report to communicate the ways that gifts were being used. The organizations included stories about those who benefited from the contributions being made and featured donors who cited their reasons for giving. The reports on giving became more than a list of names and became a way to communicate with donors about the impact of giving.

Sometimes special notes are attached or special letters are enclosed with the reports to specifically express gratitude for the donor's support in the prior year. The notes and letters may be used with all reports or may be used for a selected group or groups such as board members or major donors of a certain magnitude and above. For example, a note from the organization's president may be added to the reports going to those who made gifts of $1,000 or more and may call attention to the accomplishments cited in the report that generous gifts, such as that of the specific donor, made possible. The note may also alert the donor that a request for renewal of support will be made in the near future.

Organizations have used the gift report as a strategy to encourage renewal gifts. As the end of the year approached, an educational organization would print a "proof" copy of the section of the report that included the class list of the donor who had given the prior year but not in the current year. An arrow or a circle may be added to show where the donor's name would fit in the list. The organization would send the proof copy of the list to the donor with a message pointing out the absence of the donor's name and reminding the donor to send a contribution by a certain date to assure that the donor's name is included in the report. Similar strategies were used by other organizations.

One way organizations have evaluated the effectiveness of a gift report is by enclosing a remittance envelope that is coded to indicate it came from the report. As gifts are received in those envelopes, the gifts are coded accordingly and a report can be generated on the number and amount of the gifts that were returned in those envelopes. Having that information can help to substantiate the value of the gift report in generating immediate revenue.

Other ways to measure the impact of the report are conducting a survey specifically about the annual report, including questions about the gift report in the annual donor satisfaction survey, and having gift officers ask donors with whom they meet for feedback on the report.

Questions such as the following may be helpful:

- Did the donor receive the annual report on giving? *It is important to note if the donor is not sure whether the annual report on giving was received or is not sure which publication is being referenced. If the donor remembers the report, she may indicate her reaction without further questions.*

- Did the donor read the stories in the report about the ways contributions were used?

- What does the donor think about the report on giving? Is it helpful? Is it informative? How could it be improved?

Not only does the discussion with donors provide feedback that can be helpful in making decisions about the annual report on giving, but the conversation gives donors an opportunity to express themselves and gives the staff the chance to learn more about the donor's preferences for recognition. The donor's comments about the report will indicate his feeling about names being listed and his interest in reading stories about those who benefit from their gifts.

Contents of the Annual Report

Some organizations choose a theme for each year's report and the report's content is focused on that theme. Themes such as "Unity," "Together," "The Power of Your Gift," and "The Power of One" are just a few of the ideas for annual reports.

 **TIPS AND TECHNIQUES**

Kivi Leroux Miller, president of EcoScribe Communications, on the website www.NonprofitAnnualReports.net addresses the use of a theme for an annual report.

Ms. Miller notes that a nonprofit may organize its annual report to reflect the organization's structure. For example, the annual report may have three sections to describe the three programs implemented in the past year. While she acknowledges that this may be one of the easiest ways to structure an annual report, she points out that it is not the most compelling way to tell the story of the organization.

Ms. Miller advocates for using a creative theme to organize an annual report and to tell the organization's story in a convincing way. To be effective, the theme for the year must flow throughout the document and it may also appear as the title on the report's cover.

The following are three themes that Ms. Miller suggests that any nonprofit can adapt for its annual report:

❶ *Results That Speak for Themselves.* Having people who greatly benefit from the work of an organization talk about the organization's accomplishments is much more effective than speaking about those accomplishments

TIPS AND TECHNIQUES (CONTINUED)

directly. The inclusion of personal profiles or anecdotes is a great way of showcasing how the organization's accomplishments are improving lives.

❷ *Step by Step*. Showing annual progress is important even if the goals of the organization will take years to actualize. The organization wants to showcase how all of its achievements, even small ones, are stepping stones along the path to something greater. Using text and graphics is an excellent way to highlight achievements, no matter how small.

❸ *Reaping What We Sow*. A creative approach is to use a garden analogy to describe the organization's accomplishments, from planting seeds (the origin of projects), to pulling weeds (overcoming obstacles), to harvesting the fruits as the organization's labor (enjoying its achievements).

Other resources are:

- *How to Write a Nonprofit Annual Report: The E-Book*, at www.NonprofitAnnualReports.net

  Chapters of the E-Book are also available at the website:
  - *Creative Themes for Nonprofit Annual Reports*

  - *Sharing Financial Information in Your Nonprofit Annual Report*

  - *Writing the Executive Message for a Nonprofit Annual Report*
- *Publishing the Nonprofit Annual Report: Tips, Traps, and Tricks of the Trade*, by Caroline Taylor.[1]

The annual report for a nonprofit organization will have many of the same components as the corporate annual report. A typical annual report for a nonprofit organization may include:

- Letter or report from chairperson of the organization's board of trustees

  When an organization has a foundation that raises private support for the organization, the letter or report may be from the chairperson of the foundation board rather than or in addition to the letter from the chairperson of the organization's board.

- Letter or report from organization's CEO

If the organization has a foundation, the letter or report may be from the president or executive director of the foundation rather than or in addition to the letter from the organization's CEO.

- Stories and photos about the organization
  - About the organization's mission
  - About the achievements of the past year
  - About those who contribute to the organization
  - About those served by the organization
- List of names of the organization's board members

  If the organization has a foundation, the names of the foundation board members may be listed rather than or in addition to the members of the organization's board.

- Group photo of the organization's and/or organization's foundation board members
- Financials
  - Balance sheet
  - Statement of revenue and expenses
  - Pie charts to illustrate sources of revenue and uses of revenue
  - Charts to demonstrate trends over period of five or more years
- Information on philanthropic support
  - Summary of gifts by purpose
  - Summary of gifts by source
  - Names and amounts of recognition levels, listed from highest to lowest level
  - List of names of donors by recognition levels, listed from highest to lowest level (Names within each recognition group are listed in alphabetical order.)
  - Listing of members of Legacy Society (New members during the past year may be distinguished from others with an asterisk or other

indicator and likewise those who are deceased may be indicated in a specific way.)

- Article about a person who has included the organization in her will during the past year

- List of those persons from which bequests or other gifts have been realized in the past year

- Suggested wording for including the organization in a person's will

- Information on becoming a member of the Legacy Society

- Other lists may include:

  - Memorial gifts listed by the name of the person in whose memory gifts were made

  - Tribute gifts listed by the name of the person in whose honor the gifts were made

  - Major sponsors of special events

  - Companies from whom matching gifts were received

Page after page of lists of names can be boring. To make the lists more interesting, many organizations break up the pages with photographs and text to highlight recognition events or significant donors or volunteers. Another way to add interest is to use quotes from those making contributions or from those who benefit from the contributions as design elements throughout the lists of names.

 TIPS AND TECHNIQUES

Listing of Names

The question of how to list names in an annual report, in a booklet, on a website, or on a recognition display is frequently asked. Many feel that the names should be listed in a consistent manner. Some think it should always be "Mr. and Mrs. Frank Smith" or "Dr. and Mrs. Charles Jones." Others will argue that the names should be "Sarah and Frank Smith" and "Margaret and Charles Jones."

The organization that is donor centered will ask donors how they wish to have their names listed. Donors have different preferences, and whereas having one style of listing may be aesthetically pleasing, organizations that want to have positive relationships with donors recognize that preferences vary from donor to donor. Age, gender, and other factors influence what people like and want.

Some couples want "Dr. and Mrs. William Smith," some want "Dr. William and Mrs. Sharon Smith," or it may be "Dr. Sharon and Mr. William Smith." You may also have "Drs. William and Sharon Smith." Younger women prefer "Ms." and older unmarried women want "Miss" as their titles. Some women prefer that a title not be used. A woman, especially a younger one, will often request being listed as "Susan Smith."

The way that women's names are listed when they are widowed or divorced varies. One etiquette expert (Crane and Co.) indicates that a widow keeps her husband's name and is listed as "Mrs. John Smith." *Etiquette Now*, another etiquette reference, says either "Mrs. John Smith" or "Mrs. Susan Smith" is acceptable. When the widow is older, the suggestion is to use "Mrs. John Smith" and, if the widow is younger, "Mrs. Susan Smith" is advised. Formal etiquette calls for a divorced woman to use "Mrs." followed by her first, maiden, and married names.

With the multitude of possibilities, the way to keep donors happy is to ask them for their preferences.

Many databases have a specific place (field) for "recognition name." If a database system does not have a field so designated, creating a field that can be used when lists of names are produced is a way to keep track of the donors' preferences.

If all pledge forms or response pieces have a space for the donor to print name or names as desired for recognition lists, the information can be captured on an ongoing basis and is ready when needed.

When completing a recognition display, which can involve a major investment of time and money, or developing a campaign report, sending a confirmation of the listings to donors can assure that donors know how their names will be listed. Asking a donor to review the way a name is listed when other wording is included, such as "In memory of Mr. and Mrs. James Johnson," is a good practice. Asking a donor how a name should be listed also provides an opportunity for the organization to say "thank you" to the donor again.

One method for getting a donor to approve the way a name will be listed is to prepare and send a statement to the donor that indicates the proposed

---

TIPS AND TECHNIQUES (CONTINUED)

wording for the display or report, asking the donor to approve the wording or make changes and to sign and return the form by a specific date. When the forms are returned, each can be filed in alpha order in a notebook or scanned for reference when a donor has a question in the future. The notebook or scanned documents can be helpful when a donor decides the wording on a plaque is not acceptable and has forgotten giving approval to the wording. Likewise, maintaining or scanning the pledge forms or other response devices that the donor completed to indicate the listing of the name can be helpful.

Electronic Reports on Giving

At the turn of the twentieth century, as development programs grew, the publication of the annual report required increasingly more resources, including staffing, time, and money. The cost of printing and postage continued to climb. Organizations were getting angry messages from their constituents saying the report was a waste of money. Volunteer groups were suggesting the elimination of the published report.

The concern was whether donors actually read the report. While offering listing in the annual report was perceived to be important to the donor, organizations challenged that premise and started looking at other ways to provide information to donors on giving. In conversations with donors, organizations learned that when donors received the report on giving, they looked for their own names in the lists and little more. Some donors may have placed an especially attractive report on the coffee table for several weeks, but many reports were being discarded almost immediately upon receipt. With the reality of the rising costs and shrinking interest in the report itself, organizations have carefully reevaluated the importance of the giving report.

Some organizations began moving away from the printed annual report and started using their websites as a way to distribute the information at a much lower cost. Some organizations discontinued the report on giving totally. Those who changed the format to electronic and those who eliminated the reports indicated that little change in giving occurred and that the cost savings were tremendous. In fact, education organizations have reported continued growth in participation and in amounts given following the elimination of the printed report.

Educational organizations have created websites for their gift reports that allow their supporters to select the content they want to see, whether it is the list of donors for a specific class or the summary report on sources of contributions. Some organizations report that donors who Google their own names like finding references to their names in the online donor lists. Other types of organizations, including medical centers, have created interactive reports on their websites that give various aspects of information depending on the person's interest.

After the giving report goes online, some organizations continue to provide printed copies to those who request it. In that case, the document is printed from the online version and is mailed to those individuals.

Having the giving list online has advantages beyond the cost savings. The practice is more environmentally responsible, corrections to name spellings and other edits can be made to the online report, and each year's report can be archived.

Many organizations will continue to use written publications to report on philanthropic giving in the years to come. However, the trend is to evaluate the written report and to explore other options to make information available at lower costs. The keys to assessing the value of the report are to evaluate the gifts that result directly from the report, and to discuss the report with donors. Both approaches give insights that can be used to make the best decision for the respective organizations.

Recognition Displays

Recognition displays come in all shapes and sizes. Organizations may have the more traditional bronze plaques where name plates are added each year, trees that have names on the leaves, displays made of Corian or acrylic, freestanding displays with waterfalls, or electronic kiosks that feature the names of the donors to the organization. Some displays are uniquely designed for the organization and others are more generic. Displays may be colorful, may feature photographs, and may use wood, tiles, or other materials. Displays may include video and audio.

Recognition displays are often called *donor walls*. They may include the names of those who supported a specific fundraising effort in the past or they may be updated each year with the names of annual donors.

IN THE REAL WORLD

Johns Hopkins Founders Wall

When Johns Hopkins Institutions, which include the university (its nine academic and research divisions, and numerous centers, institutes, and affiliated entities) and the Johns Hopkins Health System, decided to create a recognition display for its most generous donors, the decision on the level that would be recognized was creative and meaningful to the organization and its history.

Rather than recognizing those whose cumulative lifetime total for giving was $1 million or more, which was the popular starting point for major universities, Johns Hopkins decided to start at $7 million in recognition that in 1873, Mr. Johns Hopkins, a Baltimore businessman, made a bequest of $7 million to create the University and Hospital that bear his name today.

The planning of the Founders Wall began in December 2006, and the wall was completed more than two years later when it was unveiled on May 2, 2009, as a part of the celebration at the end of a major fundraising campaign.

Unlike most recognition displays that list names in alphabetical order, the Founders Wall at Johns Hopkins lists names in chronological order, according to the date at which the donors reached the $7 million mark, beginning with Johns Hopkins in 1873. (The year they reached the mark appears next to each name.)

The director of institutional donor relations for Johns Hopkins Institutions, Susan T. deMuth, managed the process that included a multitude of decisions that involved a number of individuals, including senior leadership of the organization. More than a year prior to the unveiling, deMuth developed a list of questions and answers for the members of the development team that described the details of the plan. These questions reflect the many issues that need to be considered when creating a recognition display for an organization, and cover the following topics:

- Location of the wall; the reasons for the chosen location; the persons who approved the location. *Location: On the northern end of the new Decker Quad—the welcoming gateway to Johns Hopkins—just in front of Garland Hall, facing Mason Hall on the Homewood campus. The location was approved by the Board of Trustees and the President.*

- The cutoff date for persons to reach the $7 million mark to be listed on the wall for the unveiling: *December 31, 2008.*

- Plans for the donors who reach the $7 million mark after December 31, 2008. *The names of the donors who meet the threshold would be added and an annual event would be held to unveil the newly engraved names.*

- The types of gifts that would be included in calculating the $7 million lifetime total. *Estate gifts would not be included—only planned gifts. Outright gifts, pledge payments, and all planned gifts where the assets have changed hands (i.e., an annuity) would be counted toward the $7 million mark.*

- The inclusion of both living and deceased donors. *In some displays the names of deceased donors are distinguished by an asterisk beside the name. At Johns Hopkins, neither an asterisk nor other distinction for the deceased was used.*

- The inclusion of foundations, corporations, and organizations as well as individuals and families. *All were included on the wall.*

- The listing of corporations whose names had changed or that were bought by other companies. *The current company was asked how to list its name.*

- Whether the amount of $7 million would be referenced on the wall. *No. A plaque refers to the transformational gifts, but does not include the exact amount.*

- The way anonymous donors would be handled. *Anonymous donors were not included in the chronological list. However, they were acknowledged on a second plaque. All anonymous donors were asked if they wished to be included on the wall by name.*

- The method for donors to approve the way their names would be listed. *Donors received a letter and a form. Institutional Donor Relations provided draft letters to the primary relations managers or gift officers for the donors. The primary relations manager worked with other development officers as needed and sent the letters to the donors. Institutional Donor Relations tracked and managed the letters that were sent.*

- The timeline for donors to approve the way their names would be listed.
  - *List of names final in March/April 2008*
  - *Letters to donors in May/June 2008*
  - *Deadline for confirmation by donors: October 1, 2008*
- The availability of materials on the Founders Wall. *In February 2008, the development offices received folders that included a brochure, artist's rendering, and guidelines.*
- The capacity of the wall for additional names and the length of time before the wall would reach its capacity. *Approximately 185 names and approximately 10 years of growth.*
- Size of the wall and the lettering. *The marble and brick wall is 36 inches tall and 104 feet long. The letters are one inch tall.*

Source: Susan T. deMuth, Director of Institutional Donor Relations for Johns Hopkins Institutions in Baltimore, Maryland.

The process of creating a donor display is one that takes time and requires attention to detail. To maximize the benefits of a donor display in a fundraising effort, getting started on the display should begin early. Showing potential donors a sketch of the donor display can be helpful in talking to them about their gifts and the recognition that they will receive.

Tips and Techniques

Donor Recognition Displays

Top Ten Do's and Don'ts

In planning a donor recognition display, experts suggest keeping the following things in mind:

❶ *Plan ahead*—including budget and time requirements. A donor wall cannot be a last-minute decision.

❷ Communicate upfront with those who will be involved in the project—board members, marketing department, even maintenance people—and keep them involved throughout the process.

❸ If a committee is put in charge of the project, be careful about its makeup. Make sure the group has real responsibility. Do not let them just sit and hear themselves talk.

❹ Do not order a cookie-cutter wall. The display's design should fit the organization's mission and programs and complement its architecture and aesthetics.

❺ Recognize donors in a way that will motivate them to continue giving and will inspire others to support the organization.

❻ Make the display attractive. The more eye-catching it is, the more attention it will receive.

❼ The donor wall conveys a message about the organization and should serve as an introduction to visitors, so make sure it is in a high-traffic area.

❽ If the donor recognition will be updated regularly, be sure the design permits changes and maintenance at minimal cost.

❾ Do not make the project's deadline your primary focus. Good decisions cannot be made when time is the most critical factor. If the wall will be on display for years to come, do not worry about its being completed in a few weeks. You can always display a mockup and tell donors and prospects to watch for the real thing.

❿ Do not schedule a dedication or special event with an unveiling until the display has actually been installed.

Source: Advancing Philanthropy, May 2005.

When planning a donor display, consideration should be given to the following:

- Location of the display

- Size of the space and lighting in the space

- Approximate number of names in each level of giving

- Need to add or rearrange names after the display is installed

- Ease of updating the display

- Cost of design, fabrication, installation, and maintenance of display

- Approval process for donors to confirm the way names are listed

- Schedule for the project

Additional information on recognition displays is included in this chapter and a list of vendors that create donor displays appears in Appendix B.

IN THE REAL WORLD

St. Christopher's Hospital for Children began serving children in Philadelphia, Pennsylvania, in 1875 as one of the first children's hospitals in the nation. When the hospital moved into a new facility in the early 1990s, recognizing its donors and celebrating the history of the hospital were important.

To recognize those donors making significant contributions to the capital campaign that secured support for the new building and for those making annual gifts of $1,000 or more, a large wall in the main entrance of the hospital was reserved. The recognition display was designed around a motif of marbles with colorful cat's-eyes in each recognition piece.

The center of the display featured three circles, one to recognize gifts of $1,000 to $4,999, one for gifts of $5,000 to $9,999, and one for gifts of $10,000 or more. The name of each donor (or couple) was in a half-sphere that resembled a large cat's-eye marble, which was positioned in the circle appropriate to the donor's annual gift size.

On the outside of the annual recognition, a series of square-shaped acrylic pieces were arranged. The name of a donor floated in each square and three colorful marbles were embedded in the lower-right corner of each clear acrylic piece. The squares were the same size, but the background material of each square was gold, silver, or bronze in color, according to the size of the donor's campaign contribution. Half of the recognition pieces were on each side of the annual recognition display.

The acrylic squares were repeated in the specific areas throughout the hospital where recognition was given for gifts exceeding a minimum amount. While these squares were larger than those in the central display and included wording, such as "In recognition of the generous support of [NAME OF DONOR]," the area recognition plaques were all the same size and the background color again indicated the size of the gift.

In addition to the display for annual and capital campaign donors, two other walls in the entrance to the facility were used to tell the history of the hospital. One was a timeline for the hospital and featured the various buildings in which the hospital had been located through the years. Photos and significant events

In the Real World (continued)

were used along the timeline to relate key events over the years. Included in the timeline were several very ornate plaques from the original hospital building. These plaques and many others were stored in the basement of the old hospital building for years and required some professional cleaning. Many of the plaques were much larger than the plaques that would be in place today.

On the other wall was a collage of the plaques from the old building and from the basement of the old building. They were cleaned and arranged at various depths across the wall in chronological order. The materials used to make the plaques, the typefaces, and the sizes of the plaques changed as the eye traveled from left to right. Most notable were a group of plaques made of aluminum during World War II.

Pictures of the individual plaques were taken and sent to the donors or their families when addresses could be found to let them know that their past generosity was not forgotten.

The unique recognition display, area recognition plaques, history wall, and collage of plaques from the past facilities were designed, created, and installed by Mitchell Associates in Wilmington, Delaware.

 Tips and Techniques

RecognitionArt, located in Sarasota, Florida, provides a planning tool on its website. The RecognitionMap Planning Tool asks some questions that are vital but often overlooked in the donor recognition planning process. The questions regard purpose, key dates, and the location, style, and budget for the project.

Key components include:

- Whether the display will be used to recognize donors who have already made contributions or will be a marketing tool to promote contributions
- The dates of the specific campaign and the anticipated date of an event or opening at the conclusion of the campaign
- Number of donors anticipated in specific dollar ranges
- Size and materials of the wall where the display will be located
- Type and texture of the display that would complement the facility
- Budget guidelines

Naming Opportunities

Another form of recognition is naming opportunities. The opportunity to have one's name on a fund, on a facility, or on a room or other space in a facility often provides the incentive for a person to make a gift of a specific amount. Just as with recognition gift clubs, the donor first needs to have the desire to support the organization. The naming opportunity may be the catalyst for the donor completing the gift at a specific time and may influence the size of the gift.

While naming opportunities historically were used mainly to recognize donors after they have made large gifts, naming opportunities are more often used today as a strategy for increasing gifts and for offering potential donors a way to step forward to take a leadership role in a fundraising effort. To define naming opportunities, an organization needs to determine those things that make a difference in the organization and package them to be attractive to an individual donor. For example, a donor to public television could make a gift to endow a fund to support the development of documentaries, to create a fund for new equipment, or to provide outreach services in the community. All of these could be naming opportunities. A donor who has an interest may be motivated to give more to fund one of these naming opportunities where the impact of the gift will be significant.

 IN THE REAL WORLD

A name other than the donor's may be the one used for recognition purposes. The person whose name is listed may be the person the donor wants to honor or memorialize. Following are two examples of this type of recognition.

❶ Cedars-Sinai Medical Center in Los Angeles, California, has created a "Baby Tribute Gallery." For a contribution of $5,000, a baby's name and birth date will be displayed on a colorful tile in a permanent display on a wall prominently located outside of the maternity unit at the hospital. The donor may choose an aqua, lavender, maize, periwinkle, green, or coral tile. Tiles for gifts in memoriam are designated with a heart. One of the pieces of information requested on the form that accompanies the contribution is whether the donor is parent, grandparent, other family, or friend.

❷ In June 2002, the recently built medical research building on the campus of the University of Massachusetts Medical School in Worcester, Massachusetts, was officially named the "Aaron Lazare Medical Research Building." The donor, entrepreneur and philanthropist Jack Blais and his wife, Shelly, whose name would have gone on the building by virtue of the size of their gift, asked that the research building be named to honor Dr. Aaron Lazare, who served as chancellor and dean of the UMass Medical School from 1991 to 2007. The Blais contribution of $21 million dollars for the construction of the building was at that time the largest gift from an individual in the history of the University of Massachusetts.

When donors make gifts to name buildings, rooms, or programs, the organization has both the opportunity and the responsibility to involve them in its work and to help them see the impact of their giving. When people give, they want to feel connected and that they belong. Having their names on physical places or on funds and programs gives them a sense of ownership. If donors feel a sense of ownership, they are definitely connected.

TIPS AND TECHNIQUES

An organization should include in its policies and procedures for naming what will occur when a named entity (i.e., a building, department, or other facility) has reached the end of its useful life or the original function of the named entity changes.

In policies and procedures, as well as in naming agreements, a provision may be made that a representative of the organization, such as the vice president for development, will make a good-faith effort to contact the donor or other interested parties to whom a plan shall be presented to continue the recognition of the naming gift.

Following are possible plans for continued recognition of the naming gift:

- Place memorabilia or original naming plaques in a place of honor in the successor building.
- Place memorabilia or original naming plaques in another specified location at the organization.

TIPS AND TECHNIQUES (CONTINUED)

- Create a special plaque in the general area where the designated space was located, marking it as the site of the former [NAME] Room (or Wing).
- Create a donor sign retirement wall and arrange the old plaques on that wall.
- Create a single plaque that lists all donors of spaces that were "lost" during renovation. (If named spaces transfer from one building to another building, as a result of renovation or relocation of a function, existing plaques may need to be updated to reflect the design of the new location.)
- When an organization moves from one location to another, set aside a special location where the plaques from the prior location can be displayed.

One of the simplest examples of a naming opportunity and its role in giving is a fundraising effort that offers those who contribute the opportunity to have their names on individual bricks in a walkway or in a wall. For example, the American Heart Association encouraged donors to purchase bricks engraved with their own names or the names of their choosing for the Heritage Brick Walk at the American Heart Association National Center in Dallas, Texas. Each brick required a contribution of a given amount.

In some cases, organizations offer bricks of different sizes with differing gift amounts. When new buildings are built, the selling of bricks for a walkway or a wall is a common way to secure funds of modest size from a large number of donors. Brick campaigns are used in gardens and atriums of various facilities, as well. The program is usually most successful when the donor will see the brick at a future time. A similar program may be used to put names on seats in a new auditorium. The emphasis in these programs is usually the enduring nature of the recognition.

The enduring nature of the recognition is also one of the disadvantages of the campaign for a brick walk or wall. If the donor has recognition on a brick or on a seat in an auditorium for decades, the donor has little incentive to continue to make annual gifts.

An organization may have a multitude of naming opportunities. These opportunities may include programs, departments, rooms, parts of buildings, and entire buildings. Many organizations have named physical spaces and programs to honor individuals for reasons other than philanthropic support. Those reasons may include outstanding service to the organization or other significant affiliations with the organization.

IN THE REAL WORLD

Recognition for major gifts often includes naming opportunities. The following is an example of a list of naming opportunities for a college:

Named endowed fund:	$10,000
Named program:	$25,000–$50,000
Named study lounge:	$50,000–$99,999
Residence room or suite:	$100,000–$149,999
Classroom or laboratory:	$150,000–$249,999
Endowed lectureship:	$150,000–$249,999
Lecture hall:	$250,000–$499,999
Auditorium:	$500,000–$799,999
Named endowed professorship:	$500,000–$799,999
Electronic teaching classroom:	$800,000–$999,999
Named endowed chair:	$1,000,000 and above
Entry foyer or courtyard:	$1,000,000 and above

Offering naming opportunities requires considerable thought and planning. There are ten steps in the process:

1. Conduct an inventory and create a list of existing named funds and named buildings, rooms, and other spaces. The list would include the following:

- Name of donor (or honoree); address and other contact information, if available

- Name and contact information for donor's (or honoree's) next of kin, if available (Information on next of kin is important when donor or honoree is deceased.)

- Amount of donation recognized (Or the reason for naming, if other than philanthropic support.)

- Date of donation recognized (Or date of decision to name for other reasons.)

- Fund or space named

- Type of display for recognition (Size, material, wording; photograph of recognition plaque or other display is suggested.)

- Location of plaques or other displays (When buildings are renovated, plaques are often removed and are put in storage spaces. Asking those in facilities management if plaques might be stored can result in finding older plaques that have been removed over time.)

2. Develop a plan for keeping the inventory current, including the process for indicating when a plaque or other display has been retired or relocated.

3. Develop policies and procedures for naming facilities and programs.

- The policies and procedures would include the purpose of the policies, naming criteria, and the process for establishing and getting approval for naming opportunities (see Exhibit 4.3).

4. Create a list of named gift opportunities and the appropriate gift amounts.

IN THE REAL WORLD

The naming policy for an organization may include the steps that are taken in developing the list of naming opportunities. Following is an example of that section in a naming policy for a college:

NAMING OPPORTUNITY DEVELOPMENT

❶ Proposals for naming opportunities will be developed by or in consultation with the vice president for college relations.

❷ The creation of naming opportunities for buildings and spaces is based on a financial analysis of the college's donor prospect base. The decision to name new construction or existing buildings will be considered on a case-by-case basis, subject to the following guidelines:

a. The preference for new construction is 50% of total cost of construction, but consideration will be given starting at 25% of the cost of the building.

c. The naming of an existing building will require a minimum of 25% of replacement cost at current value.

e. The naming of outdoor facilities with high visibility, such as courtyards, athletic fields, and quadrangles, will require a minimum gift of not less than 50% of construction costs or $250,000, whichever is greater.

❸ Using the established naming opportunity formula, the vice president for college relations, in consultation with the development staff and architectural staff, will develop gift ranges for naming opportunities. This includes the naming or renaming of all buildings, as well as interior and exterior spaces such as additions to buildings, parts of buildings, individual items or features within larger naming opportunities/spaces, terraces, courtyards, and fields.

❹ Naming opportunities will be consistent with the mission of the college and the purpose of the building. A clear distinction will be made between naming the building and naming the program housed in a building or space within a building. Since a program may not necessarily remain in a particular building, the college, in order to maintain its flexibility, will not approve the naming of a building that requires or implies that a particular program will remain there.

❺ In cases of naming or renaming existing buildings or spaces, the Office of Donor Relations will be responsible for researching the history and current use of the space to determine whether the site is available and the naming is appropriate. Donor Relations will maintain an inventory of named spaces in existing buildings and on the grounds.

❻ If the named building or space has reached its life expectancy, due to new construction or renovation, every consideration will be given to transferring the original name to the replacement space, either individually (''Smith Hall'') or in conjunction with the name of the new donor (''Smith-Jones Hall''). At the time of replacement, the original donor will have the first right of refusal to provide a new gift to continue the naming opportunity as a single entity.

❼ The campaign director is responsible for maintaining the inventory of naming opportunities for new construction and will keep development staff up-to-date on available naming opportunities.

8 Factors that may influence a naming opportunity include the donor's or honoree's relationship to the college, prominence/visibility of the space, and nature of gift assets (convertible to cash, multiyear pledge, or deferred).

Other provisions of a naming policy may include:

SOLICITATION PROCEDURES

1 Development staff will adhere to the policy of the college on questions of naming or renaming college facilities. All negotiations with donors will take into consideration the ultimate authority of the board of trustees or the president to make exceptions to the policy in special circumstances.

2 When discussing the naming of a physical space with a donor, development staff will refer to published naming opportunities, respecting the need of the college to build, renovate, and reallocate space according to its master plan.

3 All artists' renderings, construction models, or other plans should be identified as conceptual and not a literal depiction of what the facility will ultimately be. In negotiating with donors, development staff should ensure that donors understand that even when a space will be named for them, they do not control the details of construction, furnishings, and so forth.

4 The solicitor will notify the campaign director when a gift or signed pledge for a facility's naming opportunity has been secured. The campaign director will confirm whether the naming opportunity selected by the donor is available and will adjust the naming inventory accordingly.

RECOGNITION OF GIFTS

1 Recognition plaques will respect the style of existing signage throughout the college, as well as the architecture and design of the building in which the space is named, keeping in mind the desires and satisfaction of the donor. The Office of Donor Relations will be responsible for drafting wording for the recognition plaque and will oversee the ordering, production, and placement of the plaque.

2 In the case of new buildings or complete renovation of buildings, the cost of recognition devices will be included in the project budget. In cases of new plaques in preexisting spaces, the cost will be covered in the development/donor relations budget.

Source: Naming Policy for College Facilities, Saint Mary's College, Notre Dame, Indiana.

EXHIBIT 4.3

Naming Policies and Procedures for ABC Organization

1. Purpose

   1.1 These policies and procedures have been developed to ensure that those who support ABC Organization through contributions receive recognition that is appropriate, equitable, and consistent.

   1.2 ABC Organization welcomes the opportunity to name its buildings, rooms, and other facilities; its programs; and the funds to support its programs to honor those whose generous financial support has contributed to ABC's fulfillment of its mission.

   1.3 This policy sets forth the criteria and procedures for naming facilities and programs at ABC Organization.

   1.4 The term *facilities* includes buildings, rooms, interior spaces, open spaces, and all other areas owned, operated, or controlled by ABC Organization.

   1.5 The term *program* includes specific activities or units associated with fulfilling the mission of ABC Organization.

2. Naming Criteria

   2.1 ABC Organization will name facilities and programs as follows:

   - To recognize benefactors who have made substantial financial contributions to ABC Organization. The term *benefactors* includes individuals, corporations, and other organizations.

   - *Policy may include criteria for naming a facility or program to recognize individuals who have attained achievements of extraordinary and lasting distinction. Generally, these will be individuals who have direct, substantial, and active association with the organization.*

   - *Policy may include criteria for naming a facility or program to recognize an organization with historical and exceptional ties to the organization; an event or date significant in the organization's history; a place, program, or symbol with significant meaning for or ties to the organization.*

2.2 Contributions to name a facility or program shall be in accordance with the following minimum contribution amounts or an amount agreed on by the president and the Board of Trustees of ABC Organization.

2.2.1. Renaming ABC Organization requires an endowment of $75 million, of which at least three-quarters must be unrestricted to ensure flexibility for the overall enhancement of the organization.

2.2.2. Naming a new building under construction or an existing building under renovation requires a current gift of 50% or more of the construction cost announced at the beginning of the construction or renovation project.

- *The minimum contribution required for naming varies from organization to organization. The amount is usually at least 50% of the cost, but may be two-thirds, or 100%.*
- *Policy also may include minimum amounts for naming a center of excellence, institute, or program.*
- *Possible addition to this section:* ABC Organization encourages donors naming buildings to consider endowing the maintenance of the building to prevent the need for renovation and possible renaming.
- *Policy may distinguish between naming opportunities for significant gifts and the recognition afforded individuals who make gifts of smaller magnitude for tangible items. To recognize the gifts for the purchase of tangible items, the organization may attach small plaques bearing the names of the donors or the names of the person in whose honor or memory the gifts are made.*

2.3 A named building or facility (or part thereof or other designated space) will retain the name for the useful life of the building or facility (or part thereof or other designated space) or until the designated use or activity of the named building or facility (or part thereof or other designated space) changes unless (a) the building or facility (or part thereof or other designated space) is named for a term of years or (b) an exception is made by the Board of Trustees based on the recommendation of the president of ABC Organization. Replacement or substantial renovation will be considered the end of the useful life of the building or facility (or part thereof or other designated space).

2.3.1. Any proposal to rename a building or facility (or part thereof or other designated space) or to add a second name in recognition of a gift will be reviewed by the Board of Trustees.

2.3.2. When a building or facility (or part thereof or other designated space) is proposed for renaming, representatives of ABC Organization will make all reasonable efforts to inform in advance the original donors or honorees and their immediate families. A plan for continued recognition of the naming gift will be presented to the donors or honorees and their immediate families. Following contact with the donors or honorees and their immediate families, or, if no interested parties can be identified, the president of ABC Organization, in consultation with the chair of the Board of Trustees and the chair of the Development Committee, may approve the recognition plan proposed by the vice president of Development.

- *Another way that this may be written:* If the named building or space has reached its life expectancy, due to new construction or renovation, every consideration will be given to transferring the original name to the replacement space, either individually (''Smith Hall'') or in conjunction with the name of the new donor (''Smith-Jones Hall''). At the time of replacement, the original donor will have first right of refusal to provide a new gift to continue the naming opportunity as a single entity.

2.3.3. In all cases, ABC Organization will provide tasteful and appropriate recognition of past philanthropy while honoring those whose more recent gifts are integral to the future of the mission of ABC.

2.4 An agreement to name a building or facility (or part thereof or other designated space) for a benefactor must be in writing and signed by the benefactor and ABC Organization. The agreement will include provisions addressing the following:

2.4.1. That the name of the building or facility (or part thereof or other designated space) exists only for the useful life of the facility or a term of years approved by the Board of Trustees, as applicable, unless an exception has been approved pursuant to 2.3, above. Replacement or substantial renovation of the building or facility (or part thereof or other designated space) will be considered the end of the useful life of the building or facility (or part thereof or other designated space).

2.4.2. That the name may be changed if a benefactor ceases payment on a pledged donation for naming the building or facility (or part thereof or other designated space), after a pro rata period of time that reflects the number of pledge payments made, given the estimated useful life of the building or facility (or part thereof or other designated space) or the term of years covered by the naming agreement, as applicable.

2.4.3. The types of signage, including logos and images if applicable, that will be used by ABC Organization in connection with the naming. Signage must be consistent with the guidelines for signage for the organization.

2.4.4. In the case of corporate donors, the circumstances under which the name of the building or facility (or part thereof or other designated space) and related signage may be changed in the event that a corporate name change occurs as a result of a corporate action, such as a merger.

- *Many organizations include in their policies that any naming for a corporate donor will be limited to a defined number of years.*

3. General Provisions

3.1 If at any time following the approval of a naming, circumstances change substantially so that the continued use of that name may compromise the public trust, the president and general counsel shall be consulted regarding future action.

- *Other ways this provision may be worded include:*
  - Notwithstanding any other provisions of this policy, no naming will be approved or (once approved) continued that will call into serious question the public respect of ABC Organization.

- ABC Organization reserves the right to withdraw recognition and naming agreements should such withdrawal be deemed in the best interest of ABC Organization.

3.2 No name will be approved that will imply ABC Organization's endorsement of a partisan political or ideological position or of a commercial product. This does not preclude a naming with a name of an individual or company that manufactures or distributes commercial products.

3.3 ABC Organization reserves naming opportunities for current gifts. ABC Organization will treat estate and planned gifts with naming elements as a request. ABC will honor the request at the final distribution of the gift when the name is appropriate and where the gift meets the minimum funding for the named opportunity at the time of distribution. ABC reserves the right to decline gifts with naming restrictions.

3.4 The authority to name does not extend to the decision to erect a building, establish a program, or otherwise proceed with that which is being named. Such decisions will be made on the basis of the usual criteria established by and in the manner described by the Board of Trustees.

Each organization should develop a list of standards for named recognition and should update the list on a periodic basis.

The standards for named gift opportunities will vary from organization to organization and the minimum amounts for naming rights will change over time just as the cost of everything increases.

When an organization prepares its list, talking with similar organizations to determine the standards for naming at those organizations can be helpful. However, factors beyond type and size of organization will come into play.

The maturity of the overall development program may be a factor in defining minimum amounts for naming opportunities. If the development program is relatively new, the minimum amounts for naming may be lower than those for an organization with a more mature program. For example, some colleges and universities may require gifts of $500,000 for a named professorship and $1 million for an endowed chair. However, at Yale University, with its long tradition of fundraising, endowing a professorship requires a minimum gift of $3 million and a deanship requires a gift of $5 million.

Assigning naming amounts to various spaces requires consideration of additional factors, including the overall size of the fundraising initiative for those spaces. The key factors to consider in assigning amounts to spaces are:

- *Visibility.* How many people will see the space? Who will see the space? For example, a conference room is more visible than a staff lounge.

- *Size of the space.* How large is the space? For example, if two spaces have comparable visibility, the larger of the two would have a higher gift amount associated with it.

- *Use of the space.* Is the space integral to the mission of the organization? For example, in a hospital, an operating room may have a higher gift amount than the workroom for the nursing staff.

5. Develop strategies for using named-gift opportunities in cultivating and soliciting gifts.

6. Define a process for tracking those gift opportunities and determine who will track them. Categories or status may include:

- *Reserved.* When staff determines a specific opportunity is appropriate for a prospect that is being cultivated, the opportunity may be reserved for that prospect for a defined period of time.

- *Pending.* When a specific gift opportunity has been offered to a prospect for consideration and the prospect's decision is pending.

- *Confirmed (or funded).* When a donor has made a commitment to make a gift for a specific named-gift opportunity, the opportunity is confirmed or funded. (A gift agreement that defines the specific details of the gift and the naming should be developed and signed by the donor and the organization at this point.)

While many organizations are tempted to keep the information on named-gift opportunities in a spreadsheet, maintaining the information on the development database is advised. A list of gift opportunities and the corresponding amounts can be created in the database and used as prospects are cultivated and solicited.

7. Define the steps and the persons responsible for:

- Logistics involved in creating, ordering, and installing signage
- Coordinating publicity, such as news releases and feature stories, when the gift is made and when the naming occurs
- Planning any events, such as a ribbon cutting or unveiling of a plaque

8. Implement the strategies defined.

9. Evaluate the strategies and revise as needed.

10. Update the list of opportunities periodically.

When developing naming opportunities, consideration should be given to the number of opportunities provided. If naming is available for gifts of every size and recognition plaques are in every room, hallway, and other available spaces, the advantage of naming opportunities is lost. Naming opportunities should provide opportunities for donors to step up to make significant gifts and the number of naming opportunities should be small enough to make the *privilege* of naming a space special.

IN THE REAL WORLD

For many years, museums, zoos, libraries, hospitals, and other nonprofit organizations carried names that reflected where they were located or what they did. If a nonprofit had another name, it usually belonged to an individual patron, a particularly common occurrence at universities.

However, in recent years, the names of companies are appearing frequently at nonprofit organizations. In the *New York Times*, on February 18, 2001, Julie Edelson Halpert writes in her article "Dr. Pepper Hospital? Perhaps, for a Price; Company Names Are Busting Out All Over," that "Now, the nonprofit sector is starting to go the way of sports arenas, adopting corporate names for big donations." The article addresses the reasons for this change and explains that companies view their support of nonprofits as an alternative means of advertising. Associating a company's name with a nonprofit helps strengthen the image of the company, building loyalty among its employees and with the public. Mattel, the maker of Fisher Price, Hot Wheels, and Barbie, contributed $25 million to the Children's Hospital at UCLA to put its name on the hospital in 1998.

The trend continues to grow and the price for having a company's name on a high-visibility organization continues to increase. For example, the Columbus Children's Hospital was renamed the Nationwide Children's Hospital after receiving a $50 million gift from Nationwide Foundation in 2006. The Nationwide Foundation is an independent corporation in Columbus, Ohio, that is funded by the Nationwide Companies and is dedicated to making strategic philanthropic investments to meet the most critical needs in the communities where Nationwide associates, agents, and their families live and work.

Concern has been expressed about the possible influence of corporations on nonprofit organizations. Andrew Hagelshaw, executive director of the Center for Commercial-Free Public Education in Oakland, California, expressed his concern about putting a company name on a nonprofit, saying it "takes a public space and uses it inappropriately to advertise a brand-name product to the community."

Alex Molnar, professor of education in the division of Educational Leadership & Policy Studies and director of the Education Policy Studies Laboratory at Arizona State University, noted that putting the name of a corporation on a building was quite different from and far worse than naming a building for an individual. The distinction, according to Professor Molnar, is that an individual is not interested in promoting a particular product or service. He views naming an organization or its building for a corporation as "no longer a personal statement of honor, but a commercial decision to promote."

Ann Bitter, former president of the Minnesota Children's Museum, said she felt that children were confused when the content of an exhibit was connected with the purpose of a for-profit organization. She added that "the line between for-profit and nonprofit has blurred" and said that nonprofit organizations need to be cautious when they agree to corporate sponsorship because managing the balance between the content and the commercial can be a "slippery slope."

But advocates say that corporate sponsorship can work given proper safeguards. Many organizations are making the new trend work for their programs.

Recognition Events

Having an event where donors can be recognized can contribute to the donor's feeling of being appreciated. In addition, recognition events provide donors with the opportunity to become more engaged and involved in the organization. Donors have a chance to meet others associated with the organization, including board members, administrators, other donors, and, on occasion, those served by the organization. For example, at educational institutions, donors who have established endowed scholarship funds often have the opportunity at recognition events to meet the students who have received the respective named scholarships. Recognition events also provide the development staff with opportunities to introduce donors to key individuals and to discuss the organization and its future plans.

 IN THE REAL WORLD

Christopher J. Krizek, executive director at All Saints Health Care Foundation in Racine, Wisconsin, while in a position with a health-care organization in another area, developed an annual event for members of the Legacy Society that was held on Arbor Day.

Based on the following quote, a tree-planting ceremony was the setting for recognition of those who had made planned gifts.

> The true meaning of life is to plant trees, under whose shade you do not expect to sit.
>
> —Nelson Henderson (Adaptation of a Greek proverb)

Those individuals who had notified the organization of bequest intents or who had made other planned gifts were invited to the event. The group would go to a site on the campus where a hole in which to plant a tree was pre-dug. Several leaders, including the organization's president and the board's chair, would say a few words about the significance of the ceremony and students from a local elementary school were invited to plant the tree in honor of the members of the Legacy Society.

Following the presentation and the tree planting, the students and the members of the Legacy Society shared light refreshments. A plaque was placed at the base of the tree explaining its significance in recognition of the Legacy Society.

Other features of the event included a master gardener speaking on the meaning of Arbor Day and a local nursery donating small trees for the students to plant at their homes.

The objectives for the event were twofold. First, the ceremony was a thank-you for and recognition of the commitment of the Legacy Society members to the mission of the organization. In essence, the event was an acknowledgment that these individuals were planting trees under which they did not expect to sit or making gifts from which they did not expect to derive benefit, but that would benefit future generations. The second objective was to teach the young students about the importance of philanthropy in society and the significant role they could play in the future.

Many organizations have events exclusively for those who make gifts at or above a specific level. However, the limits defined by the Internal Revenue Service for *insubstantial* goods and services comes into play when recognition events are "benefits" for giving. (In 2007, the goods and services were considered insubstantial if the fair market value of the benefits received did not exceed the lesser of 2 percent of the payment or $89.)

With the IRS requirements in mind, organizations have changed the way recognition events are conducted. For many organizations, receiving the

 TIPS AND TECHNIQUES

Honorcraft Inc., located in Stoughton, Massachusetts, offers a checklist for organizations that are developing donor recognition plans. The company refers to its checklist and questions as "Your Guide to a Stress-Free Experience" and in its introduction points out that donor recognition "can be a very rewarding—and a very challenging experience." Organizations are advised that preparation is the key to a smooth process and that preparation needs to start as soon as possible by answering some important fundamental questions.

TIPS AND TECHNIQUES (CONTINUED)

Following are the suggested questions in the guide:

☐ Goals

What do I want my donor recognition program to achieve?

What, if anything, has been promised to the donors?

☐ Scope of the program

How many elements will my program have?

- Central recognition display

- Area recognition plaques

- Mementos

- Printed materials

- Others

☐ The team

Who will help me make this happen? Have I contacted them?

- Development staff members

- Campaign consultant

- Administrators

- Facilities planners

- Architects

- Designers

- Board members, past and present

- Donors

- Volunteers

☐ Names

Will I need to add more names on a regular basis?

Will I need additional room on the display to add names?

Can my staff add those names easily and efficiently?

Have I double- and triple-checked the names? Dates? Headings? Have I had somebody else check the names?

Will I need to and, if so, be able to revise the names already on the plaque?

Is the material flexible enough to allow changes?

Will the changes affect or disrupt the design of the display?

☐ Placement

Exactly where will the display be located?

What is the lighting in that location?

Will additional lighting be needed?

Is construction going on around that location?

☐ Fabrication

Am I prepared to confirm any changes in the schedule?

Have I prepared the area for installation?

☐ Approval

Do I have an approved concept?

Have I specified all of these items for approval?

- Dimensions

- Materials

- Colors

- Finishes

- Copy

- Mechanical items

Have I finalized costs?

Have I arranged for fabrication?

Do I fully understand what we have approved?

Does it cover our short-term and long-term goals?

Who must approve the budget? The placement? The list of donors? The design?

Can I make all of the decisions, or are committees involved?

How long do these committees take with their decisions?

Am I prepared to guide a committee into making the right decision?

If not, whom can I enlist to help me persuade the committee?

☐ Budget

What is my budget for the program?

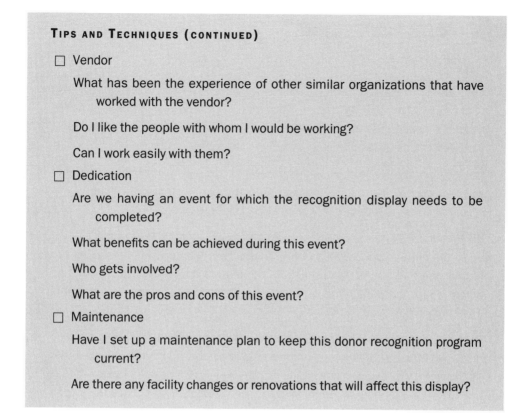

invitation to the event is the benefit for the donor and those attending are paying to cover the fair market value of the food and beverage. In this case, the organization needs to have an extraordinary event that donors want to attend. Again, creativity is the key to making the event successful. Choosing interesting venues can add appeal to the event. For example, an organization may ask a donor, who is giving at the minimum amount or above, to host the event in the donor's home or yard. Another interesting element might be the program for the event, such as a renowned speaker, author, or explorer.

Events may be entirely social or they may be educational about some facet of the organization. A hospital may have a physician speak on a new program or on research that is being conducted. A social service organization may have an authority speak on a topic of particular interest to the donors.

Some organizations have developed events where the cost per person is insignificant. For example, a religious organization may hold a special religious

IN THE REAL WORLD

The Hudson Hoagland Society was established in 1985 to recognize individuals who make annual gifts of $1,000 or more to the Worcester Foundation for Biomedical Research at the University of Massachusetts Medical School in Worcester, Massachusetts.

Each spring, the Hudson Hoagland Society convenes to hear from a speaker who "embodies the spirit of exploration, the same spirit that drives basic research." The following guest speakers have appeared:

Sir Edmund Hillary, mountaineer and explorer, recounted the events leading up to the day in 1953 when he and Sherpa mountaineer Norgay became the first climbers known to have reached the summit of Mount Everest. He also talked about his commitment to the Sherpa people of Nepal following his ascent to Everest.

Peter Hillary, mountaineer, explorer, and son of Sir Edmund Hillary, discussed his experiences, including two summits on Everest, including one with his father as the first father-and-son duo to achieve the feat, an 84-day trek across Antarctica to the South Pole, and the first-ever ascent, which he and two companions completed, of the Shackelton Glacier, establishing a new route to the South Pole.

Eugene Kranz, former NASA director of mission operations, discussed his role as leader of the "Tiger Team" who brought the Apollo 13 crew safely back to Earth in April 1970.

Brian Jones, British balloonist, recounted his history-making adventure as co-pilot of the Breitling Orbiter 3 as one of the first men successfully to circumnavigate the globe in a hot-air balloon.

Phil Buck, explorer, shared the details of his planned 10-year expedition to traverse the world's oceans, and discussed the ancient art of reed ship construction and his amazing journey from the coast of Chile to Easter Island, the initial leg of the expedition. Buck's is the first-known reed ship expedition to circumnavigate the globe, supporting the theory that civilizations of antiquity could have crossed ocean expanses in primitive boats.

Robert D. Ballard, Ph.D, oceanographer, renowned for undersea discoveries of shipwrecks, including the *Titanic*, *Bismarck*, and *Lusitania*, reported on his expedition to comb the floor of the Black Sea in search of artifacts that would support the theory that a cataclysmic flood struck the region some 7,000 years ago, a possible basis of the Biblical story of Noah and his Ark.

Michael Novacek, senior vice president, curator of paleontology, and provost of science at the American Museum of Natural History, talked about his book, *Dinosaurs of the Flaming Cliffs*, the story of six years of expeditions into the Gobi Desert of Mongolia. The team he led unearthed a trove of dinosaur skeletons, eggs, and embryos and the fossils of early mammals, some new to science.

Jean-Michel Cousteau, explorer, environmentalist, and son of Jacques Cousteau, discussed the changes needed to preserve the beauty and abundance of the oceans and the tropical coral reefs and showed videos, including a world-premiere look at scenes from his film about the country's marine sanctuaries.

service for its donors. For other organizations, the separate recognition event has been replaced by giving recognition to donors at other nonexclusive events that are already scheduled, such as annual meetings.

Other events that provide opportunities for recognition include ground-breakings, ribbon cuttings, and open houses. At the time of the groundbreaking

A religious organization sponsored a mass for its benefactors to recognize them for their generosity and support:

Mark your calendar!

Please join us for the

Sisters of Mercy

BENEFACTORS' MASS

Followed immediately by Brunch

In the ABC gymnasium

Sunday, October 12, 2000

10:00 A.M.

The ABC Motherhouse Chapel

for a new building, the capital campaign may be ready to move from its quiet phase to its public phase. If so, the event is an excellent opportunity to give public recognition to the leadership donors to the campaign.

Even if the organization is not ready to move into the public phase of its campaign, the groundbreaking can still provide a recognition opportunity. Following the groundbreaking, the organization may host a reception for the leadership donors and the board of trustees as a recognition event for those donors who have made it possible to break ground.

When a building opens, organizations often have ribbon cuttings and open houses to mark the occasion. If possible, the organization should have its recognition displays and area recognition plaques in place for the opening of a facility. If the display and the plaques are not in place, creating attractive facsimiles of the display and the plaques and putting them in place can be meaningful to donors. Donors not only want to see the recognition themselves, they want others who attend the event to see the display and plaques. Some organizations conduct a pre-event for donors and their families to see the facility and the recognition display and plaques prior to the ribbon cutting and open house. By holding a pre-event, the organization gives special recognition to its donors. The other advantage of the pre-event is that the number in attendance is less than at the public event and donors can be given special attention by key persons.

As with all special events, the objectives for each event should be clearly defined and an evaluation should be conducted to determine whether the event met its objectives. Having volunteers involved in the planning of these events is a strategy for getting donors involved and engaged. Through their involvement, the volunteers can see the value the organization places on recognition and the importance of leadership giving.

Summary

Recognition is based on the human need to feel a sense of belonging and acceptance by others. Recognizing a donor goes beyond saying "thank you" and makes others aware of a donor's contribution to an organization. By recognizing those who have given, an organization expresses its gratitude to a donor in a public way and encourages others to follow the example of those who have given. Recognition is provided in a number of ways, including listing names in publications, on websites, and in recognition displays on walls in a facility. Buildings, rooms, stadiums, libraries, and specific programs and funds are often named in recognition of a donor's generosity, and press releases, celebrations, and other events are focused on the recognition of a person who has made a significant contribution to an organization.

Individuals have different views of recognition and have expectations that vary from person to person. While some want as much recognition as they can possibly get, others want an element of anonymity.

Recognition for philanthropic support includes recognition gift clubs that identify a group of persons with similar characteristics, such as size of gift, constituency type, or common interest or affinity, and provide public acknowledgment of their support. Organizations also offer recognition by listing names of donors in an annual report, sometimes called a "report on giving," by offering opportunities for donors to have their names on buildings, rooms, programs, and funds, by listing the names of donors in wall displays in the organization's facilities, and by hosting events specifically for donors.

Note

1. Jossey-Bass, San Francisco, Copyright 2002.

CHAPTER 5

Recognition: Part 2

After reading this chapter, you will be able to:

- Define the recognition gift club and its characteristics.
- Create, expand, and enhance recognition gift clubs.
- Plan, implement, and evaluate a recognition gift club program.
- Develop guidelines for the recognition gift club program.
- Know IRS standards for recognition.

More on Recognition Gift Clubs

Creating gift clubs is a way in which many organizations provide recognition to their donors. A gift club is a recognition program for a group of donors with similar characteristics. The common thread may be the level of giving, the type of giving, the frequency of giving, the constituency type, or a specific interest or affinity.

The three most common recognition gift club programs are:

1. *Annual giving.* Recognition is provided based on the giving during a one-year period. The recognition may be based on the total of all gifts during that timeframe or on a defined type or types of gifts over the 12-month period.

2. *Cumulative lifetime giving.* Donors receive recognition for the total of all gifts, possibly with some exclusions, to an organization over time.

3. *Planned giving.* Recognition is extended to those who have included a provision for the organization in their wills or other estate plans and/or those who have made planned gift arrangements, such as charitable gift annuities, charitable remainder trusts, pooled income funds, and charitable lead trusts.

Many other recognition gift club programs exist (see Exhibit 5.1), but those for annual, cumulative lifetime, and planned giving are the most prevalent in organizations of all types and sizes.

EXHIBIT 5.1

Categories of Gift Clubs

By Constituency or Specific Interest

- Young alumna or alumnus; GOLD (Graduates of the *Last Decade*)
- Person born at hospital
- Interested in outdoors (Public Broadcasting)
- Employee
- Youth (age XX or younger)

By Type of Gift or Frequency of Giving

- Monthly giving: automatic monthly donations from credit cards or checking accounts
- Years of giving
- Years of consecutive giving
- Gift every year since graduation
- Bequest intents
- Planned gifts, regardless of amount

By Amount of Gift

- Total of unrestricted annual giving
- Total of all giving in a 12-month period
- Lifetime total giving
- Irrevocable gifts (with minimum amount stated)

Creating a Gift Club Program

An organization may have just one gift club, but is likely to have more than one club in its overall recognition program. An organization should determine the number of gifts clubs that are optimal for its program. Each gift club should provide donors with meaningful recognition and should encourage giving. Having one or two gift clubs and making them meaningful for donors is better than having a dozen gift clubs that are not utilized well to build relationships with donors. The organization that begins with one or two gift clubs can use what it learns from its initial experience in adding other gift clubs as deemed appropriate.

Before beginning a gift club program, researching what other organizations have done and asking questions about their programs can provide valuable information. The organization should learn what others have found successful, as well as what others wish they had done differently in the beginning.

IN THE REAL WORLD

To establish some recognition gift club groups, an organization may need to identify those who share a common bond before asking for the gift.

In the following article, Mellissa E. Gayer, Director of Development at Evangelical Community Hospital in Lewisburg, Pennsylvania, recounts how the hospital identified a group of potential donors by establishing a common link.

HOSPITAL LOOKS FOR EVAN BABIES

Do you know where you were born? Can you recall the name of the hospital where you first entered the world? Most people can tell you right away because there is a strong connection between their identity and their birthplace.

At Evangelical Community Hospital (ECH) in Lewisburg, Pennsylvania, the Development Department worked extensively with the Public Relations Department to identify people in the community who have a connection to the hospital.

IN THE REAL WORLD (CONTINUED)

In the spring of 2006 the hospital kicked off a community-wide marketing campaign to promote the hospital and to identify those people in the community who were born at Evangelical.

The purpose of the campaign was to:

- Form a bond with those who were born at ECH.
- Promote Evangelical's name in the community.
- Attract new visitors to the hospital website.
- Encourage Evan Babies to "give back."

As part of the campaign, radio ads broadcast Brahms' lullaby followed by adults and children taking turns saying, "I'm an Evan Baby!" Next a sweet child's voice asks, "Are you an Evan Baby, too?"

Listeners were asked to call the hospital or visit the website to register if they were born at Evangelical Hospital. Evan Baby ads were placed in the newspaper and registration forms were placed throughout the hospital and other local areas including the local shopping mall and physician offices. Billboards depicted cute babies with the tagline, "Are you an Evan Baby?"

Those who registered received a letter from the hospital's CEO along with a free gift (a baby footprint magnet with "I'm an Evan Baby!" printed on it). A contest was held to choose the oldest, youngest, most famous, most unique, person living farthest away, and the family with the most Evan Babies. A local obstetrician provided prizes for the winners. Winners were featured in the newspaper and in the hospital's newsletter.

The community response was huge. More than 2,200 people responded by letting the hospital know about their Evan Baby status. Many mothers and grandmothers registered their children and grandchildren. One Evan Baby was living in Thailand and found the Evan Baby registration form on the hospital's website.

For the second phase of the marketing campaign, several Evan Babies were selected and were featured in radio, newspaper, and billboard ads. One newspaper ad showed a happy grandmother and her five Evan grandbabies gathered around her, while another ad featured a physician who delivered her own granddaughter at Evan. A second wave of Evan Baby names were collected during this campaign.

Evan Babies ages 18 and older and their parents and grandparents were added to the hospital's database so they would receive regular hospital updates, news of events, and opportunities to support the hospital. By establishing a connection between the individual and the place of his or her birth, the hospital hopes to establish a bond that will last a lifetime.

The group is also a source of potential donors and when Evan Babies give to the hospital, they will be recognized as Evan Babies. In this case, the recognition group for giving was used as the vehicle to identify potential donors.

Regardless of the type of gift clubs, the steps for creating them are the same. Basically, establishing each gift club in the program involves six steps (see Exhibit 5.2):

1. Defining criteria for membership. The first step in establishing a gift club is determining the criteria for membership. Criteria vary from organization to organization and no set of criteria is right or wrong. Each organization decides its own criteria for membership based on the organization's culture, history, and goals. For some organizations, gift club recognition levels may begin at $50, while other organizations may begin their recognition levels at $1,000 or more and may include gift club levels as high as a million dollars or more.

EXHIBIT 5.2

Six Steps to Establishing a Recognition Gift Club

1. Define criteria for membership.
2. Develop benefits for membership.
3. Choose an appropriate name.
4. Develop a plan.
5. Implement the plan.
6. Evaluate the program.

TIPS AND TECHNIQUES

Announcing a New Recognition Gift Club/Society

The following letter is an example of one method that may be used to announce the creation of a new recognition gift society. Depending on the number of persons who qualify for the new recognition gift club program, which begins at lifetime giving of $1 million, phone calls from the president prior to the letter or calls to follow up the president's letter from members of the development staff who had relationships with the individuals may also be used.

If the volume of persons who qualified at all levels was too large to make personal calls from the president feasible, perhaps the president should call all of those at the $10 million level. The call would provide yet another opportunity for the president to say "thank you" to the donor.

May 5, 20XX

Name

Address

City, State, ZIP

Dear_____:

On March 14, 2009, during the celebration of the 70th Anniversary of the founding of ORGANIZATION XYZ, we will be announcing the creation of the XYZ Lifetime Giving Societies, which recognize individuals and organizations whose contributions over the past 70 years total one million dollars or more. The societies reflect all gifts (current, planned, and in-kind) to XYZ. The program will continue in perpetuity and others will be recognized as their giving reaches this significant threshold.

Three levels of recognition have been established:

- The Founder's Society—$10 million
- The President's Society—$5 million
- The 1938 Society—$1 million

Our research indicates that your lifetime giving in support of XYZ qualifies you for recognition in the *1938 Society*. We are extremely grateful for your generous support and welcome you as a charter member of this special group of individuals and organizations that have been essential to our success in our first 70 years. Your leadership in giving is an inspiration to us and we look forward to a continued relationship with you in the days ahead.

We would like to list your name in recognition of your generosity in our publications and on our website. Recognizing you and the other members of these societies will give others an example to follow and will communicate the importance of philanthropy to XYZ. Please complete and return the enclosed form to make sure that we list your name as you wish.

Thank you for your generous support over the years. You have made a difference in the lives of those served by ORGANIZATION XYZ.

Sincerely,

John A. Doe

President

Answering the following questions will provide direction in determining the criteria for membership.

- What is the key factor for qualification for membership in this gift club?
  - Does the donor need to make a gift or gifts of a certain magnitude? If so, what is the amount required for membership? Over what period of time?
  - Does the donor need to make a specific type of gift, such as bequest intent or planned gift? If so, what types of gifts will be included?
  - Does the donor need to belong to a specific constituency, such as physicians or alumni of the past decade? If so, what groups are included?
- Who will be included as members of the gift club?
  - Will the membership be limited to individuals?

    Many annual giving recognition programs are limited to individuals. Most will also include the persons who direct gifts from family foundations or donor-advised funds to the organization. A contribution from a small business may be handled in a similar way if the gift is clearly at the direction of the owner of the business. Making that option available is at the discretion of the organization.

- Will membership include spouses and partners?

    Most organizations include the donor and the donor's spouse or partner as members for a gift of a certain magnitude.

- Will businesses, corporations, foundations, and/or organizations be included?

    Some organizations include businesses and corporations in the same recognition program for annual gifts as that for individuals. Others have a separate giving program for businesses and corporations. The decision is one the organization makes on the basis of the goals and objectives of the program. Whether organizations, associations, and foundations are included in annual recognition gift club programs is a matter for the organization to decide.

- For gift clubs where magnitude or type of giving is the basic criteria for membership, what gifts will be included in determining membership?

    - Will support for special events count toward the amount needed for membership? If so, will the full amount be counted or will the amount that exceeded the fair market value of the tangible benefits that the donor received be used?

    - Will corporate matching gifts that are made by the donor's employer be counted toward the donor's gift club membership?

    - Will the value of in-kind contributions be included? If so, how will that value be determined?

    - Will recognition be given at the time of a pledge or when the gift is paid?

- For gift clubs for cumulative lifetime giving, what gifts will be included in determining membership?

    - Will the value of planned gifts and/or bequest intents be included in the cumulative lifetime total? If so, what amount will be used? Face value, future value, or other value?

- If the accuracy of development records prior to a specific date are incomplete or questionable in their accuracy, will the organization set a specific date and count only gifts made from that time forward in the cumulative lifetime total? What will that date be and how will it be communicated to donors?

- For gift clubs for bequest intents and/or planned gifts, what gifts will be included in determining membership?

  - Will a minimum-size gift be required for membership?

    - If so, how will membership be handled for bequest intents where the amount cannot be determined, such as those where a percentage of the residue of the estate is bequeathed to the organization?

    - If so, how will planned gifts, such as charitable gift annuities and charitable trusts, be valued? Face value, future value, or other value?

  - To qualify for membership, what type of documentation, if any, will donors making provisions in their wills be required to provide?

2. Developing benefits for membership. The next step in establishing a gift club is developing the benefits for membership. The benefit that is most frequently offered for membership in a gift club is the donor's name listed in publications and/or in a recognition display. Other benefits may include invitations to events, access to the resources of the organization, and/or conversations and/or gatherings with the organization's administrative and volunteer leadership.

IN THE REAL WORLD

"Membership Has Its Privileges"

Organizations, whether commercial or nonprofit, may call what is given in return for membership benefits, *privileges or rewards*, but basically they are the tangible and intangible "carrots on the end of the stick" that are used to entice people to become members of a defined group.

As development programs at nonprofits have matured, the trend has been to move from the tangible to the intangible, from the item the organization gives to

IN THE REAL WORLD (CONTINUED)

the experience that the donor shares with the organization or those affiliated with the organization.

The intangible benefit of "satisfaction" or "pleasure" for the donor may be described as a benefit in words such as the following:

The satisfaction of knowing you are making a difference in the lives of [*those served by the organization*].

Following are other benefits, privileges, or rewards that organizations provide to those in their recognition gift clubs:

- Special membership card
- Car decal featuring name of club
- Invitations to XYZ Society Weekend, a weekend of activities that focus on recognition of members of the recognition gift club
- Access to members-only section of website
  - Discussion forums
  - Photo gallery
- Special newsletter (or other publication) specifically for the ABC Circle, with appropriate name such as *The ABC Circle Gazette*
- Advanced notice of events
  - Events with limited tickets
  - Access to preferred seating
  - Travel opportunities
- Lunch with the president or senior administrator
- Gift announced at a board meeting
- Poinsettia or wreath delivered by an appropriate member of the staff or other person (In educational institutions, the gift may be delivered by a student; for top donors, the poinsettia or wreath may be delivered by the president of the organization or another member of the senior leadership staff at the organization.)

One popular benefit of membership in a gift club is an exclusive reception and dinner for members of that gift club. Some organizations host exclusive events that members of the recognition gift club attend at no cost. Membership at other organizations in the same types of recognition gift clubs may provide donors with invitations to these exclusive events, but the donors are charged a fee to cover the cost of the event, if they choose to attend. These receptions and dinners can be quite elaborate, with entertainment and live music for dancing. If donors are not paying to attend these events, organizations need to be aware of the regulations established by the Internal Revenue Service as they relate to benefits provided in return for gifts (see Exhibit 5.3).

EXHIBIT 5.3

IRS Substantiation and Disclosure Requirements for Charitable Contributions

Good and services are considered to be *insubstantial* if the payment occurs in the context of a fundraising campaign in which a charitable organization informs the donor of the amount of the contribution that is a deductible contribution, and:

- The fair market value of the benefits received does not exceed the lesser of 2 percent of the payment or $89, or
- The payment is at least $44.50, the only items provided bear the organization's name or logo (e.g., calendars, mugs, or posters), and the cost of these items is within the limit for "low-cost articles," which is $8.90.

Free, unordered low-cost articles are also considered to be insubstantial.

The IRS requirements include a membership benefits exemption that stipulates:

An annual membership benefit is also considered to be insubstantial if it is provided in exchange for *an annual payment of $75 or less* and consists of annual recurring rights or privileges, such as:

- Free or discounted admissions to the charitable organization's facilities or events
- Discounts on purchases from the organization's gift shop
- Free or discounted parking
- Free or discounted admission to member-only events sponsored by an organization, where a per-person cost (not including overhead) is within the "low-cost articles" limits.

Note: The dollar amounts above are for 2007. Guideline amounts are adjusted for inflation. Contact IRS Exempt Organizations Customer Account Services at (877) 829–5500 for annual inflation adjustment information.

Special Gift Clubs at Hospitals:
Concierge Programs

Many hospitals have developed VIP programs, or what one might call *concierge* programs, for donors who make annual gifts of a certain magnitude. Some programs require annual gifts of $1,000 and others are based on annual gifts of $5,000 or more. The names of the programs vary from organization to organization.

Names include "Friends of the Hospital," which is used at Northern Michigan Regional Hospital in Petoskey, Michigan; "Lightkeeper's Society" at Cape Cod Hospital in Massachusetts; and others at various hospitals.

While the specific elements of the various programs may differ, these programs have similar features. First and most important, potential members are told clearly that they will not receive a different level of care. In appreciation and gratitude for the donor's support, the donor will receive assistance from the development staff when coming to the emergency room, being admitted to the hospital, or needing to locate a physician. The assistance is available 24 hours a day, seven days a week.

These programs are extremely popular in resort communities. In the case of Northern Michigan Regional Hospital and Cape Cod Hospital, many individuals using the hospitals are summer residents with resort homes in those areas. Since these individuals have primary physicians elsewhere, many donors like having easy access to a physician if one is needed.

In some cases, the donor receives a card with a phone number on it that the donor may call for assistance. Some facilities decided to eliminate the card as it was often lost, was used by friends of the donor, and was used in subsequent years when the gift was not renewed.

An important part of the success with these programs is having the names of the members of the groups entered on the databases at the hospitals. Even those programs that distribute membership cards also use this methodology. When the person goes to the emergency department, the staff member registering the patient sees the code on the donor's record and calls the appropriate person in the development office.

A designated member of the development staff or an administrator of the hospital is available at all times. That person will receive the call and will go to

IN THE REAL WORLD (CONTINUED)

the hospital to meet the patient and assist as needed. Sometimes, assistance involves sitting with the spouse of the patient, making a phone call for the patient, or getting a blanket or drink of water for the waiting family member.

Physicians, nurses, and other staff need to understand the program and its value to the organization. They must know that these donors are not receiving a different level of care and that the program is about gratitude for the gifts that the person has made to the organization. The success of the program requires cooperation from many persons in the organization.

Hospitals have found these concierge programs to be effective not just in encouraging increased giving, but also in giving the development staff and others the opportunity to meet those persons who can potentially make major gifts to the hospitals and the hospitals' programs.

The benefits for gift clubs should be designed to build the relationship with the donor. Giving donors trinkets, like coffee cups, umbrellas, and paperweights, is not as meaningful as giving the donor access to the organization. In developing benefits for recognition gift clubs, the organization should look for benefits that are opportunities for the donor to become more involved and engaged with the organization.

3. Choosing an appropriate name. The third step in creating the gift club program is choosing a name for the gift club. While some organizations actually

TIPS AND TECHNIQUES

Tangible or Intangible Gifts for Recognition Gift Clubs

Many organizations feel that tangible items are essential for recognition gift clubs. In some cases, specially designed items may be meaningful for donors who have made significant gifts to an organization over a period of time. Such gifts usually have a meaning that relates to the organization and its mission. For example, members of the Einstein Society at the National Academies (Advisors to the Nation on Science, Engineering, and Medicine), which means

IN THE REAL WORLD (CONTINUED)

those with cumulative lifetime giving of at least $100,000, receive small replicas of sculptor Robert Berks' Einstein Monument, which is located in front of the National Academies Headquarters in Washington, DC. For many donors the most meaningful benefits of gift clubs are those that are intangible and related to events and activities that give the donor the opportunity for involvement and engagement with the organization. These benefits would include invitations to events, such as annual meetings or small group forums, or meetings with key administrative and volunteer leaders of the organization. These intangible benefits are also contributing to the growth of the relationship with the donor by educating and engaging the donor in the organization's mission. Through these activities the donor gets to know more about the organization and the donor's confidence in the organization grows stronger. These are the steps that are required to develop loyalty and set the stage for continued support.

call their recognition groups *clubs*, many have chosen *society, council,* or *circle*. Some organizations consider *society* to be elitist and prefer *circle* as warmer and more inclusive.

The name of a gift club may be generic or it may be unique to the organization. Generic names include *Century Club* or *Century Circle* for annual gifts of $100 and *Heritage Circle* or *Legacy Society* for planned gifts. Names like *President's Associates* or *Founder's Society* are also generic names, as are various hierarchal names like *bronze, silver, gold,* and *platinum,* or *friend, patron,* and *sponsor*.

Some organizations choose unique names that are meaningful to that organization for their gift clubs (see Exhibit 5.4). The American Red Cross in Central Massachusetts has its Clara Barton Society for those who make annual gifts of $1,000 or more, Pennsylvania State University (Penn State) has its Mount Nittany Society for those whose cumulative gifts total $250,000 or more. Names of founders or early presidents, or names of persons having made significant contributions, including but not restricted to monetary gifts, to the organization are also possibilities for unique names. Gift clubs named for individuals are usually named for persons who are deceased.

EXHIBIT 5.4

Establishing Names for Recognition Gift Clubs

Every organization has numerous possibilities for the names of its recognition gift clubs. If the nonprofit wishes to consider names that have special meaning for the organization, a number of options exist.

Following are possible sources of unique names:

Motto and/or Notable Quote

- *Lux Libertas Society:* Taken from the *University of North Carolina*'s motto etched in its official seal—*Lux libertas*, Latin for "light and liberty." Also noted is a former president's description of the university as "an outpost of light and liberty."

- *Res Publica Society: Res publica* is Latin for "public affairs" and is used to describe "a dedicated group of leaders of the community" at *Claremont McKenna College* in California.

Landmark

- *Mount Nittany Society:* Mount Nittany is the common name for Nittany Mountain, a prominent geographic feature and landmark for *Pennsylvania State University*.

- *Fort Hill Legacy:* Fort Hill was the beloved home of John C. Calhoun, which his son-in-law Thomas Green Clemson gave to the people of South Carolina; Fort Hill is in the center of the current campus of *Clemson University*.

- *Clocktower Society:* Westlake Hall clocktower at *Bradley University* in Peoria, Illinois, described as "a sentinel overlooking the Quad," has been a landmark on the campus for more than a century.

Significant Years

- *1845 Society:* The year that the Republic of Texas granted a charter to found *Baylor University*.
- *1911 Society: Reed College*'s first classes were held in 1911.
- *Benefactors of 1889:* The year that Thomas Green Clemson's will, endowing *Clemson College*, was accepted by South Carolina.

Mascot, Symbol, Colors

- *William Society:* Named for "William," sometimes referred to as the museum's unofficial mascot, a statuette of a hippopotamus, which is one of the most popular ancient Egyptian figures in the museum's collection: *Metropolitan Museum of Art, New York.*
- *Scarlet and Black Circle:* Grinnell College colors.
- *Maroon & Gold Donors:* University of Minnesota colors.

Names of Founders

- *Clark Society:* Brothers Addison and Randolph Clark were the founders of *Texas Christian University.*
- *Christensen Society:* Three brothers whose artistic vision pioneered the *San Francisco Ballet.*

Names of Persons Connected to Mission

- *Clara Barton Society:* American Red Cross (chapters throughout the United States).
- *Marlin Perkins Society:* Director of the Saint Louis Zoo from 1962 to 1970 and the renowned host of *Mutual of Omaha's Wild Kingdom: Saint Louis Zoo.*
- *Brahms Club; Debussy Club; Mozart Society; Beethoven Society: Las Vegas Philharmonic.*

Terms Associated with the Organization's History or Core Mission

- *Golden Horseshoe:* The section of the old Metropolitan Opera House with its golden auditorium, a sunburst chandelier, and gold damask stage curtains that was reserved for the wealthy families of New York who owned the opera house until 1940: *Metropolitan Opera, New York.*
- *Overture Club; Concerto Club; Virtuoso Circle; Conductor's Circle: Cincinnati Symphony Orchestra.*

The name of a person who made a significant gift in the past through a will or other estate plan is often chosen as the name of the planned giving recognition club. For example, Kansas University named its planned giving

---

EXHIBIT 5.5

The Watkins Society

Kansas University

The *Watkins Society* recognizes individuals who have developed an estate plan or other deferred gift arrangement with KU Endowment that will ultimately benefit the University of Kansas, KU Medical Center, the School of Medicine—Wichita, or the KU Edwards Campus.

Elizabeth M. Watkins, for whom the society is named, donated generously to KU through her will. In the 1930s, she bequeathed her home, which became the residence for KU chancellors. She also funded the construction of Watkins Memorial Health Center (now Twente Hall), Watkins Scholarship Hall, and Miller Scholarship Hall, among many other initiatives.

> I . . . wish to provide a bequest in aid . . . of the University of Kansas.
> . . . The best way to do this is to make use of . . . the Kansas University Endowment Association.
>
> —Elizabeth M. Watkins, 1930

Source: www.kuendowment.org/donor_recognition/giving_societies/watkins_society.aspx.

---

recognition club the Elizabeth M. Watkins Society in honor of a donor who generously supported KU through her will in the 1930s (see Exhibit 5.5).

The mistake is frequently made that a gift club is named for a person but the organization fails to explain who the person was and why the recognition club was named for that person. The power of using a person's name is the story that accompanies the name. Names of logos, mascots, physical structures, or stated values can also provide names that are meaningful to the organization.

If an appropriate name that is specific to the organization is not readily identified, the organization may choose to give the recognition gift club a generic name to move ahead with launching the program. Later, if a more distinctive name emerges, the club can be given a new name. Renaming a recognition gift club provides a marketing opportunity later when the new name is announced.

4. Developing a plan. The next step is developing the plan for launching the gift club or possibly a group of clubs. To begin this step, the organization needs to establish its objectives for the gift club. For example, if a club for gifts of $1,000 or more is being introduced, determine the outcome that is desired from implementing the gift club. The organization may want to review the number of gifts of that size and the total amount given through those gifts in two or three prior years. On the basis of prior giving and expectations for the gift club, goals for number of gifts at that level and the total amount of those gifts can be established.

IN THE REAL WORLD

Organizations with a large number of donors who tend to make small gifts multiple times each year encourage donors to make automatic monthly contributions through their credit cards or checking accounts and provide recognition to those who choose this method of giving.

Following are three examples of monthly giving recognition programs. Included are excerpts from each organization's website that promote the monthly giving programs:

❶ Habitat for Humanity International

Recognition group: HopeBuilders

From website: http://www.habitat.org/donation/hopebuilder/

Join our monthly giving program for as little as $5 a month. You'll provide the consistent support needed to end poverty housing.

HopeBuilders are the foundation of each home we build. HopeBuilders provide Habitat a stable and reliable source of funding that allows us to plan ahead.

Won't you join this special group? For less than the cost of one dinner out each month, you can become a HopeBuilder. Please join us today.

Become a HopeBuilder today and enjoy:

- Hassle-free monthly donations
- Automatic donation from your *credit card* or *checking account*
- Knowing your donation is put to work immediately

- Complete statements provided for tax purposes
- Bimonthly newsletter updating our progress
- The ability to change or suspend your donation at any time

Your love goes a long way. Become a HopeBuilder today! Whatever amount you would like to share, your generosity will earn you the gratitude of thousands of people in need of a decent place to live.

❷ Dana-Farber Cancer Institute

Recognition group: Partners in Courage

From website: http://www.dana-farber.org/how/gifts/monthly/

The fight against cancer is continuous and ongoing with no pauses allowed. Partners in Courage is a very special group of loyal Dana-Farber supporters who make monthly gifts to support that continuous battle.

Their generosity provides dependable funding for groundbreaking cancer research, and helps provide our patients with the highest level of patient care. Join *Partners in Courage* and become a partner in our quest to find cures for cancer.

Benefits

In addition to the personal satisfaction that you will gain from your membership in *Partners in Courage*, we have a variety of ways to thank you for your outstanding support, including:

- Special updates about research findings and treatment advances that your gifts have made possible.
- A subscription to our quarterly newsletter, *Impact*.
- Bi-annual issues of our full-color magazine, *Paths of Progress*.
- Fewer solicitations: Because we can rely on your monthly contributions, the amount of mail you receive from us will be limited, if you wish.
- Annual Summary Statement: To aid in your tax preparations, in January of each year you will receive a consolidated statement of your *Partners in Courage* gifts.

❸ KPBS (Public Broadcasting Station affiliated with San Diego State University)

Recognition group: Sustaining Members

From website: http://www.kpbs.org/give/sustaining_member_program

Simplify your Life! Simplify your Giving! Become a KPBS Sustaining Member.

IN THE REAL WORLD (CONTINUED)

- Join the growing family of KPBS members who generously give monthly or quarterly gifts to the station. KPBS Sustaining Members provide a dependable, ongoing source of funding that allows us to concentrate on airing the great programs that you enjoy, year after year. Thank you for your support!

- It's so easy with convenient and secure withdrawals from your credit card or checking account. You save time and money since you never have to write another check or find a stamp.

- Enjoy the satisfaction of knowing your support is helping reduce KPBS' administrative costs—that makes your contribution a full investment in the unique and outstanding programs you expect from public broadcasting.

- You're in control. You can change or stop your payments at any time by calling us.

- Your membership is always active. You never have to look back and see when you last gave to KPBS.

- You receive fewer mailings asking for support and you have more time to enjoy all the programs that make KPBS a valuable resource for you and everyone else in your household.

- It's affordable. Spreading your support throughout the year is easier on your budget. Plus it gives KPBS the security of a steady, reliable stream of income.

SUSTAINING CONTRIBUTION

- $5 per month
- $10 per month
- Dollar-a-Day Club: $30.42 per month
- Producers Club: $100 per month
- Other: $_____ per month

INFLATION GUARD

_____ I authorize KPBS to increase my monthly gift by 10% on December 31 of each year.

After measurable objectives are determined for each gift club, the specific ways to introduce each gift club are determined and described in writing. At this step, a marketing plan for each gift club should be developed. The plan should define the target audiences and the strategies that will be used to promote the gift clubs to each audience. The use of appeal letters, phone calls, publications, and websites to inform and solicit the members of the target audience needs to be described and a timeline for implementing these strategies should be developed. Volunteer committees can be organized to assist in the promotion, solicitation, and acknowledgment of gifts at gift club levels.

IN THE REAL WORLD

Launching an annual giving recognition society with permanent recognition is not the most effective way to assure continued success.

EXAMPLE 1

A recognition program called the "President's Circle" was established for an organization with the minimum amount for membership being a commitment of $5,000 or more to be paid over five years. The benefits of membership included an annual reception and dinner and listing each year in the annual report. No provisions for renewal or for length of membership were established. The members of the President's Circle viewed their membership as lifetime membership.

After a number of years passed, most of the members of the President's Circle were no longer making contributions, although their names were listed in the annual report and they were invited to a dinner and a reception each year. The reception and dinner were eliminated but the names were always listed in the annual report.

To reactivate the giving of the members of the President's Circle, who were the most capable donors associated with the organization, a decision was made to get the group together for a reception and a presentation on the organization. Each attendee at the reception would receive a packet of materials and a pledge card when they left. The reception was to be followed by individual meetings to ask each member for continued support.

Unfortunately, although a number of years had passed, the members were expecting a reception and dinner as had occurred in the past. Upon arrival, the attendees were not pleased to find a "cash bar" although the invitation had clearly indicated that a cash bar would be provided. Quickly, the cash bar became an "open bar" and questions were being asked about the location of the dinner. At the end of the evening, the packets were distributed to the attendees, but follow-up was fruitless. Those who had given $5,000 over five years were members of the President's Circle and felt any request for additional funding was inappropriate.

EXAMPLE 2

An organization decided to launch its annual giving program for gifts of $1,000 or more to coincide with the opening of a new building that included a performance auditorium. To encourage donors to become members of the Inner Circle, those who made gifts of $1,000 or more would have their names put on seats in the auditorium. Many joined the Inner Circle in the first year, but renewal efforts were difficult. When members were contacted, they indicated that they made a gift to get their names on the seats and did not plan on continuing to support the organization at that level. While the materials on the Inner Circle were explicit that the program was an annual giving program, the benefit of getting one's name on a seat was not consistent with the annual nature of recognition. To complicate the situation even more, some donors believed that they would sit in their named seats when they attended events in the auditorium.

The recognition gift club program is designed to encourage donors to increase their levels of giving. To maximize that opportunity, donors need to be reminded of gift clubs on a continuous basis. In appeal letters, phone calls, and face-to-face contacts, asking a donor to consider increasing an annual contribution to $1,000 to become a member of the President's Circle is an effective way to secure increased gifts. That request should be supported by articles in newsletters, by information on response slips and envelopes, and on the organization's website.

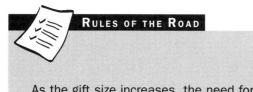

RULES OF THE ROAD

As the gift size increases, the need for personalized recognition grows.

The plan needs to be developed in alignment with the rest of the development plan for the organization. To be effective, the gift club program must be integrated with the overall donor relations program and the overall development plan for the nonprofit. The gift club program needs to fit with and complement direct mail, phone-a-thons, telethons, special events, major giving, planned giving, capital campaigns, and other fundraising efforts.

One strategy for introducing a new gift club is to establish a time period for *charter* or *founding* membership. If the club is launched in March 2009, announcing that those who qualify for membership by December 31, 2009 will become charter or founding members encourages donors to take action more quickly. Many persons like having the special status of being among the first to become members. The additional benefit that these persons receive would be the designation as a charter or founding member for as long as they continue to qualify for that level in annual giving programs and for perpetuity in cumulative lifetime and planned giving clubs.

Plans for implementing a program include putting the systems and processes in place to record and acknowledge the members of the club appropriately, to provide the benefits that have been promoted, and to measure attainment of goals. Determining how the desired listing of names will be obtained from donors and how the information will be stored in and retrieved from the database, establishing protocol for drafting and preparing appropriate letters for those meeting the criteria for membership, and setting up a system for putting the names of these persons on appropriate mailing lists for information and events are important steps in getting ready to implement the plan.

TIPS AND TECHNIQUES

Name Verification Form

One method for getting donors to verify that they approve of having their names listed as members of recognition societies and to verify the way they wish their names to be listed is to request completion of a name verification form, such as the following:

[NAME OF RECOGNITION SOCIETY]

By allowing ORGANIZATION XYZ to list your name among those who generously support XYZ, you will be providing us with the opportunity to recognize you for your leadership in giving, and others may be influenced by your generosity and encouraged to follow your example in supporting XYZ.

Please complete the following to indicate your willingness to have ORGANIZATION XYZ recognize you for your generosity with the purpose of encouraging others to support XYZ.

LISTING AUTHORIZATION FORM

ORGANIZATION XYZ has my/our permission to list the following name(s) in the appropriate recognition categories in its annual report on giving (or honor roll of donors), in other XYZ publications, and on the XYZ website, as deemed appropriate.

Name as it currently appears in XYZ records:
Dr. and Mrs. William Jones
If you desire an alternative listing to the one above, please print your name as you wish it to appear for recognition purposes.

_____

(Please Print)

_____   _____

(Signature)   (Date)

Please return this form in the enclosed envelope, or mail to:
Jane Doe
Director of Donor Relations
Organization XYZ
500 Main Street
City/Town, State 00000

Please contact Jane Doe at jd@xyz.org or (555) 555-5555 with any questions.

The plan should include the strategies for evaluating the success of the program. The evaluation should include an assessment of both quantitative and qualitative information (see Exhibit 5.6).

In addition, the plan should include a budget that addresses the additional costs that will be incurred as the strategies for promoting, implementing, and evaluating the gift club program are actualized.

EXHIBIT 5.6

Evaluation of Gift Club Programs

Quantitative

1. Determine the following:
   - Number of new members at each level this year
     - Number of *new* members this year (never having given at a gift club level)
     - Number of *reactivated* members this year (having given at a gift club level, but not in the last 12 months)
   - Number of members who renewed this year at same gift amount as last year
   - Number of members who renewed and increased gift size this year
     - Total dollars of increases in giving by members this year
     - Average increase in giving by those giving more than in the prior year
   - Number of members who renewed but decreased gift size this year
     - Total of decreases in giving by members this year
     - Average decrease in giving by those giving less than in the prior year
   - Number of donors who did not renew membership
     - Number who did not give this year
     - Dollars given in prior year by those who did not give this year
   - Increase (decrease) in total number of members at each level this year
   - Increase (decrease) of total dollars given by members at each level this year
2. Develop graphs with trendlines to illustrate above information over multiple-year timeframes (three, five, and ten years).

Qualitative

1. Administer surveys with questions about gift club recognition:
   - Mail the survey to selected groups of donors. (Code the surveys to indicate the specific group receiving the survey.) Include postage-paid return envelope.
   - Send the survey with an email message.
   - Meet individually with major donors and administer the survey in person.
2. Conduct focus groups with donors to discuss gift recognition clubs; each focus group may represent a specific constituency or type of donor. For example, a focus group may include first-time donors, donors who are employed by the organization, grateful patients from a health-care organization, or alumni from a specific decade for an educational organization.

At this stage, a written document for the gift club program should be developed and the key information from the document should be included in the donor relations manual for the organization. The document should include the criteria for membership (from step 1); the benefits of membership (from step 2); any significant information about the name of the clubs (from step 3); and the plan (from this step), including objectives, strategies for promoting, implementing, and evaluating the program, the timeline, and the budget. The document should be reviewed and updated annually or more frequently in the early stages of the program.

IN THE REAL WORLD

The Seattle Symphony describes its Musical Legacy Society in one sentence on its website:

> The Musical Legacy Society welcomes as members those who have provided for the Seattle Symphony in their estate plans.

The benefits of membership are described as follows:

> In addition to receiving the tremendous satisfaction of helping to secure the Symphony's future, Musical Legacy Society members receive

IN THE REAL WORLD (CONTINUED)

many benefits and special opportunities to interact with the Orchestra, including:

- Invitation to a Spring Luncheon and Recital hosted by Maestro and Mrs. Gerard Schwarz

- Access to the Norcliffe Founders Room, Seattle Symphony's exclusive donor lounge, for complimentary refreshments during concert intermissions

- Invitation to the Closing Night Party

- Invitation to a Behind the Scenes event featuring a guest artist and/or Symphony musicians

- Invitations to selected open rehearsals and receptions

- Personalized ticketing assistance

- A Musical Legacy Society lapel pin

Following the list of benefits, information about planned giving is included:

If you believe in the joyous power of music, you should be aware that numerous provisions of the Internal Revenue Code make deferred gifts attractive, even for those who never thought they could make a sizeable contribution to a charitable organization such as the Symphony. For more information, contact: *[Name, title, phone number, and email address are provided.]*

5. *Implementing the plan.* Implementation of the program, using the plan, timeline, and budget that have been developed, is the next step. The preparation is completed and the strategies that have been developed are put into action. Throughout the implementation phase, the development staff will monitor the results of each strategy and will modify the plan as needed.

TIPS AND TECHNIQUES

Guidelines for Recognition Gift Clubs

An organization should have a written set of guidelines for its recognition gift clubs that is updated on a regular basis. The guidelines should reflect any changes as clubs are added, deleted, combined, expanded, or enhanced.

TIPS AND TECHNIQUES (CONTINUED)

Following is a checklist for the guidelines:

☐ The definition of a year for recognition purposes:

    ☐ January 1–December 31

    ☐ July 1–June 30

    ☐ Other

☐ Types of gift clubs that the program will include:

    ☐ Annual giving

    ☐ Lifetime giving

    ☐ Planned giving

    ☐ Other

☐ Criteria for membership in the various recognition gift club programs:

    ☐ Constituencies that are included in each recognition gift club

        ☐ Individuals

            ☐ Persons who direct gifts from family foundations or donor-advised funds to the organization

            ☐ Owners of small businesses who direct gifts from the business to the organization

        ☐ Businesses and corporations

        (Businesses and corporations may be in a separate recognition gift club.)

        ☐ Organizations, associations, and foundations

        ☐ Other

    ☐ Types of gifts included in determining membership in each recognition gift club:

        ☐ Corporate matching gifts

        If a donor works for an employer that matches the gifts of employees to charitable organizations, the gift from the company may be included in determining gift club membership. Donor A works for Company B and when Donor A makes an annual contribution of $500, a matching gift form that is completed by the charitable organization is forwarded to Company B. Company B then sends a gift of $500 to the organization to match the gift of Donor A. An organization may decide to include Donor A as a member of the recognition program for gifts of $1,000 or may choose to exclude Donor A.

TIPS AND TECHNIQUES (CONTINUED)

☐ Sponsorship of special events

    ☐ Total contributed by sponsor

    ☐ Amount of sponsorship minus fair market value of benefits received

☐ Tickets purchased for special events

    ☐ Total contributed by sponsor

    ☐ Amount of sponsorship minus fair market value of benefits received

        Some organizations choose not to include support of special events in their recognition gift clubs. Others count either the full amount provided by the donor or the amount that exceeds the value of what the donor receives in exchange for the sponsorship or ticket purchase. If a donor is a sponsor for an event or purchases tickets for an event, the complete amount provided by the donor may not be tax-deductible, depending on the fair market value of what the donor receives in return for the sponsorship or for the tickets. Whether the full amount provided by the donor or the part that is tax-deductible is included in determining gift club recognition depends on the organization.

☐ In-kind gifts

    If a donor makes a non-cash gift of either goods or services, the organization may or may not include the gift in its recognition program. The fair market value or the amount of the charitable deduction, which is the responsibility of the donor to determine, may be used for recognition purposes, if the organization decides to include these in-kind gifts in the recognition program.

☐ Restricted gifts

    An organization may decide that only unrestricted gifts are included in the annual giving recognition program or the organization may decide to count both unrestricted and restricted gifts. Most organizations include both restricted and unrestricted contributions, but either choice is acceptable.

☐ Campaign gifts

    Many organizations make the distinction between annual and capital gifts for recognition purposes. Other organizations consider all gifts made over the stated period of time (January 1–December 31 or July 1–June 30) as the total for recognition.

NOTE: Donors are often confused to see their names not included in recognition for a specific year in which a gift of a significant amount was made. This can occur if the recognition is specifically for annual giving and does not include gifts for a campaign or other restricted gifts.

☐ Pledges

An organization may decide to include a donor in an annual recognition gift club program at the time of the pledge or at the time of the gift. For a multiyear pledge, the organization will need to decide whether the person is listed in the year of the pledge at the level that reflects the entire commitment or whether the donor is listed in each year at the level of that year's payment.

☐ The benefits of membership in the various recognition gift clubs:

    ☐ Benefits for donor only

    ☐ Benefits for donor and spouse/partner/guest

    ☐ List of benefits

        ☐ Invitations to events

        ☐ Publications

            ☐ Annual report

            ☐ Newsletters

            ☐ Special letter from the president

        ☐ Parking pass

        ☐ Tangible items

        ☐ Others

    ☐ Fair market value of benefits

6. *Evaluating the program.* At regular intervals through the course of the year, the progress in meeting goals will be measured. Assessment should occur at least quarterly and should provide the opportunity to examine what strategies are being successful and what strategies need to be altered or eliminated. The evaluation should include both quantitative and qualitative information as previously outlined in the planning phase. The review should include an analysis of the responses to the various aspects of the program. Donors, volunteers, and staff should be invited to give feedback on the program and questions about the program should be noted.

IN THE REAL WORLD

People often form their giving habits when they take their first job in the first few years after completing college. The organizations that people initially support are often the ones that they will continue to support.

To make sure that young alumni are giving to their alma maters, which is important for assuring long-term support from those alumni, colleges and universities have developed programs to encourage younger graduates to give to the school they attended.

Educational institutions also are establishing recognition programs for members of the senior class to educate students on the reasons to give and to establish the habit of giving to their alma maters even earlier.

Colleges and universities have established special giving societies for recent graduates and for members of the senior class. For example, at the University of Mary Washington in Fredericksburg, Virginia, the President's Council recognizes annual unrestricted gifts and includes three gift societies.

$10,000+	Washington Society
$5,000–$9,999	Monroe Society
$2,008–$4,999	Centennial Society

In addition, the President's Council is available to the classes that graduated from the university in the past ten years as follows:

$1,000–$2,007 (Classes out 10 years)	Gold Eagle Club
$500–$2,007 (Classes out 5–9 years)	Silver Eagle Club
$250–$2,007 (Past four classes)	Bronze Eagle Club

Members of the senior class who make gifts of $50 are members of the Eagle Club, which is in a group of recognition societies that begins at the $250 level for others.

Likewise at the University of North Carolina at Chapel Hill, the annual membership requirement for the Chancellors' Club is $2,000, except for those who have graduated in the past ten years.

Following the evaluation of the program, the success of the program should be celebrated and donors participating in the gift club program should be made aware of its success and the difference their participation has made in the giving program and in fulfilling the mission of the organization.

Counting Gifts and Recording Gifts

Counting a gift for gift club recognition should not be confused with how the gift is recorded in the database system. Often a gift is recorded on one account but is counted for gift club recognition in another account.

For example, a contribution from a family foundation or a donor-advised fund is entered in the database system as coming from the family foundation or the entity that administers the donor-advised fund. To count the gift toward gift club membership for the person directing that gift to the organization, that person receives "soft credit" for the gift to indicate that the gift was the result of that person's instructions. Many database systems have a feature called "soft credit" that allows the individual to receive gift club recognition for the gift although it is officially recorded as coming from the issuing entity.

Likewise, to include the matching gift from a donor's employer in the donor's total for gift club membership requires giving the donor soft credit for the gift in the database system, while the company is actually the donor of record for the matching gift. The gift from Donor A is recorded as a gift from Donor A. The gift from Company B is recorded as a gift from Company B. However, Donor A receives soft credit for the matching gift from Company B and receives recognition for the two gifts added together since Donor A made the gift from Company B occur.

Working with the person who oversees gift entry is required for gifts other than those made directly by the donor to be counted toward recognition gift clubs. Many organizations use the soft credit feature for this purpose.

The Impact of IRS Guidelines on Benefits

When organizations began to use gift clubs to encourage increased giving, the standard recognition for those who gave $1,000 or more was the annual reception and dinner, often called the ABC Circle Annual Dinner, for those who were members of the ABC Circle by virtue of their gifts that year. The invitation to the event was extended only to those who gave at the specific level or above.

Some organizations continue to have these recognition benefits. However, some organizations have changed the nature of these events in response to the IRS regulations on goods and services. A donor cannot claim a tax deduction for any single contribution of $250 or more unless the donor obtains a contemporaneous, written acknowledgment of the contribution from the recipient organization. That acknowledgment must describe goods or services an organization provides in exchange for a contribution of $250 or more. It must also provide a good-faith estimate of the value of such goods or services, because *a donor must generally reduce the amount of the contribution deduction by the fair market value of the goods and services provided by the organization.* Goods or services include cash, property, services, and *benefits or privileges.*

One exception is when the goods or services the charitable organization provides in exchange for contributions are "insubstantial." In that case, the goods and services do not have to be described in the acknowledgment and thus the donor is not required to reduce the amount of the deduction.

These regulations have implications for organizations that provide benefits to the members of their recognition gift clubs. The *limit on insubstantial goods and services* means that an organization can provide benefits with a fair market value of no more than $20 (the lesser of 2% or $89) to a donor who makes a gift of $1,000 without diminishing the donor's tax deduction. Providing a reception and dinner for a donor and guest/spouse with a *fair market value of $20 or less* is virtually impossible. Providing dinner for two at some fast-food restaurants can easily exceed $20.

The determination of the value of the goods and services provided is based on the fair market value of what the donor receives, regardless of whether the organization or another entity covers the cost. If a corporate donor underwrites the cost or contributes the food and beverage for the reception and/or dinner, the value of the goods and services, which is based on the fair market value, remains the same.

If those attending the event are making gifts of $10,000 or more, the maximum fair market value of the food and beverage would be $89 (the lesser of 2% or $89). It may be possible to provide a reception and dinner for that amount. However, if the donor and a guest/spouse attend the event, the $89 would need to cover the fair market value of the goods and services that both receive.

Many organizations have modified the "exclusive," members-only event in light of the IRS regulations. One alternative to the exclusive dinner as a benefit for those who give at certain magnitudes is having a non-annual event to which a broader group of persons are invited. While the donors of a certain magnitude are invited, others such as potential donors who do not make gifts at those levels are also invited. The event is no longer goods and services received in exchange for the gift. The event is no longer the Annual ABC Circle Dinner.

The event may become a "Celebration of Philanthropy," perhaps held in November about the time of National Philanthropy Day. It may become a Founder's Day event to coincide with the anniversary of the organization's establishment. In either case, the dinner is no longer *exclusive* to those who give at a specific level.

Another alternative to the ABC Circle Dinner as it has been in the past is an event to which only members of the ABC Circle are invited but for which the members pay the cost of the event. For example, the organizations may bring in a nationally known speaker for a presentation to the ABC Circle. The evening may include a dinner before or after the speaker's presentation. But the members of the ABC Circle would pay to cover the fair market value of their food and beverages.

If an organization has been holding such an event for a number of years as a benefit for making gifts of a certain magnitude, making a change is difficult. However, the alternative is to include in the acknowledgment letter that the fair market value of goods and services that the donor receives, which includes the ABC Circle Dinner, is $X. Thus, the tax deduction for the donors' gifts would be diminished by that amount.[1]

The Other Side of Recognition Gift Clubs

While recognition gift clubs are helpful in encouraging donors to give at higher levels, organizations often rely on the gift club program to determine the *standard* for recognition for every donor, regardless of the specific likes and dislikes of the donor. If a donor has made a gift that qualifies the donor and the donor's spouse for recognition at a specific level, the development staff needs to be sure that the donor receives the benefits for that level gift, if those benefits are appropriate for the donor. Recognition may need to be modified according to the donor's preferences.

Unfortunately, as recognition programs are put in place for gifts at higher and higher levels, organizations often attempt to standardize those things that need to be *individualized*. Organizations need to recognize that the benefits provided for donors through recognition clubs for cumulative lifetime giving at significant levels must be approached carefully. As gift levels get higher, organizations need to approach gift recognition as being different for each donor. The interests and desires of each donor must be considered when designing recognition plans for these donors, many of whom have long–term relationships with the organization. Understanding what the donor expects and wants is essential in making recognition meaningful.

TIPS AND TECHNIQUES

Planned Giving Societies

When an individual tells an organization that a provision has been made in the person's will or estate plan for the charity, that individual has elevated the nonprofit to the status of family. These individuals are important to the organization as bequests tend to be far larger than outright gifts. However, when a gift is not immediately forthcoming, the organization sometimes overlooks the importance of donor relations.

In "Planned Giving Tomorrow" (Winter 2008), a newsletter published by PlannedGiving, Inc., Mindy Aleman, CFRE, APR, writes in her article, "You Had Me at Bequest!,"

> Too often, once a prospect has documented his/her bequest intentions, the donor acknowledgment period lasts through several months of standard thank-you letters, a holiday greeting or goodie, and perhaps a recognition dinner, depending on level of gift.

> The donor's name is summarily noted in recognition reports, on walls of fame, etched onto a plaque or mug, whisked away into a legacy giving society.

> Then, drops off the crevice into the deep, dark hole of *no further action* required.

Ms. Aleman tells of a panel of donors at a conference who were discussing their pet peeves of fundraising:

> One older donor stunned the audience as she recounted how her multi-million-dollar bequest went largely ignored.
> "I was virtually forgotten . . . tucked away in someone's file," she explained, "I wasn't on anyone's invitation list, never received a call, never even got a simple birthday card. In short, when I updated my Trust, I took them out. They probably still don't realize, but when I pass, they'll discover what I did, and it will be far too late for anyone to make amends."

TIPS AND TECHNIQUES (CONTINUED)

Those who have informed an organization of a bequest are as important, if not more important, as any major gift donor. For most organizations, realized bequests are much greater than the typical major gift the organization receives. By informing the organization of the bequest provision, the donor is conveying a passion for the organization and its mission. The acknowledgment, recognition, and stewardship of these donors needs to be as well planned and implemented as any other aspect of donor relations.

The legacy or heritage giving society exists for just that purpose. How should these donors be acknowledged, recognized, and stewarded? Following are some suggestions:

- An annual luncheon for all members of the Heritage Society.
  - As individuals get older, they often are hesitant to drive at night. Since members of the Heritage Society tend to be retired and older than the average donor, organizations have found that these individuals prefer a luncheon to a dinner. A luncheon on a Saturday may be good both for the older generation and for those younger donors who are still employed.
- Educational organizations often schedule their recognition event for their Heritage Societies to occur during reunion weekends.
  - In educational organizations, the recognition for the Heritage Society members may be combined with the recognition event for scholarship donors or other major donors. Those who have made bequest intentions have the opportunity to meet students or faculty who are deriving benefit from the gifts that have been made by the donors in the room. Inviting a student or faculty member who is the recipient of a scholarship or receives funding as the result of a bequest made in the past is also a nice touch. The donors can see how bequests such as theirs will make a difference.
- Invitations to special events, seminars, lectures, annual meetings of the board.
- An annual update on the Heritage Society, including numbers of new members, total members, and gifts realized.
  - Include the amount of endowment funding that the organization has as a result of bequests over the years and quantify the number of persons being served by the income from that endowment.
- Send birthday cards; invite donors to lunch on their birthdays; call or visit them on their birthdays.

TIPS AND TECHNIQUES (CONTINUED)

- As donors get older and their families dwindle in size, the importance of being remembered on a birthday is especially meaningful, especially for those who never married, those whose spouses are deceased, and those with no immediate family in the area where they live.
- Personal notes on the cards are appreciated by donors.
- Birthday cards that feature pictures that relate to the organization or to the special interests of the donor are thoughtful gestures.
  - A hospital that has a large number of babies born each year features a different baby each year on its birthday cards for donors.
  - A university has a beautiful picture of its campus or a group of students on its birthday card.
- Send other appropriate greeting cards and/or call the donor on holidays or special occasions.
- Design a special lapel pin for members of the Heritage Society, or a tie for the men and a scarf for the women.
- Onetime gifts, like the pin or tie and scarf can be presented to new members at the Heritage Society Luncheon each year.
- Invitations to serve on advisory councils, committees, or boards.
- Invitations to assist the development staff in thanking those making bequest gifts and in visiting with other potential bequest donors.

A donor may not welcome some of the benefits that are offered in the gift club program. If a conversation or other communication should suggest that a donor might not want to receive anything tangible, it should be recorded in the database and should alert the staff to question whether to send the donor the special calendar that all donors at that level are receiving. If the staff is not certain whether to send that item, the donor should be asked. A donor prefers to be asked and given a choice than to receive an item that the donor perceives as a waste of money or not to receive an item when the donor's neighbors and friends have received it.

IN THE REAL WORLD

Tokens of Appreciation

Andy Nulman, noted entrepreneur, public speaker, and blogger, indicated in his blog, entitled "Theory 18—Digital Love vs. Physical Gifts," that he wanted to share something that had been on his mind for a while:

> . . . I public speak often, and each time I do, the kind people for whom I do usually express gratitude by loading me up with well-meaning branded gifts like t-shirts, business card holders, digital clocks, tote bags and the like.
>
> And while these tokens of appreciation are indeed appreciated, I have two confessions to make:
>
> ❶ I don't need them.
>
> ❷ I don't want them.
>
> And I suspect most other speakers would say the same thing about the parting gifts imparted upon them, as well.
>
> Harsh? Perhaps, but stay with me for a second.
>
> Let's face it, despite my gratitude for my hosts' kind offerings, there aren't enough days in the year to wear all the promo clothing I get from these engagements, I have more business card cases than I do business cards . . . well, you get my drift. So if I may be so bold, to all those for whom I speak in the future, may I suggest the following: Show me the love.
>
> What I mean by that is instead of giving me a tangible *tchotchke*, give a donation to a charity of my choice. Or one of your choice. Or one at random. Whichever way you choose, people continue to benefit from my words and your fine decision of sharing them with your audience.
>
> Wait. I'm not done.
>
> Not to be greedy, but in this digital day and age, you can continue to spread warmth by sending some link love my way. Tell your email list what a great job I did (if I did). Share the news about the exciting breakthroughs at Airborne Mobile on the front page of your website. Post some photos of our time together and send your folks to learn more about me at either *Airborne* or *right here*.

IN THE REAL WORLD (CONTINUED)

Everyone wins. You keep your costs down, I get to interact with your logo and company spirit long after a t-shirt would've frayed into nothingness, and buzz builds for all of us.

Many of an organization's donors have similar feelings about the tokens of gratitude they receive in return for their contributions. Since philanthropic people give to multiple organizations, they may be receiving items from a number of organizations. If an organization (recipient) tells others about Mr. Nulman's presentation (gift), that sharing of information has an advantage for Mr. Nulman and his company (giver). When a nonprofit (recipient) shares with others its appreciation for its donors' gifts (gift), the organization (recipient) derives benefits. While the donor does not derive benefit from the organization's telling others about the gift in the way that Mr. Nulman does when others hear about his presentations, the donor may benefit in an intangible way. The donor may be relieved not to receive another token gift and may be pleased to have the organization share its gratitude for his gift with others to encourage them to also give—especially when those who learn of his gift choose to support the organization.

What would you prefer as an expression of gratitude? Would you want an umbrella, paperweight, or coffee mug? How would you feel about the organization telling others about its gratitude for your gift if the organization thought telling others may lead them to give?

Source: Andy Nulman, President and Chief Marketing Officer Airborne Mobile, "Pow! Right Between the Eyes! Andy Nulman's Blog About Surprise," March 25, 2008.

Depending on the level that the donor has achieved, both on an annual basis and on a lifetime basis, and on the donor's potential for continued support, the donor relations plan, which includes acknowledgment, recognition, and stewardship, should be developed as individually as possible (see Exhibit 5.7).

While guidelines and policies are important to the administration of a recognition gift club program, special circumstances may require some adjustments to those policies. When an organization launches a capital campaign, thought should be given to how campaign gifts will be recognized in the context of the successful annual giving recognition gift club program.

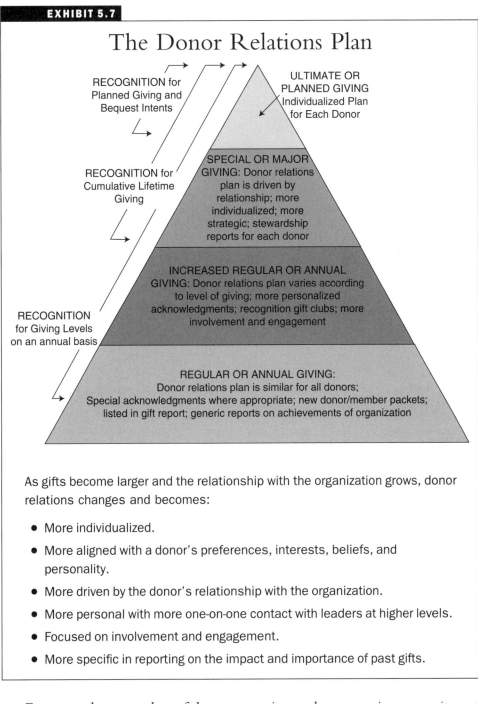

EXHIBIT 5.7

The Donor Relations Plan

RECOGNITION for Planned Giving and Bequest Intents

ULTIMATE OR PLANNED GIVING Individualized Plan for Each Donor

RECOGNITION for Cumulative Lifetime Giving

SPECIAL OR MAJOR GIVING: Donor relations plan is driven by relationship; more individualized; more strategic; stewardship reports for each donor

INCREASED REGULAR OR ANNUAL GIVING: Donor relations plan varies according to level of giving; more personalized acknowledgments; recognition gift clubs; more involvement and engagement

RECOGNITION for Giving Levels on an annual basis

REGULAR OR ANNUAL GIVING: Donor relations plan is similar for all donors; Special acknowledgments where appropriate; new donor/member packets; listed in gift report; generic reports on achievements of organization

As gifts become larger and the relationship with the organization grows, donor relations changes and becomes:

- More individualized.
- More aligned with a donor's preferences, interests, beliefs, and personality.
- More driven by the donor's relationship with the organization.
- More personal with more one-on-one contact with leaders at higher levels.
- Focused on involvement and engagement.
- More specific in reporting on the impact and importance of past gifts.

For example, a member of the community made a campaign commitment in the prior year for a gift of $250,000 and paid the first of five annual payments. The donor walks into the organization and sees a recognition display on the wall. The absence of the donor's name on the wall where annual gifts of $1,000 or more are recognized may raise some questions for the donor.

IN THE REAL WORLD

Organizations may have recognition programs for multiyear giving and for multiyear commitments. For example, the Metropolitan Opera has a recognition program that includes recognition for major giving over three years.

Recognition for major gifts to the Met begins with Major Gift Patrons for annual gifts of $25,000 or more and a group of benefits are offered to everyone who gives at this level or higher. At each increased level, additional benefits are offered. Levels for annual gifts include $25,000, $35,000, $50,000, $100,000, $250,000, and $500,000 or more.

However, within its recognition program for major gifts, multiyear giving is recognized in two instances. At the $50,000 level, the donor receives an added benefit in the third year of membership and The Golden Horseshoe recognizes a multiyear commitment totaling $200,000.

To become a member of The Golden Horseshoe, a donor makes a commitment of $200,000 or more over three years or $70,000 annually. *(The nondeductible base amount is $645 per year; additional optional benefits will increase the nondeductible portion of the gift.)*

Members of The Golden Horseshoe help guarantee the Metropolitan Opera's financial stability through their multiyear pledges. During the course of their membership term, in addition to all the privileges listed above, they receive:

- Dedication of a performance in their honor, including a prominent listing on the cast page of the program, a special dinner at The Grand Tier Restaurant, and a center parterre box
- Invitation to the Met's annual Golden Horseshoe dinner, with guest artists
- Inscription of the member's name on the Golden Horseshoe plaque on the Mercedes T. Bass Grand Tier of the Opera House
- Dining privileges at the private Metropolitan Opera Club

Of course, the donor will receive special recognition for the campaign gift on the special display in the entrance to the new building, when the facility is completed in the next two to three years. Certainly, the names that the donor saw do not include campaign gifts, just gifts to the annual fund. But the donor may not know these facts.

What seems simple can be complex. The donor knows that a check for $50,000 was mailed to the organization in December and sees that recognition is being given for gifts of $1,000 or more. Unfortunately not every donor who sees the perceived discrepancy will take time to ask about it. If the person does not ask and leaves the organization feeling slighted after making a gift of $250,000, the relationship may have been damaged beyond repair. Not only will future gifts be at risk, but the donor may decide not to honor the remaining pledge. Even when the donor asks and the difference in annual and capital giving is explained, the donor will often continue to focus on the fact that a donor of $1,000 is receiving recognition when his gift of $50,000 is not being recognized.

Organizations that are donor-focused may consider not limiting annual recognition to just those gifts earmarked for annual giving. During the campaign, the organization may wish to modify its guidelines for the annual giving program to include all gifts, annual and capital, actually given to the organization during the year. In other words, the amount used to qualify a donor for membership would be the cumulative total of all gifts paid from January 1 to December 31, regardless of the purpose of those gifts. If the modification makes donors feel valued and appreciated, it will support the overall program.

Expanding and Enhancing a Gift Club Program

One key ingredient in making a gift club program effective is to make it fresh and exciting by expanding or enhancing the program from time to time. If the annual evaluation of the gift club program shows that the program's growth has slowed and that gifts are not increasing, a closer look at the program is needed. To know whether a gift club program needs to be expanded or enhanced, the organization needs to observe trends in numbers of members at various levels and in total dollars given by members from year to year.

Expanding a gift club program may include adding new gift levels or creating levels within an existing recognition gift club. Enhancement of a gift club may include new levels, new names, modification of benefits, or the introduction of a new logo for one or more of the clubs within the program. Expanding or enhancing a gift club program gives the organization an opportunity to market the changes and to call attention to the program.

 IN THE REAL WORLD

Affinity–Based Recognition Gift Clubs

In *Secrets of Successful Fundraising: The Best from the Non-Profit Pros*, compiled and edited by Carol Weisman, in the chapter on donor recognition, written by Cecile W. Garrett, a number of examples are given for affinity-based clubs.[2]

Ms. Garrett highlights recognition clubs that are offshoots of larger donor groups, such as the program- or genre-related clubs for donors that public television stations promote. A group of individuals within the larger donor group, which in this case is members or annual donors, join together around a theme or interest that resonates with them. Many public television stations have family memberships or kids' club memberships that feature program-related benefits such as ''Arthur'' stickers or *Sesame Street* balloons, or, for the parents, educational materials to supplement lessons taught in the broadcast of certain programs. Kids' clubs may offer discounts to local museums or may sponsor special events for their members and their families.

IN THE REAL WORLD (CONTINUED)

Milwaukee public television station WMVS, which broadcasts *Outdoor Wisconsin*, a popular local television series, has the Outdoor Wisconsin Club. The benefits of membership include a newsletter about program highlights and advanced notice for ticket sales to the Outdoor Wisconsin Banquet, a fundraising event that the station has been holding since before the club was initiated. As Ms. Garrett notes, the Outdoor Wisconsin Club is not labor intensive to administer. Other affinity clubs at the station include the Kids Club, the Saturday Morning Breakfast Club, and the Tea Time at 10 Club. The contribution required for membership in these clubs is slightly higher at $75 than the contribution of $40 for basic membership.

Affinity clubs can also be used with mid-level and major donors. The members of the groups share a common ethnic, cultural, age, professional, lifestyle, or community interest. Ms. Garrett cites the example of the University of Virginia Law School. When a capital campaign was launched to renovate the school's new Law Grounds and Withers Hall Lobby, a new affinity group was formed: female graduates of the law school. The group had not been previously identified and targeted for major gifts cultivation to the same degree as had the male graduates. A special plaque in the main lobby provided an opportunity for these individuals to be recognized publicly. In part motivated by the visibility they would receive as individuals and as a group, 200 women, many of whom had never given to the University of Virginia Law School, made four- and five-figure gifts. The effort "paved the way for future giving from the law school's current 40 percent women student population."

Expanding a Gift Club Program

Example 1: An organization started its gift club program for annual giving with its top level at the $1,000 level. As time goes by, the need for higher giving levels becomes clear as $1,000 has become the ceiling for annual giving and few donors are making gifts above that amount.

If an identity has been created for the $1,000 group, which is called the President's Society, the gift clubs above the $1,000 level could also be included in the President's Society. The strategy would be to continue to have those persons who make gifts of $1,000 or more as members of the President's Society and to create levels within the President's Society. For example, those making gifts of $1,000 to $2,499 would be Associates in the President's Society. Those making gifts of $2,500 to $4,999 would be Partners, those making gifts of $5,000 to $9,999 would be Fellows, those making gifts of $10,000 to $24,999 would be Ambassadors, and those making gifts of $25,000 and above would be Founders. All of these donors would be members of the President's Society, but also would be Associates, Partners, Fellows, Ambassadors, or Founders depending on the size of the gifts:

Current program. President's Society: Gifts totaling $1,000 or more between January 1 and December 31 in a given year

Expanded program. President's Society: Gifts totaling $1,000 or more between January 1 and December 31 in a given year

President's Society Associates: $1,000–$2,499

President's Society Partners: $2,500–$4,999

President's Society Fellows: $5,000–$9,999

President's Society Ambassadors: $10,000–$24,999

President's Society Founders: $25,000 and above

Example 2: An organization's first step in creating its gift club program was with a club for annual gifts of $1,000 or more. Expanding the program may include introducing a gift club for cumulative giving or for bequest intents. The organization may choose to expand its program by adding gift clubs for gifts totaling $500 and $250 to provide levels leading to the $1,000 level. For organizations with direct-mail programs and with donors at lower gift levels, adding these gift clubs may be appropriate for moving smaller donors to increased levels.

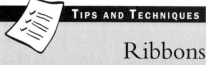

TIPS AND TECHNIQUES

Ribbons on Name Tags

At professional conferences, the number of ribbons that can be attached to a name tag is ever increasing. Some of the ribbons, such as those that identify

"speakers" or "sponsors," are helpful while others, like "tired feet" and "party animal," serve more as icebreakers.

A strategy for recognizing members of a recognition gift club is to have special ribbons printed that can be attached to name tags. For example, a nonprofit with a recognition gift club at the $1,000-and-above level called the Founder's Society would have ribbons printed in an appropriate color, saying "The Founder's Society." At various events, when members of the Founder's Society are attending, these ribbons would be added to the name tags of those individuals. The ribbon makes members of the Founder's Society feel special and all those attending the event are aware of those persons who are generously supporting the organization.

An organization that used this strategy introduced the ribbons at its annual meeting. All of the members of the Founder Society were invited to the meeting and those who attended wore "The Founder's Society" ribbons on their name tags. When the meeting began, the president of the organization explained the meaning of the ribbons and asked the members of the Founder's Society to stand to be recognized.

Having too many ribbons takes away from their significance. An organization may consider limiting the number of ribbons used for recognition to one or two for an event. Depending on the event, the ribbons might identify those in the top tier of giving for the prior year, those who have achieved the defined thresholds for cumulative lifetime giving, and/or those who are members of the planned giving recognition program.

Enhancing a Gift Club Program

Example 1: At the turn of the twenty-first century, a number of organizations changed the basic level of membership for leadership annual giving from $1,000 to $2,000. Others have chosen numbers with historical significance for the organization, such as the year in which the nonprofit celebrates its 100th anniversary, as the minimum amount for membership in the gift club program. For example, an educational institution has its centennial in 2008 and establishes $2,008 as its new minimum level of giving for its leadership gift club recognition.

EXHIBIT 5.8

A Message to Organization ABC's Supporters

For decades, Organization ABC has recognized its most generous supporters by inviting them to become members of giving societies: the *President's Club*, the *Circle of 1,000*, and the *Lifetime Giving Club*. These groups were created to honor the important role that donors play in the success of Organization ABC and to inspire new levels of philanthropy.

For the first time in more than ten years, the requirements for membership are being changed. These changes reflect careful study by a task force of donors, volunteers, and staff, benchmarking with peer organizations, and increases in the cost of fulfilling the mission of Organization ABC, as well as inflation.

LIFETIME GIVING CLUB

Effective January 1, 2010, cumulative gifts of $250,000 or more will qualify donors for membership. There will be no increase in the requirement for membership to the *Founders Circle*, which will continue to honor donors whose cumulative gifts exceed $1 million. Current members and donors who qualify at the current $100,000 minimum level by December 31, 2009, will retain their membership after the increase goes into effect.

Example 2: If the lifetime giving program was established with $100,000 as the minimum amount for membership and a decision is made to increase that amount to $250,000, a date should be established for the new minimum level. In this case, the accepted practice is to leave everyone in the program that has qualified to date using the original level and to establish a date when the new criteria will be used for membership qualification. An announcement about the change should be made six months or more prior to the change (see Exhibit 5.8).

Example 3: When the gift club for those making bequest intents was established, the recognition group was named the Heritage Society or the Legacy Society. The organization decides to personalize the program. A person who made a bequest that provided significant benefit to the organization is identified and the name of the recognition program is changed to honor that person. By making the change, the organization has the opportunity to tell a story and to promote making bequest provisions in a different way.

To make the expansion or enhancement of a gift club program meaningful, a plan must be developed for marketing the "new" gift club program. The objective is to bring attention to the gift club program and to promote increased giving. As when establishing a gift club program, measurable goals should be established and an evaluation should be conducted to determine whether those goals are achieved.

Summary

Recognition clubs for gifts of various sizes and types are used effectively by organizations to promote increased giving. The three common types of gift clubs are those for annual giving, for cumulative lifetime giving, and for planned giving. In addition to the gift clubs that are based on type and level of giving, others are defined by the specific constituency, frequency of giving, or specific interest or affinity. Establishing a gift club involves establishing criteria for membership, defining the benefits of membership, choosing an appropriate name, and developing, implementing, and evaluating a plan for the gift club. Benefits of membership are designed to bring donors closer to the organization and to build the relationship with the donor. When developing benefits for membership in gift clubs, IRS guidelines limiting the amount spent on benefits need to be considered. Names for gift clubs can be generic or they can have special significance to the organization. The plan for using the gift clubs should be aligned with the overall plan for the development program and should be integrated into the various aspects of the program. Gift clubs should be evaluated against the goals and objectives established for the program using both quantitative and qualitative information. Evaluation may lead to expansion and enhancement of gift clubs over time to keep the program exciting and to focus attention on it.

Notes

1. The source for the information on the requirements of the Internal Revenue Service for substantiation and disclosure was Department of the Treasury, Internal Revenue Service, Publication 1771(Rev.52007) Catalog Number 20054Q.

   Detailed rules for contemporaneous written acknowledgments are contained in Section 170(f)(8) of the Internal Revenue Code and Section 1.170A-13(f) of the Income Tax Regulations.

   The "low-cost article" rules are set forth in Section 513(h)(2) of the Code.

   Information can be found on the IRS website at www.irs.gov.

2. F.E. Robbins & Sons Press, St. Louis, Missouri. Copyright 2000 by Board Builders; Second printing 2002, revised.

CHAPTER 6

Stewardship

After reading this chapter, you will be able to:

- Define stewardship.
- Describe the four components of stewardship.
- Distinguish stewardship from other components of donor relations.
- Understand the role of stewardship in development.
- Create a stewardship report.

The Definition of Stewardship

Stewardship means acting as a steward or caretaker. The word *steward* is defined by http://dictionary.reference.com as:

1. A person who manages another's property or financial affairs; one who administers anything as the agent of another or others.

2. A person who has charge of the household of another, buying or obtaining food, directing the servants, etc.

3. An employee who has charge of the table, wine, servants, etc., in a club, restaurant, or the like.

4. A person who attends to the domestic concerns of persons on board a vessel, as in overseeing maids and waiters.

5. An employee on a ship, train, or bus who waits on and is responsible for the comfort of passengers, takes orders for or distributes food, etc.

6. A flight attendant.

7. A person appointed by an organization or group to supervise the affairs of that group at certain functions.

8. *U.S. Navy.* A petty officer in charge of officers' quarters and mess.

9. To act as steward of; manage. (Verb used with object)

10. To act or serve as steward. (Verb used without object)

Steward was the title of a class of high officers of state in early England and Scotland, meaning "one who manages affairs of an estate on behalf of his employer" (c.1386). The use of the word to mean "overseer of workmen" dates back to approximately 1300. The use of *steward* to describe the "officer on a ship in charge of provisions and meals" is first recorded about 1450 and was extended to trains about 1906. *Stewardess* to mean the "female attendant on passenger aircraft" was first used about 1931. But the term had been used on ships (where she waited on the female passengers) from 1837.

The term *stewardship* is often used in churches as the principle on which tithing is based. "Guard what has been entrusted to your care" (1 Timothy 6:20) is one of the biblical references that is quoted to support the concept of stewardship. While the various religious denominations have different views of stewardship, the basic biblical principle is that God has given all things to men and women and that giving back and taking care of that which has been given is an "acknowledgment of God's blessings." Stewardship involves understanding what God requires and acting in accordance with those requirements. In many ways, stewardship in its religious context means being responsible and accountable to God.

Active concerns for the environment are also referred to as *stewardship* in a religious context. "The earth is the Lord's and everything in it" (Psalm 24:1) is cited when talking about the responsibility that men and women have for protecting the environment for future generations.

Whether in a religious context or not, the word *stewardship* is used frequently in discussing environmental issues, such as pollution, global warming, destruction of habitats, and massive extinctions. Each spring, the nation celebrates Earth Day and calls attention to the importance of good *stewardship* of the earth. In the speeches on Earth Day, which began in 1970 and is observed annually on April 22, the importance of protecting the environment is noted as the personal responsibility of each individual in America. A video on YouTube, called "Stewardship of Earth," begins by describing the planet as a gift received billions of years ago and asks the question of how that gift has been used. With striking pictures of the pollution and the destruction of the environment, the conclusion of the video is that attempts at stewardship of earth have failed.

When stewardship is defined for a nonprofit organization, it also means taking charge, managing, and using wisely that which has been given to the organization. By virtue of an organization accepting a monetary or other gift, the nonprofit is taking responsibility for that gift on behalf of the donor and is using the gift on behalf of the donor. The organization is the conduit between the donor and those served by the organization. In the broadest sense of the word, stewardship may include acknowledgment and recognition, but its essence is that the organization is taking charge of a gift on behalf of the donor and is responsible and accountable for its wise use in accordance with the donor's wishes.

TIPS AND TECHNIQUES

Consent to the Release of Information

Sharing information about the person who benefits from a gift, such as a scholarship recipient at an educational institution, is an effective means of stewardship. By telling the donor about the recipient, the organization can put a face on the value of the gift for the donor. If an organization wishes to use this strategy, a consent form should be developed for the signature of the person whose information is being shared. A consent form is also appropriate for other organizations, such as health-care and social service organizations, where information about an individual is being given to another person or persons as part of stewardship. Making individuals aware that you are sharing information about them with others is always a sound practice, and having a signed consent form eliminates problems that may arise:

SAMPLE LANGUAGE FOR A CONSENT FORM

I understand that XYZ College reports to those who make philanthropic contributions for financial aid about the activities, graduate school plans, and career goals of the recipients of the funds they have contributed. I further understand that XYZ needs my permission to release this information to them.

I understand that by signing this form I am giving permission to Financial Aid, the Office of Institutional Advancement, and the Office of the Registrar of XYZ College to provide donors of financial aid funds the following information: (a) information on my academic progress, including grade point average; (b) biographical and extracurricular information as stated on this and subsequent forms; (c) directory information, such as name, home address, and field of study; and (d) amount of aid received from all sources.

Some organizations also include the expectation that the recipient of the scholarship will write a letter of appreciation to the donor that will be provided to the Development or Institutional Advancement Office to share with the donor or the donor's family. In these cases, the consent form may also include:

I agree to release the contents of my scholarship appreciation letter to the Office of Institutional Advancement. I understand that the entire letter or a portion of the letter could be used in publications or on the XYZ College website, or shared with friends or alumni of the college.

The Components of Stewardship

When a board of directors of an organization was asked to define *stewardship*, their answers included the honoring of donor intent, prudent investment of gifts, and the effective and efficient use of funds to further the mission of the organization. When the group was asked to go beyond that response, their faces were blank. The one aspect of stewardship that is often forgotten is "reporting back". An organization needs to tell a donor that the donor's intent was honored, the gift was invested prudently, and the funds were used effectively and efficiently to advance the mission of the organization.

Stewardship is that aspect of donor relations where an organization demonstrates its gratitude by being accountable for the use of the gift and by reporting back to the donor. Stewardship has four components:

1. Honoring donor intent

2. Investing gifts prudently

3. Using contributions effectively and efficiently to advance the organization and make a difference in the lives of those served by the organization

4. Reporting back to the donor on the first three components of stewardship

Acknowledgment, or the thank-you letter, phone call, or other communication, may address the potential impact of the gift. However, at that point in time, the organization can merely cite the impact of prior gifts from that donor or other donors, and address what impact the current or recent gift is expected to have. Likewise, recognition may reference the impact that a gift is expected to have.

IN THE REAL WORLD

Lisa Hillman, Fellow of the Association for Healthcare Philanthropy (FAHP), senior vice president, and chief development officer at Anne Arundel Health System in Annapolis, Maryland, provided meaningful acknowledgment and stewardship to a generous woman who wished to remain anonymous.

A ROOFTOP PICNIC

She was the widow of a prominent surgeon. Mother to three grown daughters, grandmother to two, world traveler, pianist, and engaging conversationalist, she is one of the most memorable donors I have known.

Intensely private about her giving, she shared a favorite quote: "The best thing money can buy is privacy." When she gave—always no less than a six-figure gift—she prefaced it with a phone call, a request that it be put to use for any one of the programs she favored, and an insistence that only I and the CEO know about it.

We honored her requests. We both adored her.

When the time came to build our replacement hospital, it was clear that she would be a major—and anonymous—donor to this project. She intimated that at some point we would receive a very large contribution. There was the slightest hint of a serious illness.

How to thank and recognize such a marvelous woman during her lifetime? And at the same time, how to respect her intense wish for privacy?

On our campus, cranes were erecting the 9-story patient tower adjacent to a recently opened 5-level parking garage. The rooftop of the garage looked over the construction site, alive with work crews, steel and beams—site of the future hospital. An idea struck. With the secret aid of two staff members, we arranged a surprise "rooftop picnic" for two. She knew only that I was picking her up for lunch. As we drove back to the hospital campus, my colleagues were roping off a section on the rooftop level of the garage, setting up a table and two chairs, complete with linen and elegant boxed lunches. They were long gone when my car drove up to the roof. Slowly, she took in the elegant table-setting, realized where we would be having lunch that day, and shrieked with delight. The sunlit May day was backdrop to her sunlit joy at such a lovely surprise.

Two years later, after she passed away, two separate gifts arrived via an attorney in a far-away state. The donor had taken great pains to ensure anonymity. The gift was $1 million.

Stewardship is the aspect of donor relations that comes after the gift has been used and the impact of the gift can be reported. Stewardship is illustrating that what was said would happen in the acknowledgment and the recognition has happened and the impact was what the donor anticipated or, in some cases, is beyond what the donor anticipated. For example, if one of the outcomes of a leadership gift to an annual giving program or a capital campaign was to encourage others to give, reporting back to the donor how many did subsequently give can be stewardship. Reporting that the number of anticipated gifts exceeded projections can be meaningful to the donor and can make the donor feel that the gift was used wisely.

The Role of Stewardship

Stewardship is sometimes called "proof of performance," because it verifies that the organization did use the gift as the donor was told the gift would be used or as the donor asked that the gift be used.

In business, proof of performance is not so different. Those who market products want to be able to measure the impact of marketing on their visibility and sales. In addition, photos and quotes from others provide evidence of the marketing campaign. Proof of performance for a product may involve a demonstration or testimony from another user of the product.

Stewardship is often required by those who make grants to organizations. In the grant application, information may need to be provided on how outcomes will be measured and acceptance of a grant may include a commitment to submit an annual report on the funded project. While most contributions are not made with an explicit requirement for reporting, the organization that embraces a donor-centered approach to philanthropy recognizes the importance of reporting back to the donor. Stewardship can include written reports, photos, and quotes. Telling a donor that a gift has made a difference in the way the organization fulfills its mission is a critical step in building a relationship. Having those persons served by the organization express gratitude is one way to acknowledge a gift and having those served by the organization convey how the organization has made a difference in their lives is an excellent way to provide stewardship. With major gifts that support specific programs, the opportunities for stewardship may be more direct. The person who funds a scholarship can meet the students who benefit from the scholarship and can receive reports on the success of that student.

IN THE REAL WORLD

A certain man relates with great pride that each fall he and his wife visit the campus of their alma mater and have a picture taken with the students they are supporting through their endowed scholarship fund. In their home, a special shelf on the bookcase is lined with the photographs from each year. The annual photograph is described by the couple as essential to their continued support.

The couple, who met one another at the university, gathers with the students each year, shares their story of success after graduation, and tells the students what has motivated them to establish the fund. Many of the students are from the couple's hometowns because they requested that preference be given to students from those towns.

The donors see their gift as having a broader meaning than just the scholarships. They feel that they are setting an example for future alumni, encouraging them to give back to the university in appreciation for what they received in scholarship support.

For example, a couple reports that they provided tuition for a young man from a family who lived in poverty to attend a private high school. The couple proudly displays pictures of the young man and talks about his success in college and after college.

The key to stewardship is communication about the outcomes from a gift. Regardless of whether the achievements of the organization are reported in a newsletter or publication or in an individualized report on a specific project or fund that a donor has supported, the objective is to tell donors what their gifts have accomplished. Those who are philanthropic make investments, and stewardship is reporting on the return on their investments.

IN THE REAL WORLD

One morning, as I walked into the office of the local chapter of the American Red Cross, I commented to the volunteer opening the mail about the large pile of envelopes that had been sent back after the Clara Barton appeal for gifts of $1,000 or more. The volunteer agreed and noted that one check was for $50,000. I stopped in my tracks and asked the volunteer to repeat what she had just said. She replied, "We have a check for $50,000 in this group of responses." In shock and amazement, I asked to see the check. I quickly took the check to the chief financial officer and proudly showed him the check. He was delighted to get an unrestricted gift for that amount. I proceeded to find the executive director of the organization, who was also pleasantly surprised.

In conversation, I learned that the person making the significant gift in response to a mail request for $1,000 had replied to a planned giving mailing and had asked for information about making a bequest. The executive director had followed up with the gentleman and had discussed his making a provision in his will for the organization. After the discussion, the gentleman indicated that he was not sure he wanted to make any changes to his plans. That conversation had taken place about six months before this check was received.

The executive director asked what she should do to say "thank you" for such a special gift. I recommended that she visit the gentleman, who lived nearby, and take him a basket of fruit. I also suggested that she tell the donor how his gift would be used. The executive director paused and said the gift was un-restricted and would be used for operations. I suggested that perhaps some-thing that costs $50,000 or more that was in the budget could be earmarked for this contribution. After some thought, the executive director agreed and several options for using the gift were identified.

The executive director visited the gentleman, delivered the basket of fruit, and told the donor how appreciative the organization was. She also asked the donor whether he would like his gift to be used to support one of three different programs. He indicated he had no specific preference among the items suggested. The executive director told him that the gift would be used for a specific program among the three and told him how his gift would make a difference.

After several months, the executive director went back to visit the donor and reported on the use of the $50,000 gift and how that gift made an impact in the lives of those served by the organization.

Stewardship for unrestricted gifts is usually broad and gives an overall look at an organization's accomplishments. However, being able to link a gift to a specific program provides an opportunity for more targeted stewardship.

The Stewardship Report

An organization has the responsibility for stewardship of every gift. For smaller gifts, the stewardship report may be less specific than it is for the major gift restricted to a specific purpose.

For endowed funds, the organization should make a report to the donor on at least an annual basis (see Exhibit 6.1).

The components of a stewardship report would include the following:

EXHIBIT 6.1

Letter from the President

Dear [SALUTATION USED BY PRESIDENT FOR SPECIFIC DONOR],

On behalf of ABC Organization and its Board of Trustees, I want to thank you for investing in the mission of ABC. By establishing an endowment, you are allowing us to provide [health care, education, cultural opportunities, or OTHER SPECIFIC SERVICE] today and are assuring our ability to continue to offer tomorrow's [patients, students, community, or OTHER SPECIFIC CONSTITUENCY] with these programs. Your generosity contributes significantly to the growth and success of ABC Organization.

As a part of our commitment to provide good stewardship and accountability to our investors, we proudly present your annual personal endowment fund report. This past year has been very successful as you and other donors made contributions of more than [TOTAL DOLLARS].

I am pleased to provide an update on the [NAME OF FUND]. At the close of our last fiscal year, June 30, [YEAR], the fund had a balance of [AMOUNT]. An overview of the investment practice and performance for ABC is enclosed in your personalized packet. Should you have any questions, please contact me or [NAME, TITLE] at [PHONE NUMBER] or [EMAIL ADDRESS].

We deeply appreciate your ongoing support as we continue to move toward accomplishing our mission of [MISSION OF ORGANIZATION].

Sincerely,

[SIGNATURE]

[NAME OF PRESIDENT]

Enclosures: *Fiscal Year [YEAR] Endowment Fund Financial Activity Report

*Overview of Investment Practice and Performance

Endowment Fund Financial Activity Report

Name of Fund

Fiscal Year [YEAR]

July 1, [YEAR]–June 30, [YEAR]

ENDOWMENT FUND

Fund Balance as of 7-01-XX	$ AMOUNT
New Gifts	AMOUNT
Investment Income	AMOUNT
*Earnings Available for Expenditure	(AMOUNT)
Endowment Fund Balance as of 6-30-XX	$ AMOUNT

*Policy for determining the amount of distributable monies is set by ABC Organization Board of Trustees based on a percentage of the three-year moving book average of the Endowment balance.

Overview of Investment Practice and Performance

Endowment gifts to ABC Organization are placed in ABC's Endowment Fund for investment and oversight purposes. By approving Investment Objectives and Policies, the Board of Trustees has set in place a plan to preserve and augment the value of the endowment. The Trustees have adopted the broad objective of investing endowment assets so as to preserve both the real value and the long-range purchasing power of the endowment income.

The Board seeks superior returns through a diversified, professionally managed portfolio absent imprudent risks. To achieve its objectives, the Board retains independent investment firms that were selected on the basis of a number of factors, including investment expertise, cost of service, and history of producing returns consistent with or exceeding benchmarks for their respective asset class. ABC's Investment Objectives and Policies govern the overall allocation considerations and ranges of investment in equities and fixed-rate securities.

How does this translate into performance for ABC's investments in general and for your endowment fund balance in particular?

The answer is *quite positively*. The portfolio in general and your endowment in particular increased in value during the year ended June 30, 20XX. We are pleased to report that actions taken by the Board of Trustees to diversify and rebalance its investments produced returns exceeding benchmarks in all categories. The largest portion of ABC's equity investment is held in [NAME OF FUND], which returned [PERCENTAGE] percent compared to [PERCENTAGE] percent return for the S&P 500 Index, and [CITE OTHER MEASURES OF INVESTMENT PERFORMANCE]. In addition, a large portion of the reported total return was captured. This "realized" return, which represents "money in hand," not just market gain, has been posted as an increase to your fund balance. This return is the source of the spendable funds to support the purpose you intended in establishing your endowment fund.

The Board of Trustees seeks to balance the need for current endowment income against long-term investment and spending objectives by means of a spending policy that allots dollars on a percentage of the average year-end market value for the preceding years. This method smoothes out swings in market value, thereby protecting the corpus of the endowment fund and allowing ABC to more reasonably predict future distributions to benefit its mission and its needs.

The following reflects the total fund balance of ABC's Endowment, which includes all named endowment funds. The endowment balance includes investment results along with new gifts:

	Fiscal Year Ending 6/30/xx [PRIOR YEAR 3]	Fiscal Year Ending 6/30/xx [PRIOR YEAR 2]	Fiscal Year Ending 6/30/xx [PRIOR YEAR 1]
ABC Organization Endowment Fund Balance	$ [AMOUNT]	$[AMOUNT]	$ [AMOUNT]

Endowment Fund Activity Letter and Report adapted from letter and report developed by University of Arkansas Fort Smith Foundation, Inc. in Fort Smith, Arkansas.

- *Letter from the president of the organization* that thanks the donor for investing in the mission of the organization and provides a summary on the named fund

- *Report on fund activity* that includes beginning balance, new gifts, investment income, earnings allocated for expenditures, and ending balance

- *Overview of investment practice and performance* that indicates how funds are invested and what the investment performance has been over the previous year

- *Information* on adding to the endowment fund

IN THE REAL WORLD

In addition to the stewardship reports that are prepared for individual donors, organizations have identified other ways to give donors feedback on what their gifts have accomplished:

- An organization publishes a quarterly newsletter called *Impact* that reports on the achievements of the organization and links them to philanthropic support. The organization mails the newsletter to all donors of $100 or more.

- Several one-page reports are developed on key programs at the organization. The reports are sent to the people who supported the respective programs or who had expressed interest in those programs.

- A report on outcomes at a children's hospital in pediatric cardiology are shared with those donors who have supported pediatric cardiology and those who have expressed interest in pediatric cardiology.

- Copies of a newspaper or journal article about a program are sent to specific donors who have supported the program.

- Donors to a program are invited to a seminar that a faculty member is giving on the advances made in the area of study supported by the donors.

- A group of donors to a research project are invited to a reception honoring the researcher leading the project for the work being done in that specific area of research.

- A curator of a museum invites donors to attend a special program that highlights the exhibit that the donors have supported.

- Donors who supported an educational program at the local chapter of the American Red Cross are invited to the graduation ceremonies for the persons having completed the program.

Summary

Stewardship is reporting back to a donor or being accountable to the donor for the use of the contributions that the donor has made. When an organization receives a contribution, it is accepting responsibility for using the gift wisely and as the donor intended. Stewardship has four components: honoring donor intent, investing gifts prudently, using contributions effectively and efficiently to advance the organization and to make a difference in the lives of those served by the organization, and reporting back to the donor.

Stewardship, unlike acknowledgment and recognition, is about the outcomes from the gift or its impact on the organization and those served by the organization. Stewardship is proof of performance, or reporting on the return on the investment that the donor made. Donors who have funded scholarships or have established specific funds, especially endowment funds, should receive personalized stewardship reports annually. The reports should show what activity has occurred in the fund, including additional gifts, interest earned, and expenditures made, and should give an overview of investment strategies of the organization and investment results.

Stewardship is communicating with donors on the ways in which their gifts have made a difference.

CHAPTER 7

Donor Relations: Other Topics

After reading this chapter, you will be able to:

- Develop a donor relations plan for a capital campaign.
- Incorporate donor relations into prospect cultivation.
- Measure the impact of a donor relations initiative.
- Describe ways to use the Internet to support donor relations.
- Recognize differences in age, gender, and culture for donor relations.
- Describe trends in donor relations.

Donor Relations in the Capital Campaign

One of the early steps in planning for a capital campaign should be the strategies for donor relations, including acknowledgment, recognition, and stewardship. As with all donor relations programs, developing the guidelines before rather than midway through the effort will assure that the organization expresses gratitude in a timely and appropriate manner. In addition, a thoughtful, creative recognition plan that is weaved into the campaign can help maximize the gifts and pledges received.

Developing the plan for acknowledgment of gifts and pledges, which may include letters, personal notes, phone calls, and other communications, both at the time the gift or pledge is made and after the gift or pledge is made, is the first step. The acknowledgment plan should delineate which donors get what expressions of acknowledgment, from whom, and in what timeframe.

The second step is determining the way in which donors will be recognized for the commitments that they make to the campaign. Recognition may include listing of names of donors in written and online reports and newsletters. Donors may have their names included in recognition displays. Individual donors may receive recognition with the naming of a fund or of a specific area of a facility or even the facility. Other opportunities for recognition include press releases, receptions or events, announcements at board meetings or in other forums, and giving donors a special gift to display in their homes or offices.

The third step in preparation for the donor relations that will accompany the campaign is stewardship or reporting back to donors. Since campaigns are often conducted over a number of years, the importance of stewardship in keeping donors engaged is significant. Organizations have a responsibility for giving updates throughout the campaign to those persons who make gifts early in a campaign. Keeping donors advised of the progress of the project and the campaign is an important strategy for giving them a sense of making a difference.

Acknowledgments for Capital Campaign Gifts and Pledges

In preparing for a campaign, the development of the acknowledgment plan involves defining the methods that will be used to acknowledge gifts and pledges for the campaign, determining who will acknowledge which gifts, and putting a timeline on when acknowledgments will occur. Methods for acknowledging gifts can be letters, personal handwritten notes, phone calls, and email messages. Acknowledgments should come from high-level staff and volunteers at the organization. A letter signed by the president of an organization is usually more meaningful to the donor than a letter from a member of the development staff.

Likewise, a phone call from a board member is usually more significant to a donor than a call from an office assistant. As with all acknowledgments, promptness is extremely important. The initial thank-you should occur within 48 hours of receiving the gift. Subsequent letters, notes, and phone calls may come from other persons at various intervals following the pledge or gift.

Since many commitments to campaigns are multiyear pledges, thought should be given to acknowledging pledges that are made with and without an initial payment on the pledge. Thought also should be given to acknowledging a verbal pledge. In this case, a pledge form for the person to complete to formalize the pledge may be included with the letter, along with a postage-paid return envelope.

Acknowledgment of gifts and pledges will vary according to the size of the gifts and to the constituency from which the donor comes. For example, the way that an organization thanks a donor for a pledge of $5 million should differ from the approach to expressing gratitude to a donor for a gift of $500. The thank-you for an emeritus board member should differ from the thank-you for an employee of the organization.

While the objective of the plan is to know how, by whom, and when each donor will be acknowledged, flexibility for personalizing the thank-you message should be built into the plan.

Recognition for Capital Campaign Giving

Recognition has long been a component of the capital campaign. In educational organizations and hospitals, the recognition wall or display that is the oldest is usually one for a capital campaign, often one conducted near the beginning of an organization's history.

Recognition continues to be an important component of the capital campaign. Recognition may include the listing of names of donors on a wall, in a display, in a written report, or on the organization's website. In addition, one recognition practice that many organizations use exclusively during capital campaigns is that of naming spaces, rooms, or buildings in recognition of the donors.

During capital campaigns that will support the construction of buildings or other physical structures, the development of naming opportunities becomes a major focus of recognition and becomes a strategy in conducting the campaign. As the commitments to a capital campaign are usually far greater than those an organization receives on an annual basis, naming opportunities can help establish new and higher levels of giving for the campaign.

While potential campaign donors usually do not decide to make gifts to a campaign solely to have their names on the wall or in a special area, the naming opportunities may have an impact on the timing and on the size of the commitment.

Those who solicit campaign gifts, both staff and volunteers, find that talking about recognition can be helpful in asking for a significant gift. For example, asking for a gift of $25 million to name a building is easier than just asking for a commitment of $25 million. To make the gift even more feasible for a donor's consideration, it may be described as a gift of $5 million per year for five years to name the proposed building. The request to a donor that includes a naming opportunity should focus more on the building and its importance to the organization's mission rather than on the gift amount.

Developing recognition for a capital campaign can be effectively done by using the gift table for the campaign. If the gift table has gifts of $5 million, $1 million, and $500,000 at the top, determining naming opportunities for those top gifts can be helpful in talking to potential donors about their gifts (see Exhibit 7.1). Using the gift table and the architectural plans for the building, the staff or a committee can review the various spaces available for naming. Considering the size of the spaces, the prominences of the spaces, and the uses of the spaces, a process can begin to match spaces to the gifts needed for campaign success.

Setting prices for naming opportunities can be challenging. The amounts for the gifts should reflect what the market can bear and what the organization needs in its campaign. The gift amounts need to be proportionate to one another and should tie to the overall campaign goals. If the top gift-naming opportunity for a campaign is set at $30 million and a lead gift of $5 million is

EXHIBIT 7.1

Gift Table for $7.5 Million Capital Campaign

Number of Gifts	Average Size	Total Gifts	Cumulative Total
1	$1,500,000	$1,500,000	$1,500,000
2	$500,000	$1,000,000	$2,500,000
4	$250,000	$1,000,000	$3,500,000
8	$100,000	$800,000	$4,300,000
20	$50,000	$1,000,000	$5,300,000
35	$25,000	$875,000	$6,175,000
70	$10,000	$700,000	$6,875,000
Many	<**$10,000**	**$625,000**	**$7,500,000**
140			**$7,500,000**

Recognition for a campaign of $7.5 million that is using this gift table may include the following:

- *Naming opportunities.* Donors would be given the opportunities to name a facility, room, or other space for gifts at the following levels:

  $1.5 million (2–3 options recommended)

  $1.0 million (2–3 options recommended)

  $500,000 (4–6 options recommended)

  $250,000 (8–10 options recommended)

- *Area recognition.* Rather than naming the space for the donor, the next level of recognition would be giving the donor recognition in a specific area.

  For example, a plaque may be displayed in the elevator lobby with wording such as: "In recognition of the generous support of John and Jane Jones." Rather than the elevator lobby being named "The Jones Elevator Lobby," the Joneses would receive special recognition in that specific area.

  Donors would receive recognition in specific areas for gifts of the following levels:

  $50,000, $75,000, $100,000, $150,000, $200,000

- *Recognition display.* Donors would have their names listed in a recognition display in a visible area of the facility for gifts of $25,000 or more.

   A separate recognition display may be designed for an area frequently seen by employees, such as the cafeteria, that would include the names of those employees that make campaign commitments equal to or exceeding a specific amount or a variable amount, such the value of one hour's pay per pay period for three years.
- *Published report and online report.* Donors would have their names listed in a report to be published at the conclusion of the campaign and on an online donor list for gifts of $10,000 or more.

needed to meet the campaign goal, the assignment of amounts for naming opportunities should include an opportunity at the $5 million level or higher. The determination will need to be made on what projects supported by the campaign would be appropriate for naming for a contribution of $5 million or more. More than one review of the architectural drawings and the gift table is often needed to get the amounts established for naming opportunities.

In establishing gift amounts, aiming high is the best strategy. The tendency is to set amounts lower than they should be often leading to a sense of frustration after the campaign is over. The gifts associated with naming opportunities should be the largest gifts for a campaign.

When Miami Children's Hospital began planning its campaign to establish a Children's Brain Institute, the lead gift needed to achieve the campaign goal of $25 million was $4 million. However, the opportunity to name the institute, which was to serve as a national model for the diagnosis and treatment of children with brain disorders, was considered to have value worth far more than $4 million. It was determined that the opportunity to name the Children's Brain Institute would require a gift of $15 million.

Keeping the names of specific buildings and rooms separate from the function of those buildings and rooms is an important concept in establishing naming opportunities.

In a campaign for the Millard Fillmore Health System in Buffalo, New York, to build a hospital in the suburbs of the city, two donors made gifts to name the hospital's business office and the admissions office respectively. At the time the gifts were made, the business office was a much larger space in a more prominent area while the admissions office was much smaller and occupied a space at the end of a hall where the foot traffic was minimal. The gift amount for naming the business office was three times that of the gift for the admissions office.

After ten years, the functions of the business and admissions offices had changed and the larger and more visible space became the admissions office while the smaller space at the end of the hall became the business office. The names identified with the two spaces did not change as the relative size and visibility of the two spaces did not change. However, the donor who made the smaller gift to name the admissions office was convinced that he made a gift to name the "admissions office" rather than the space in which the admission office was housed at that time and that his name should remain with that function. Despite communication that described the criteria for naming as size and visibility, the donor remained unhappy. Being clear about whether the space or the function for that space is actually what is named is an essential component of offering naming opportunities.

Planning ahead for recognition of donors to a campaign has a number of advantages. A major advantage is the role that donor recognition can play in strategies for cultivation and solicitation of capital campaign donors. If naming opportunities have been developed and approved, a strategy early in the campaign can be reserving the top-named gift opportunity in the potential donor's name, and approaching the donor to say the organization has reserved the naming rights for the building for the donor because the organization wants the potential donor to be the first person given the opportunity to make the lead gift to name the proposed facility.

When talking to a donor about a lead gift, showing the donor the architectural renderings for the building can be useful. Some organizations have gone one step further and have obtained architectural drawings of buildings with the potential donor's name on the front of the building. For example, Mr. and Mrs. Paul Smith see their names in large letters on the front of the "Smith Family Center for Women's Health." Video presentations that show three-dimensional

IN THE REAL WORLD

A community hospital in Massachusetts conducted a capital campaign to raise $1 million to construct a new entrance to the facility and a new emergency department. Physician leaders who were asked to assist with the campaign were concerned that the participation in the campaign by the physicians would be minimal as in past fundraising efforts for the hospital.

One of the strategies developed to increase participation was to have the names of those doctors who made a commitment of $10,000 or more listed in a special section of the campaign recognition display that would be placed in the entrance to the hospital. The physicians would have their names included in the overall list of donors in the appropriate category for size of gift, but also would have their names in the special section for physicians.

The physician leaders and co-chairs of the physician campaign made regular presentations at medical staff meetings on the status of the campaign and encouraged those who had not participated to complete their pledge cards. At one of the medical staff meetings, the physician that was leading the presentation mentioned the special section in the recognition display for physicians. A physician in the audience raised his hand and wanted to know the minimum-size gift for inclusion on the donor wall. A number of physicians took note of the amount and five physicians found their way to the development office the following day to make commitments of $10,000 each. Other gifts and pledges of $10,000 were made by physicians following the meeting where the minimum amount for recognition was announced. The participation by the medical staff in the capital campaign was more than double their participation in prior fundraising efforts and the total contributed far exceeded that committed by physicians in earlier campaigns.

renderings of a building from various levels and angles have been designed to share with a potential donor and have included the person's name being added to the front of the building as the potential donor watches. While many donors clearly state that they do not want to receive recognition for giving, the possibility of having one's name on a building or in another specific area has contributed to the securing of many significant gifts in campaigns.

If the recognition display can be designed early in the campaign, a conceptual drawing of the display can be a helpful tool in cultivating and soliciting the support of donors throughout the campaign. Volunteers and staff find that showing potential donors the way the display will look can be effective in discussing potential support.

Another advantage of early planning is the opportunity to work with the architects for the building or other persons involved in a project to select a location where the central recognition can be displayed for maximum visibility. Getting to know these people also can be extremely helpful in making sure that the list of gift opportunities remains up-to-date as building modifications are made. If a space on the recognition list is eliminated or the size of the space changes for an area that a donor has chosen for gift recognition, the opportunity to talk with the donor about the change goes more smoothly if the discussion occurs long before the building is completed rather than the week before the facility opens.

Another advantage of planning ahead is developing an adequate budget for recognition as part of the campaign budget. The plans for recognizing donors, whether in reports, in a donor display, or through special events, can be a significant budget item for a capital campaign.

Unfortunately, without advanced planning, a capital campaign might come to its conclusion before the question of how to pay for the recognition that was promised during the campaign arises. With the high rate of turnover in the development profession, often the chief development officer at the end of the campaign is not the same person who developed the budget for the campaign a number of years earlier. On many occasions, a development officer in place at the end of the campaign has discovered that the campaign budget did not include the costs of recognition or that the budget allocation is not adequate to meet the promises of the campaign. In addition, the development officer may learn that the campaign celebration party that the board and administration insist must occur was not included in the campaign fundraising plan or in the campaign budget.

If the campaign budget does not include adequate funding for recognition, developing the recognition for as little money as possible becomes the primary objective, rather than giving thoughtful consideration to recognition that can support an ongoing development program. When a donor recognition display is attractive and appealing to those who see it and the campaign celebration event is meaningful to donors, the recognition can convey to donors that the organization truly values philanthropy and appreciates its donors.

Donor recognition displays may include special sections for various constituencies of an organization. For example, in addition to listing all donors by size of gift, an organization may have a special section or separate panel for employees who made gifts at or above a minimum level.

While recognition during a capital campaign often focuses on a recognition wall or other recognition display, recognition can include other strategies.

IN THE REAL WORLD

A children's hospital was building a new facility and wanted to encourage the employees of the hospital to participate in the campaign. A minimum amount was established for employees to contribute to receive recognition in a special display for employees only. Each person who contributed that amount or more had his or her name on a tile in a display that was on a prominent wall in the cafeteria of the new building. The display featured tiles of various colors that complemented the décor of the room. Within the display, tiles featured the signatures and the printed names of the employees who contributed the established minimum or more to the campaign. When the display was unveiled, the nutrition services staff made cupcakes with small triangular flags on toothpicks stuck in them. The names of the employees whose names were on the tiles were written on the flags in the cupcakes.

The campaign was promoted to employees through small group sessions held on each shift. The objectives of the sessions were threefold. One objective was to make sure employees knew about the campaign for the new building in case people in the community asked them about it. The second objective was to explain the importance of employee giving to the capital campaign as requests were made to the community, including corporations and foundations. The third objective was to give employees the opportunity to participate in the campaign if they chose to do so. The recognition display for employees was highlighted and employees received a list of gift amounts broken down by the amount an employee would designate for payroll deduction each pay period over the pledge period of three years.

When employees made a pledge to the campaign, they received lapel pins that were designed specifically for the campaign. The pin was a small red oval with the initials of the hospital's name printed in gold. Employees wore them proudly throughout the campaign.

The participation of the employees in the campaign was much higher than was anticipated and the amount contributed was more than twice the goal established for them.

When lead gifts are made during the quiet phase of a campaign, the public acknowledgment of the gift may be delayed until the official kickoff of the campaign. However, recognizing that leadership donor among the donor's peers, family, and friends need not be delayed. For example, announcing the gift of a board member at a board meeting can be meaningful to a donor. Other significant gifts can also be announced at board meetings or at campaign cabinet or steering committee meetings. Inviting not only the donor, but also the members of the donor's family, to those announcements can add to the value of the recognition. Taking pictures of those events and presenting a framed photo to the donor at a later date can also contribute to the donor's feeling of being appreciated.

TIPS AND TECHNIQUES

Annual Report During the Capital Campaign

An organization is in the quiet phase of its capital campaign and is getting ready to produce its annual report for the past year. The dilemma is how to recognize those persons who have already supported the campaign without mentioning the campaign. Omitting the names of these persons would certainly be considered inappropriate when the gifts made by these lead donors are much larger than many of the gifts of many of the donors being listed in the annual report.

Tips and Techniques (continued)

The organization has at least two options:

❶ Rather than putting the names of the campaign donors in the annual report, a separate report of possibly one or two pages could be developed on campaign contributions. The report could be included with the annual report sent to those donors. In the separate report, the reason for not including them in the larger publication could be explained and special note could be made of the importance of the lead gifts made thus far in the campaign. An update on the progress with the campaign leadership phase could be included for these select donors.

❷ The campaign donors may be listed as a separate group within the recognition gift club for upper-level gifts. The group may be called "complimentary" members or "special gift" members of the recognition society for annual gifts. A note to explain the special listing may be included with the report for those donors. In this case, when donors complete their campaign pledges, they can be asked to renew their membership in the gift club with an annual gift of an appropriate amount. This strategy provides an opportunity to convert campaign donors into annual donors at the conclusion of the campaign.

A discussion with the donor of a lead gift about recognition of the gift should take place as soon as possible after the gift commitment is made. The emphasis should be on how recognition of the donor's gift will motivate others to make significant commitments. The options for recognition may include a reception for the donor and the donor's family and friends to celebrate what the gift means to the organization and those served by the organization. Recognition may include publicly announcing the gift at a future event, such as the kickoff of the overall campaign, or at a groundbreaking or other event connected to the capital campaign or project. That recognition may include a news release, a feature article in a local publication, or a photo and story on the organization's website. Recognition for the donor of a leadership gift can be positioned at key intervals throughout the campaign.

Another way to recognize donors to a capital campaign is to hold a campaign celebration when the campaign is successfully completed or when the facility that the capital campaign supported is opened. The event may be a reception, a dinner, a ribbon cutting, or a combination of events. The event may be held for a few key donors or it may be a more inclusive event. Limiting the invitees to those who made gifts of a specific amount or more is a strategy that makes the event special and also keeps the budget under control. The minimum amount used for the invitation list may reflect the levels of recognition established for the entire campaign. For example, if those donors making gifts of $10,000 or more are included in the recognition display, the invitation list for the event may be the same, including those who made commitments of $10,000 or more. An event to celebrate the successful completion of the campaign may feature a video presentation that addresses how the projects supported by the campaign will make a difference in the lives of those served by the organization. Features of the event might include the presentation of a large check for the total amount raised through the campaign, the distribution of the printed campaign report, or the presentation of a symbolic gift to donors to mark the occasion.

Stewardship for Capital Campaign Giving

Reporting back to donors about the impact of their gifts is essential during capital campaigns. When the staff is busy moving forward with cultivation and solicitation to reach the goals for a campaign, losing sight of stewardship for those who have already given can happen if plans have not been made to keep donors informed of the progress of the project and the campaign.

During a campaign, communication is essential to keeping everyone interested and involved. In addition to cultivation and solicitation of donors, plans need to be developed for stewardship visits and reports during the campaign as well as following the campaign.

Campaign newsletters that provide news on the project and progress of the campaign can be useful tools for stewardship, as can visits with leadership donors throughout the campaign. Inviting donors to see the progress being made on a building or other project can be meaningful as well. Stewardship may include periodic reports to donors on the specific aspects of the project in which each donor has an interest. Throughout the stewardship activities, the focus should be on the way the building will serve to fulfill the mission of the organization.

Following a campaign, reporting back to everyone who contributed to the campaign is important in maintaining the relationship with those donors. Too often a campaign ends and the only communication between an organization and the donor is a final report and pledge reminders until the campaign pledge is paid or until planning for another campaign begins. If stewardship is not included in the plans during and following the campaigns, donors will often begin supporting other organizations and may not be inclined to make subsequent gifts to the organization that ignored them until the campaign pledge was paid.

Donor Relations in Prospect Cultivation

Making the distinction between donor relations and cultivation is not easy, because development is not a linear process but a circular one. *Cultivation* may be defined as the process by which an organization informs, interests, and involves potential donors as it seeks gifts from them. Donor relations is the process that takes place *after* the gift is made.

However, after a donor makes an initial gift, donor relations becomes cultivation for the *next* gift (see Exhibit 7.2). If the definition of donor relations is "everything that happens between asks," donor relations becomes cultivation for the next gift and all subsequent gifts. If the first-time donor is not acknowledged and recognized and the gift is not stewarded appropriately, the first gift may be the last gift.

In prospect management, organizations track those activities that bring or "move" a potential donor closer to making a contribution. In many cases, the potential donor will be one who has made prior gifts. In that case, the acknowledgment, recognition, and stewardship for the prior gift should be included in the strategy for cultivating the next gift. Each action from the thank-you letter to the stewardship report should be recorded and tracked as "moves" toward the next gift.

The Director of Donor Relations should be a member of the prospect management team and should play a role in developing the cultivation plan for donors. Cultivation should include the activities and events that are included in the acknowledgment, recognition, and stewardship plans for the donor.

Donor Relations and Cultivation

After a *prospect* is identified and the initial cultivation leads to a gift, the prospect becomes a *donor*. From that point, stewardship and cultivation become *intertwined*.

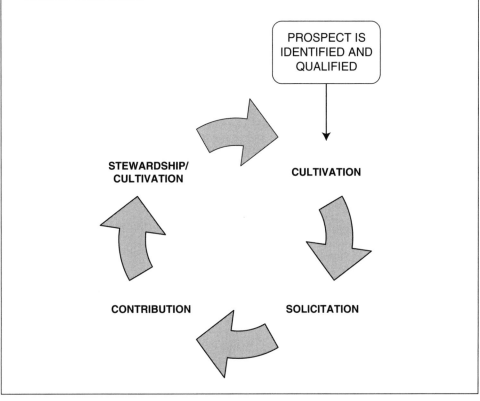

In planning the number of contacts that a prospect manager needs to schedule for a donor in active cultivation, stewardship visits should be included as well as discovery, cultivation, and solicitation visits. Some organizations require prospect managers to make stewardship calls on donors as part of the cultivation process.

Measuring the Impact of Donor Relations

In Chapters 4 and 5, the evaluation of gift clubs was discussed. Both quantitative and qualitative means of measuring the achievement of objectives were reviewed. As donor relations becomes more essential in development programs, the question is often asked about the return on investment. Unlike other aspects of development, the impact of donor relations strategies is not directly tied to revenue. In fact, directors of donor relations are often concerned that their activities are described as not "raising money." When budgets are reviewed in nonprofit organizations, justifying non-revenue-producing activities can be challenging. The question is: Can the impact of a comprehensive donor relations program be measured? The answer is yes.

Measuring success of a donor relations program is similar to the marketing slogan of Morgan Stanley: "We measure success, one investor at a time." In donor relations, success is measured one donor at a time. If the donor is happy, the donor relations program for that donor was successful. The donor's feeling about giving to an organization is the only measurement that counts.

However, development activity is measured by numbers. In addition to total gifts raised, number of donors, number of new donors, average gift size, return on investment, or cost to raise a dollar, fundraising for major gifts is focused on number of prospects in a gift officer's portfolio, number of contacts per week or per month, number of solicitations made, and percentage of solicitations that result in gifts. Defining the numbers for donor relations may be more challenging.

Before establishing the metrics by which the donor relations program will be measured, an organization should define five aspects of the program:

1. *Scope of the program.* The scope of the donor relations program will depend on the maturity of the organization's development program, its current donor relations program, and its staffing and budget. The donor relations program should include the planning, the management, and the implementation of strategies for thanking donors, recognizing donors, and/or stewarding donors.

2. *Objectives of the program.* Knowing what outcomes are expected from the program will focus the metrics on those specific aspects of the program. The objectives may include retention and/or upgrade of specific donors and may include cultivation of major and planned gifts.

3. *Methods.* Defining the methods that will be used to attain the stated objectives is also critical so that the targeted strategies are the ones measured and the data collected is reflective of the methods. Methods may include letters, phone calls, donor walls or donor displays, stewardship reports, newsletters, special events, and/or face-to-face contacts.

4. *Participants.* Determining those who will be participating in the program is also a key step. Persons within the development office, which may include chief development officer, major gift officers, and program and support staff; others in the organization, which may include administrative leaders and members of the finance or accounting staff; board members and other volunteers; and those who are beneficiaries of the organization's mission may be involved in planning, managing, and implementing the strategies for the program.

5. *Audience.* A program may be targeted to one or more groups of persons or donors. Those who are on the other side of the relationships that are being built with the organization have many characteristics and will shape the program's scope, objectives, methods, and participants. The program may be focused on individuals, corporations, foundations, and/or associations or on specific groups, such as employees, board members, or donors of a specific magnitude.

Along with definitions, an organization will need to consider how broadly the donor relations program is understood and endorsed, what resources are available, how willing various persons or groups of persons are to play a role, what policies and guidelines are and are not in place, and what training will be required for involving others in the program.

After these five parameters are established, the organization can define the outcomes that indicate success. The desired outcomes need to be measurable over a defined period of time. Examples of desired outcomes may include:

- Increase the retention rate of first-time donors by 10% in [YEAR].
- Motivate 5% of donors making gifts of $1,000 or more in [YEAR] to increase their gift size in [NEXT YEAR].

- Achieve additional gifts for endowment funds in [YEAR] from 2% of those donors who have established endowment funds in the prior five years.

- Secure more gifts of equal or greater size from those attending the recognition event than from those not attending the event.

Not only do the program components need to be realistic in scope, but also the ability to measure various aspects of a program will need to be considered:

- *Example.* The desired outcome for the coming year is to increase the retention rate of first-time donors by 10%.

Steps in determining what information is needed and how it will be gathered would include:

1. *Establish a clear understanding of what constitutes a first-time donor for this desired outcome.* A review of first-time donors may indicate that some donors should not be counted. For example, for some organizations, the number of donors whose first-time gifts are memorial gifts may vary significantly from year to year and, as many memorial gifts are made in response to a family's request, the donors who make these gifts may have a greater tendency to be onetime donors. If retaining memorial donors is subject to other factors, an organization may decide to exclude these donors from the counts to get a better assessment of the effectiveness of the strategy being used.

   - Determine whether and how specific gifts, such as memorial gifts that need to be excluded from counts, are coded in the database and determine that the coding will make it possible to exclude those gifts in counts.

   - Determine if a donor whose support has lapsed for an extended period of time will be considered a first-time donor if support is renewed and, if so, for what period the support must be lapsed to give a past donor the status of first-time donor.

2. *Establish the retention rate that is to be increased.* The retention rate in the past year against which the coming year's rate will be measured is the percentage of the donors making first-time gifts in the year before this past who made subsequent contributions in the past year.

- For example, if the retention rate in 2010 is measured against the retention rate in 2009, the percentage of persons who made first gifts in 2009 that renew in 2010 (retention in 2010) would be measured against the percentage of persons who made first gifts in 2008 that renew in 2009 (retention in 2009).

3. *Establish how the new strategy will be tracked.* For example, if the new strategy is having volunteers make follow-up phone calls to new donors within one week of the gift being made, the completed calls should be recorded in the database in such a way that reports can be generated for those donors that received calls and for those donors that did not receive calls.

   - Agreement will need to be reached on what qualifies as a completed call. A call where the volunteer speaks to somebody other than the donor or gets an answering machine and leaves a message may or may not be recorded. The decision one way or the other is not important, but the fact that everyone defines a completed call in the same way is important. The critical factor is that the information be consistent.

   - The logistics of how and in what format the information will be recorded and maintained will need to be determined. If volunteers are making calls, the way in which the volunteer tracks the information will be important in facilitating the entry of the data in the database. Using a separate spreadsheet for such information, rather than entering the information into the database, will limit an organization's ability to easily generate reports. Having all information on donors in a central location makes it possible to cross reference other information on the donor and gifts made.

- *Determine who will enter and maintain the data.*

- *Determine what reports will be generated, when, and in what format.*

Other information that may be gathered includes:

- Method by which first gift was made

- Method by which subsequent gift was made

- Size of first gift

- Size of second gift

- Interval of time between first and second gifts

- Response to phone calls on a scale of 1 to 5, with 1 being cool and aloof and 5 being very appreciative of the call

At the conclusion of the year, the retention rate can be determined and compared to the prior year's rate. In addition, the retention rate of those receiving calls versus those not receiving calls can be analyzed. Other measurements might include retention based on methods of giving, by size of gifts, by time between first and second gifts, and/or by response to the call.

Using the Internet for Donor Relations

The Internet has become a widely used resource for donor relations. The websites of organizations are effective in communicating information about giving. Organizations have recognized the value of their websites and are using email as a means of communication for many of their donors and prospects.

Websites

The websites of organizations have the potential of enhancing donor relations programs at every level. Colleges and universities have been leaders in using the Internet to convey gratitude to their donors. The information on the websites of organizations is in a variety of places and in a variety of formats.

IN THE REAL WORLD

The following is a partial list of gift opportunities for "YALE>>tomorrow—The Campaign for Yale University."

Art Scholarship	$50,000
Drama Scholarship	$50,000
Nursing Scholarship	$50,000

IN THE REAL WORLD (CONTINUED)

Student Suite	$50,000
Urban Resources Initiative	$50,000
Digital Classroom, Public Health	$60,000
Global Institute of Sustainable Forestry	$75,000
Art Studio	$100,000
Cancer Research Fund	$100,000
Center for the Study of Globalization	$100,000
Curriculum Development Fund	$100,000
Digital Media Room	$100,000
Faculty Offices	$100,000
Pottery Studio	$100,000
Seminar Room	$100,000
Women's Faculty Forum	$100,000
Librarian's Office	$150,000
Music Practice Suite	$150,000
Art Gallery	$200,000
Pavilion and Garden	$200,000
Staff Lounge	$200,000
Dance Studio	$250,000
Dean's Conference Room	$250,000
Men's Locker Room	$250,000
Registrar's Office	$250,000
Theater	$250,000
Undergraduate Program Center	$250,000
Women's Locker Room	$250,000
Bass Library Large Study Room	$300,000
Admissions Suite	$350,000
Reception Area	$350,000
Full Tuition Scholarship	$400,000
Bass Library Classroom	$500,000
Bass Library Courtyard	$500,000
Communications Suite	$500,000

In the Real World (continued)

Green Garden Roof and Terrace	$500,000
Library Annex	$500,000
Sachem Woods Plaza	$500,000
Executive-in-Residence	$600,000
Leadership Scholarship	$600,000
Atrium	$750,000
Sculpture Courtyard	$750,000
Full Merit School of Medicine Scholarship	$800,000
Associate Curator of Photography	$1,500,000
Athletics Head Coach Position	$1,500,000
Berkeley Leadership Initiative	$1,500,000
Director of Yale Sailing	$1,500,000
Junior Curator of African Art	$1,500,000
Associate Dean for the Arts	$2,000,000
International Visiting Professorship	$2,000,000
Library Directorship	$2,000,000
Bass Library Circulation Desk	$2,500,000
Dining Hall	$2,500,000
World Fellows	$2,500,000
Yale Scholar	$2,500,000
Architecture Professorship	$3,000,000
Chief of Student Medicine	$3,000,000
Director of Center for Language Study	$3,000,000
Engineering Professorship	$3,000,000
Comprehensive Medical Scholarship	$4,000,000
Environment Center	$4,000,000
Sage Courtyard	$4,000,000
Art Gallery Conservation Program	$5,000,000
Bass Library Café	$5,000,000
Deanship of the Graduate School	$5,000,000
Deanship of the School of Nursing	$5,000,000
Director of Athletics	$5,000,000

IN THE REAL WORLD (CONTINUED)

Sculpture Gallery	$5,000,000
University Librarian	$5,000,000
Varsity Strength and Conditioning Center	$5,000,000
Visual Resources Department	$5,000,000
Int'l Theologians Scholarship Program	$7,500,000
Peabody Great Hall Renovation/Exhibit	$8,000,000
Center for Study of Corporate Law	$10,000,000
China Law Center	$10,000,000
Office of Int'l Students and Scholars	$10,000,000
Varsity Team Center at Ingalls Rink	$10,000,000
Writing Center Endowment	$10,000,000
Freshman Year Program Endowment	$15,000,000
Sculpture Building	$15,000,000
A+A Building	$20,000,000
Student Affairs Program Endowment	$20,000,000
Center for Language Study Endowment	$25,000,000
Peabody Museum Expansion and Renovation	$40,000,000
Yale University Art Gallery Facilities Renovation	$40,000,000

These and many other gift opportunities are listed on Yale's website (www
.givingcatalog.yale.edu/priority/list) in a section on the site titled "Giving
Catalog." The catalog provides the ability to browse for gifts by school or
unit, by gift purpose, by campaign priority, or by gift amount.

A click on "Giving to Yale" takes the user to Yale's Campaign. The first page of
the section features a large photo that links to news on expansion of the
campaign to include the addition of two residential colleges. Three smaller
photos and introductions to other articles appear below the larger photo. The
first photo is tied to news about the residential colleges. The other two photos
which change when the website is entered more than once, highlight the
accomplishments of the campaign, such as facilities opened, programs
introduced, or researchers being supported, and donors to the campaign,
and provide profiles on students. Each photo links to an article that provides
more detail on the topic.

The page also shows a "thermometer" that depicts the progress of the
campaign. Other links include a campaign library that contains annual reports

IN THE REAL WORLD (CONTINUED)

on the campaign and case statements for the schools, units, and areas of the university. The site also links to an online scrapbook of photographs from campaign events and milestones.

In addition to the links in the menu on the left side of the page, three additional links are featured on the page:

❶ Giving Catalog

❷ Make a Gift Now

❸ Campaign Library

A link for "News Feed" also appears. A click takes the user to a page that provides the option of subscribing to the "Yale Tomorrow" site through a news feed, which provides notification when new stories and information are posted.

Exploration of the "Yale Tomorrow" site leads to messages from the president, names and contact information for development staff, slide shows, and video clips.

Some organizations make it easier than others to find information on giving. Hospitals with charitable foundations often have a menu item titled "Foundation." A person wanting to make a gift might not know that clicking on "Foundation" is the way to make contributions. Organizations that are more user-friendly have tabs on their home pages titled "Make a Gift" or "Giving." For example, the Seattle Symphony has a tab on its website called "Support the Symphony." Some organizations have a circle or other clearly indicated place on the home page that says "Make a Donation Now" and that leads directly to a site for online giving. Public broadcasting stations often have a link on their home pages that says "Become a Member Now."

IN THE REAL WORLD

While the website for "Giving to Dartmouth" changes on a frequent basis (as effective websites should), the following is a snapshot of the website for Dartmouth College on one occasion. A click on "Giving to Dartmouth" led to three choices:

IN THE REAL WORLD (CONTINUED)

❶ How to Give

- Information on making a gift online, making a gift by mail, and making a gift or pledge by phone
- Information on other ways to give, such as gifts of securities and corporate matching gifts
- A telephone number for persons with questions about giving
- A photo of students on campus with the caption, "Join the 1769 Society," followed by "Learn more about the 1769 Society giving levels," with a link to information on the levels of giving within the 1769 Society

❷ Why Give

- A page titled "Thanks to You" provided information on the impact of giving.
- A section on a student was entitled "Your Gift Makes My Dartmouth Experience" and featured a photo of the student. Information included name and class, hometown, major, Dartmouth highlight, favorite professor, extracurricular activities, recent academic achievement, postgraduate plans, and the answer to "Why I'll support Dartmouth through the Dartmouth College Fund after I graduate."
- The page also featured a small graph, with the heading "By the Numbers," and a statement about the annual cost of a Dartmouth education and the fact that 37% is paid by alumni, parents, and friends through gifts to the endowment and the Dartmouth College Fund. A link was provided to a page that provided more information on the numbers.
- Other information on the page included the percentage of financial aid that came from the Dartmouth College Fund and other college resources, a graph that showed the sources of Financial Aid, and a graph that illustrated the breakdown of what $211 (per day) provided, including the cost of faculty, the campus, financial aid, and in-classroom and out-of-classroom opportunities.

❸ Honor Roll

- The Honor Roll page had the following text, as well as links to graduating class years:

The Honor Roll is one way Dartmouth says thank you for the outpouring of generosity from loyal alumni and friends throughout the year. The list shows donors whose cash gifts were recorded between July 1, 2007 and June 30, 2008. Click on your year below to see who gave.

IN THE REAL WORLD (CONTINUED)

- The Honor Roll page also had a small note in the upper-right section:

  Join the Ranks
  Your gift to the Dartmouth College Fund makes an impact on the lives of students. Please join your classmates and friends by making a gift today.

The note was followed by a link: *Make a gift online.*

While access to making online contributions has become a major feature of the websites of charitable organizations, many organizations are providing information on their websites that goes beyond how to make a gift. Organizations have developed a number of ways to use their websites to support donor relations and enhance their development programs, including:

- Link to "Did You Know?," which includes facts on philanthropy, such as:
  - Supporters provided $2.5 million for ABC Organization in 2007.
  - A total of 2,564 individuals, corporations, foundations, and organizations made contributions to XYZ in 2008.
  - Philanthropic contributions made it possible for ABC to provide services to 489 children in 2009.
- Link to "Why We Give?":
  - Pictures of donors and text about each donor's motivation for giving, including quotes from the respective donors. Most websites include persons from various constituencies who have made many types of gifts, including bequest intents and other planned gifts. The persons featured are changed on a frequent basis to keep the website fresh and interesting.
  - Picture of a beneficiary of the organization's services and text about the importance of the organization in that person's life.
- Link to "Ways to Give":
  - Information on making non-cash gifts, such as securities.
  - Information on planned giving.

- Websites on planned giving are available from a number of vendors. These websites are integrated into the organization's website to blend into the organization's web pages. Items on planned giving websites may include:
  - Information on membership in the Legacy Society.
  - List of members of the Legacy Society.
  - Photos from the annual event for the Legacy Society.
  - Stories and photos about specific planned giving donors. Featuring a story about a planned giving donor in a newsletter or on a website is an excellent way to recognize that donor.
- Video presentations:
  - Students at a scholarship luncheon talk about their family background, why they chose the specific college, the importance of the scholarship to them, and their plans for the future.
  - A doctor at a hospital talks about a piece of equipment that was purchased with philanthropic dollars and how the equipment was used to save a person's life.
  - Testimonials from donors about their motivations for giving.
- Photo galleries from events:
  - Recognition events for planned giving donors
  - Recognition events for annual or campaign donors
  - Fundraising events

While some organizations have tabs on their home pages for "donor relations" or "donor recognition," tabs using these phrases are not as user-friendly as the tabs for "giving" or "support."

Email Communication

As organizations collect more email addresses for their donors, they are using the Internet to send email blasts to express appreciation to donors in creative ways. The messages may include photos and music as well as audio and text that give donors an update on the progress of a campaign or say "thank you" at Thanksgiving or at the end or beginning of the year.

Different Approaches for Different Donors

Donors have specific preferences regarding the ways they are acknowledged, recognized, and stewarded. Getting to know donors is the best way to learn those preferences. However, having a conversation with every donor to an organization is probably not practical. An organization will strive to know as much as possible about its most generous donors. However, many other donors may not be as well known.

In designing donor relations programs, several considerations are important. The donor's generation, gender, and cultural background may help an organization fine tune its acknowledgment, recognition, and stewardship for those donors with which it interacts.

For example, each generation has different predilections in the way it communicates. As Baby Boomers and Generation X and Y become major donors, organizations that they support need to focus on the reasons that they give and develop donor relations programs accordingly.

From its study of generational giving trends, the Center on Philanthropy at Indiana University concluded that all generations give roughly the same amount to philanthropic causes if factors such as income, education, and frequency of attendance at religious services are considered. However, the motivations for giving and types of causes differ.

Those in the Millennial generation (born after 1981) are more likely than any other generation to cite the "desire to make the world a better place to live" as a key motivation for their philanthropic giving. Members of the Silent Generation (born between 1925 and 1945) are more likely to cite "need to provide services that the government can't or won't" as one of their most important reasons for giving. The study's findings suggest that these two generations will respond in different ways not only to the messages in appeals for support, but also to the ways an organization says "thank you."

EXHIBIT 7.3

Suggestions for Working with Older Donors (Born 1945 or Earlier)

- Use notes rather than email for important correspondence; use hand-writing whenever possible.
- Address these donors formally until told otherwise.
- Tell and show donors how their giving is maintaining the respected traditions of the organization.
- Ask permission before talking about their giving in public or to other donors.
- Make sure in a face-to-face conversation that gifts are not anonymous.
- Plan to invite children and grandchildren to recognition events and make careful accommodations for all family members who attend.
- Tell them when they can expect a letter from those who benefit from their gifts and stick to the schedule.
- Arrange for them to meet with the leadership of the organization on a regular basis and include volunteers as well as staff.
- Use formal invitations for major donor recognition dinners and ceremonies, rather than planning events by phone only.
- Use special gifts and framed certificates to recognize giving, but be careful not to seem extravagant to these frugal generations.
- If an organization is publicly honoring a donor, offer to draft remarks for the donor or show the donor what others have said in the past.
- Make arrangements for somebody to drive the donor to and from events.

Source: Adapted from presentation at ADRP International Conference in 2006 given by Lisa Russell O'Shea and Susan T. deMuth of Johns Hopkins Institutions, Baltimore, Maryland.

As members of the development staff are increasingly younger and are getting further away from the GI Generation (born between 1911 and 1924) and the Silent Generation, conscious effort is required to give these donors the stewardship *they* desire, not what the development officer of today would like (see Exhibit 7.3).

In the January/February 2007 issue of *Advancing Philanthropy*, in her article titled "Appropriate Recognition," Mary Ellen Collins gives a number of examples where cultural differences are important in considering the recognition a donor should receive for supporting an organization. In the article, Susan T. deMuth, director of institutional donor relations for Johns Hopkins Institutions in Baltimore, Maryland, recalls selecting a beautiful engraved captain's clock for the president of the organization to take as a gift on a trip to China. When she conveyed to those at the Johns Hopkins program in Nanjing that she was sending a clock, she learned that it was not an appropriate gift. The word for *clock* and the word for *end* (presumably of life) in Chinese are both pronounced the same. As a result of the two words sounding the same, giving a clock as a gift is considered in poor taste and is unacceptable in Chinese culture.

The article also highlights the challenges in Mexico of getting donors to accept public recognition. The donors have issues around their security and many feel for religious reasons that it is not proper to publicize their support of charitable organizations. Wealthy individuals in Latin America shun recognition and the Hispanic population of Miami displays similar behavior. They are described as "hesitant, almost fearful."

In Russia, the type of organization that wealthy individuals support can have "political consequences." Those who make contributions to support human rights and social justice are putting their personal freedom at risk. An oil baron who gave $60 million to private, democracy-oriented projects was reported to be in a Siberian prison camp.

Trends in Donor Relations

The field of development changes rapidly and new trends constantly emerge. In the area of donor relations, five trends are evident in watching the growth of this specialty area within development:

1. *Donor-centered approach*. The field of donor relations is based on the donor-centered approach to fundraising.

2. *Donor behaviors.* In recent years, more attention has been given to the differences in donor behaviors by age or generation, by gender, and by type of giving. Cultural differences are also being recognized.

3. *Status of donor relations.* Donor relations, including acknowledgment, recognition, and stewardship, has become coordinated, collaborative, consistent, and strategic. The professional status of donor relations and stewardship officers is a recent trend that is growing with time. The number of organizations with staff members assigned specifically to donor relations increases each year.

   Professional training opportunities in donor relations and stewardship are also increasing. The Council for Advancement and Support of Education (CASE) has two conferences each year, one on Nuts and Bolts of Donor Relations in the fall and the other for Donor Relations Officers in the early summer. The Association for Donor Relations Professionals (ADRP) sponsors an annual conference in the fall and also hosts regional workshops. Other organizations that provide training and education for development professionals are also adding sessions and tracks on donor relations.

4. *Websites.* Organizations are using their websites to provide information on donor relations. The Donor Bill of Rights, information on recognition gift clubs, announcements of and photos from recognition events, profiles of donors, links with brochures, and contact information for donor relations staff are some of the features on these websites.

5. *Outcomes and impact.* Organizations are clearly reporting on the outcomes that result from a gift or group of gifts. The impact of a gift is important to donors and development staff are being more conscientious in reporting back to donors on the impact that their gifts have made on the organization and on the persons served by the organization. Reports are comprehensive and include both quantitative and qualitative information to illustrate the impact of giving.

Final Thoughts on Donor Relations

One of the first expressions we learn as children is "thank you," which often sounds more like *ta-ta* as we go from babbling to actually talking. As our parents begin to teach us social skills, the importance of saying "please" and "thank you" is emphasized time and again. When you offer something to a child, the parent will often prompt the child with "What do you say?"

However, along the way, saying "thank you" becomes automatic. For example, each day we hear "Good morning, how are you?" and we respond "Fine, thank you" without much thought. In our daily experiences, it becomes hard to remember the last time we said "thank you" or the last time somebody said "thank you" to us other than the perfunctory words of daily life.

One of the questions that I sometimes ask in presentations about donor relations is, "When was the last time that you received an especially meaningful 'thank you' from somebody?" Many participants have a difficult time recalling an example of receiving a thoughtful expression of gratitude. Those who do remember a personal experience are easily identified, because a smile comes across their faces.

Whenever someone is asked to share his or her recollection with the group, the stories are quite interesting. One that I recall was related by a woman who sings in her church choir. She had received a personal note in the mail from a member of the congregation that expressed that person's gratitude for her sharing her beautiful voice each week. The person who wrote the note explained how her worship experience was more meaningful when she heard this woman singing. The recipient said that she was touched by the person taking the time to write a personal note. She received words of appreciation each week, but the note went beyond what she had experienced before.

Knowing that my cousin was a collector like me, I gave her a monetary gift for her "significant" birthday and told her to use the gift to buy something special that she could keep. She wrote to me after she spent the money, told me what she bought, and how special the item was for her. On a subsequent visit to her home, she showed me the item that she had acquired. I was so pleased to know that she spent the money as I intended and that she took the time to show me her purchase.

If you can recall a special "thank you" from another, you can begin to understand what a sincere expression of gratitude can mean to a person.

I remember an inspiring presentation I heard about the wonderful role that we as development professionals have in working with donors to help them see their dreams come true. Not only do we have the opportunity to help donors bring their desires to reality, but we also have the opportunity to say "thank you" in a way that has meaning and brings fulfillment to those who care about the causes we represent.

Several years ago, I read a book called *Simple Abundance,* by Sarah Ban Breathnach, and shortly thereafter had the opportunity to participate in a workshop that she led at the Chautauqua Institution in Chautauqua, New York. Her book and her workshop were about experiencing life to its fullest. She believes that a sense of gratitude is essential, and that the first step to achieving "simplicity, order, harmony, beauty, and joy" is with a *gratitude journal.* I began the process she recommended, took a beautiful blank book, and at the end of each day recorded five things for which I was thankful. It was a rewarding exercise and gave me a new appreciation for what it means to *be thankful.*

Taking everything for granted is so easy in the fast pace of everyday living. But taking the time to express gratitude for the simple things in life can be powerful. I believe that each of us can better understand the value of a meaningful and sincere "thank you" if we become more grateful ourselves. Saying "thank you," recognizing those who give, and telling them how their gifts made a difference is more than a task that we have to accomplish; it is the opportunity and privilege to show those who support our organizations how their giving makes a difference.

> Gratitude unlocks the fullness of life. . . . Gratitude makes sense of our past, brings peace for today, and creates a vision for tomorrow.
>
> Melody Beattie

ABC Hospital Foundation
Director of Donor Relations/Director of Stewardship

JOB DESCRIPTION FOR: Director of Donor Relations/Director of Stewardship

GENERAL RESPONSIBILITIES: To develop, implement, monitor, and evaluate programs and events to properly acknowledge, recognize, and steward all gifts to ABC Hospital Foundation.

SPECIFIC DUTIES INCLUDE:

- Develop, implement, and monitor an overall donor relations plan for the foundation.
- Plan, coordinate, and supervise the gift acknowledgment process.
- Plan, coordinate, and supervise all donor cultivation and recognition events.
- Develop and revise, as needed, guidelines and procedures for acknowledgment, recognition, and stewardship of all gifts to the foundation.
- Coordinate the listing of names in publications and in donor displays.
- Coordinate the resolution of complaints, errors, or disputes with regard to acknowledgment, recognition, and stewardship of donors and/or their gifts.

- Develop, implement, and monitor an endowment reporting system to report to donors on the status of endowed funds, including investment income, gifts received, and expenditures.

- Coordinate with major gift officers to develop, implement, and monitor appropriate stewardship plans for each major gift.

- Participate in developing cultivation strategies for major gift donors and prospects.

- Develop and implement a plan for measuring the effectiveness of the donor relations program at the foundation.

- Provide ongoing education for the foundation staff on "best practices" in donor relations.

- Other duties as assigned.

MINIMUM QUALIFICATIONS:

- Minimum of two years' work experience in fundraising, public relations, communications, or a related field.

- Bachelor's degree from an accredited institution of higher education or equivalent experience.

- Strong communication skills (written and oral) and listening skills.

- Strong organizational and interpersonal skills.

- Willingness to travel in fulfillment of duties.

- Ability to operate personal computers and related software (word processing, spreadsheet, etc.).

PREFERRED QUALIFICATIONS:

- Five or more years' direct experience in fundraising, advancement, or public relations, preferably in a health-care setting, with an emphasis on donor relations or stewardship.

- Experience with fundraising-specific software and databases.

Donor Recognition
Vendors for Recognition Displays

Amri Studio

(Formerly known as Wallach Glass Studio)

1580 Sebastopol Road

Santa Rosa, CA 95407

(707) 527–1205

www.amristudio.com

Ascalon Studios Inc.

115 Atlantic Avenue

Berlin, NJ 08009

Toll Free: (888) 280–5656

www.ascalonstudios.com

Awards USA

24260 Greenway Avenue

Suite A1

Forest Lake, MN 55025

Toll Free: (888) 462–5008

www.donor-recognitions.com

Donorwall

Toll Free: (877) DONORWALL

www.donorwall.com

The Donor Wall

812 SW Washington

Suite 900

Portland, Oregon 97205

(503) 228–6106

www.thedonorwall.com

Honorcraft Inc.

292 Page Street

PO Box 385

Stoughton, MA 02072

In Massachusetts: (781) 341–0410

Outside MA: Toll Free: (800) 542–1235

www.honorcraft.com

Karen Singer Tileworks

90 East Church Lane

Philadelphia, PA 19144

(215) 849–7010

www.karensinger.com

Mitchell Associates

One Avenue of the Arts

Wilmington, Delaware 19801

Toll Free: (888) 594–9400

www.mitchellai.com

MD Designs by Metal Décor

2601 Colt Road

Springfield, IL 62707

Toll Free: (800) 637–8591

www.mddesigns.com

Partners in Recognition

405 South Main Street

Ft. Loramie, Ohio 45845

(937) 420–2150

www.partnersinrecognition.com

PlannedLegacy

Suite 220-309 McDermot Avenue

Winnipeg, Manitoba Canada R3A 1T3

Toll Free: (866) 882–3580

www.plannedlegacy.com

Presentation Design Group

1010 Obie Street

Eugene, OR 97402

(541) 344–0857

www.pdgdesign.net

Stobbe Design

3621 Larkspur Drive

Ponca City, OK 74604

(580) 382–1674

www.stobbedesign.com

1157 designconcepts

(Formerly known as VisionMark)

171 South Lester Avenue

Sidney, Ohio 45365

(937) 497–1157

www.1157designconcepts.com

W&E Baum

89 Bannard Street

Freehold, NJ 07728

Toll Free: (800) 922–7377

www.webaum.com

Vendors: Bookmarks

The following companies design and produce bookmarks that may be appropriate as thank-you gifts for donors:

Ameropean Corp.

7 Corporate Dr. #108

North Haven, CT 06473 USA

Phone: (800) 466–4648

Phone: (203) 239–0448

Fax: (203) 234–8820

www.leatherbookmarks.com

Email: ac@ameropean.com

David Howell & Co.

405 Adams Street

Bedford Hills, NY 10507

Phone: (800) 648–5455

Phone: (914) 666–4080

Fax: (914) 666–2721

www.davidhowell.com

Email: info@davidhowell.com

ChemArt

15 New England Way

Lincoln, RI 02865

Phone: (800) 942–8463

Fax: (800) 551–7730

www.chemart.com

Email: marketing@chemart.com

ChemArt also creates and manufactures custom ornaments.

Donor Satisfaction Survey

		Very Satisfied	Satisfied	Neutral	Dissatisfied	Very Dissatisfied
1	I was appropriately thanked for my contribution(s).	☐	☐	☐	☐	☐
2	I was thanked for my contribution(s) in a timely manner.	☐	☐	☐	☐	☐
3	The fundraising office has responded to my requests in a timely manner.	☐	☐	☐	☐	☐
4	When contacting the fundraising office I was treated with courtesy and professionalism.	☐	☐	☐	☐	☐
5	XYZ organization effectively informs me about the impact of my gift(s).	☐	☐	☐	☐	☐
6	I would recommend XYZ to my family, friends, and associates as an organization to financially support.	☐	☐	☐	☐	☐

7 In what way could we increase your level of satisfaction as a supporter of XYZ organization?

_____

_____

_____

8 Other comments:

_____

_____

_____

Checklist for Recognition and Stewardship

Name of Donor: _____

Relationship Manager: _____

Other staff to involve:

1. _____

2. _____

3. _____

Volunteers to involve:

1. _____

2. _____

3. _____

☐ Annual Letter
  ☐ Annual letter from CEO and/or from head of department or program
    to report on the impact of the gift

☐ Stewardship Visit
  ☐ Donor visits organization
  ☐ Donor tours facility
  ☐ Meeting before/after a larger event
  ☐ Travel to the donor

☐ Donor Featured in Publication or on Website
    ☐ Major publication of the organization
    ☐ Newsletter from the organization or specific program
    ☐ Independent news media
    ☐ Website

☐ Event Honoring Donor
    ☐ Award or honorary degree
    ☐ Building groundbreaking/dedication
    ☐ Chair, endowment, or program dedication
    ☐ Donor/recipient event
    ☐ Giving society event
    ☐ Legacy society event
    ☐ Lunch/dinner with leadership of organization
    ☐ Portrait or plaque unveiling
    ☐ Seminar or educational event
    ☐ Other events

☐ Involvement
    ☐ Asking donor's advice about the organization
    ☐ Board or Advisory Council membership
    ☐ Donor presentation to organization audience
    ☐ Donor states stewardship preferences and opinions
    ☐ Educational meetings with staff or other donors
    ☐ Membership on task force or ad-hoc committee

☐ Other Communications
    ☐ Convey breaking news about the organization
    ☐ Fax/email press releases and other news
    ☐ Financial report (endowment/planned giving/periodic update)
    ☐ Greeting cards
    ☐ Letter from chair holder, scholarship/fellowship recipient
    ☐ Phone call from end-user of gifts
    ☐ Progress report on an ongoing project
    ☐ Special memento for donor
    ☐ Other items of interest to donor
    ☐ Other

The checklist above is an adaptation of the standard stewardship plan and report that Johns Hopkins Institutions uses for its major donors.

Put the Donor First

Leon Leonwood Bean, who founded LL Bean in 1912, had a philosophy about the value of a customer that has withstood the test of time. LL's favorite definition of a customer is as critical to LL Bean's success today as it was in LL's day. Here is our adaptation of "What Is a Customer?" from www.llbean.com:

- The donor is the most important person.

- The donor is not dependent on us; we are dependent on the donor.

- The donor is not an interruption of our work; the donor is the reason for our work.

- We are not doing the donor a favor by serving our donor; the donor does us the favor by giving us the opportunity.

- The donor is not someone with whom to argue or match wits. Nobody ever won an argument with a donor.

- The donor is a person who brings us his or her wants. It is our job to handle them satisfactorily.

Index

"f" refers to exhibits; "n" to notes.

AAFRC. *See* American Association of Fund
    Raising Counsel (AAFRC)
ABC Hospital Foundation, 227–28
account, 5, 5f1.1, 16, 67, 179, 181, 186, 189
acknowledgment. *See also* thank-you
    for annual giving, 57–59f3.4
    critical factors for, 51–55
    defined, 4
    Donor Bill of Rights, 15–16f1.3
    donor relations, 5, 5f1.1, 16, 23, 42, 45
    first-time donors, 52, 69
    four critical factors, 52–54, 53f3.2
    gifts and gift processing, 53–54, 53f3.2
    gratitude, 6f1.2, 16, 47, 54–55, 56f3.3, 79
    by handwritten note, 47
    letter, 26–27, 40, 59
    matching-gift donor, 69
    memorial or tribute donor, 70–72
    methods of, 47–49
    multiple gift donor, 69
    by officers and staff, 49
    plan, 26, 55–62
    reactivated donor, 69
    special, 68–75
    special-constituency donor, 70
    by thank-a-thon, 63–65
Advancing Philanthropy (Collins), 230
advertising, 14, 36, 116
AFP. *See* Association of Fundraising Professionals
    (AFP)
AFP Fundraising Dictionary, 3–4
AFP Publishing Advisory Committee, vi–vii
AHP. *See* Association of Healthcare Philanthropy
    (AHP)

American Association of Fund Raising Counsel
    (AAFRC), 16f1.3
American Girl, Inc., 35–36
American Red Cross, 47, 140, 142, 184, 189
annual giving, 28, 29f2.1, 34f2.3, 57–59f3.4, 127
annual report, 10, 34f2.3, 52, 57–58f3.4, 66,
    85–95, 125, 147, 150, 156, 183, 201–2, 213
anonymous donor, 54, 81–84, 97, 125, 181
appreciate, 5–6, 5f1.1, 16, 21, 23, 45–46, 61, 66, 70,
    75
ask again, 5–6, 5f1.1, 16
Association of Fundraising Professionals (AFP),
    16f1.3, 17n1, v–vi
Association of Healthcare Philanthropy (AHP),
    16f1.3
associations, 3, 134, 154, 207
autumn months appeal, 11

bequest intents, 27, 117, 128, 133–35, 162–63,
    167f5.7, 172, 174, 216
birthday, 12, 47, 58–59, 163–64, 234
board chairperson, 25, 54, 59
bookmarks, 52, 61, 233–34
Brigham, Hank, 14, 17n2

capital campaign
    annual report and, 201–2
    donor relations, 191–204
    gift and pledge acknowledgment, 192–93
    gift table for $7.5 million, 195–96f7.1
    gifts, recognition for, 193–203, 195f7.1
    gratitude and, 191–92
    stewardship and, 192, 203–4
CASE. *See* Council for the Advancement and
    Support of Education (CASE)

CEO/executive director, 25, 49, 52, 58–59f3.4, 85, 90–91, 130, 181, 237
charitable
  deductions, 155
  foundations, 214
  gift, 3–4, 137f5.3
  gift annuities, 128, 135
  lead trusts, 128, 135
  organizations, 2, 21, 23, 73, 85, 153–54, 159, 216, 220
  remainder trusts, 128
colleges, 31f2.2, 33, 45–46, 50, 62, 67–68, 114, 157, 210, 213
Collins, Mary Ellen, 230
communications department, 29f2.1, 30
confidence, 4, 15f1.3, 24–25, 35f2.4, 80f4.1, 140
corporations, 3–4, 23, 27, 46, 59, 69, 97, 109f4.3, 116, 134, 154, 200, 207, 216
cost of donor acquisition, 22
Council for the Advancement and Support of Education (CASE), 16f1.3
Creative Themes for Nonprofit Annual Reports, 90
customer loyalty programs, 8
customer relations programs, 8–9
Customer Touchpoint Management (CTM), 14, 17n2

demographic study, 20
Developing Major Gifts: Turning Small Donors into Big Contributors (Fredricks), 81
development operations, 29f2.1
development services, 25, 30, 32, 53
direct mail, 8, 12, 21–22, 60, 72, 149, 172
Direct Mail Association, 12
Director of Donor Relations, 150, 204, 227–28
Director of Stewardship, 227–28
donor
  behaviors, 32f2.2, 221
  expectations, 23, 42, 162
  experience, 7, 14–15, 36–37, 39–42
  loyalty, 14, 20–21, 23, 116, 140
  potential lifetime value, 22
  prospects, 13, 106
  satisfaction, 10, 14, 20, 34f2.3, 88, 235–36
Donor Bill of Rights, 9–17, 15f1.3, 33, 221
donor-centered
  fundraising, 3, 9–13
  organization, 11–13
  thinking, 10–11, 13, 29, 70
  Donor-Centered Fundraising (Burke), 55
"The donor comes first," 10

donor relations. See also capital campaign; gratitude; stewardship
  acknowledgment, 5, 5f1.1, 16, 23, 42, 45
  customer relations, 8–9
  cycle, 5–6, 5f1.1, 16
  defined, 1–4
  development program and, 28–29, 29f2.1, 30, 32, 42, 94
  Donor Bill of Rights, 9–17, 33
  donor experience, 39–42
  donors, different approaches for different, 218–20
  donors, working with older, 219f7.3
  elements of surprise, 37–39, 42
  email communication and, 217–18
  emergence of, 19–23
  final thoughts on, 223–25
  impact of, measuring the, 205–10
  Internet and, 210
  manual, 33–34f2.3
  mission statement, sample, 34–35f2.4
  new donors, cost to acquire, 21–22
  philanthropic dollar, competition for, 21
  power of words, 3–7
  in prospect cultivation, 204–5
  prospect cultivation and, 205f7.2
  purpose of, 23–25
  recognition and, 2–4, 6–7, 16, 25, 163, 166, 167f5.7, 191, 204, 218, 221
  stewardship and, 3, 6–7, 19, 22, 25, 28, 162–63, 166, 167f5.7, 181–82, 191, 205f7.2, 218, 221
  sticky ideas, six common principles of, 38f2.5
  trends in, 220–21
  websites and, 210–17
  where it fits, 28–37, 29f2.1
Donor Relations Manual, 33–34f2.3
donor relations program. See also stewardship
  Bill of Rights and, 17
  cycle, 5–7, 5f1.1
  defined, 3
  donor communication, 4, 6–7, 13–14, 29f2.1, 30, 40, 42–44, 46, 62, 69, 76, 164, 181, 192, 197, 203–4, 210, 217–18
  Experience the Mission program, 41
  gratitude and, 7–8
  inventory of current, 25–26, 105–8
  steps in planning a, 31–32f2.3
  three functions of, 30, 32
Donor TouchPoint Management (DTM), 14
Drucker, Peter, 35

educational institutions, 20, 117, 136, 157, 173, 179. *See also* colleges; universities
element of surprise, 37–39, 42
email, 4, 8, 45, 48–49, 52, 55, 68, 76, 152f5.6, 192, 210, 217–18, 219f7.3
end-of-year giving, 11–12
executive director. *See* CEO/executive director
Experience the Mission program, 41

face-to-face contact, 6–7, 148, 207, 219f7.3
first gifts, 21, 24, 32, 55, 204, 209–10
first-time donors, 26, 33, 52, 63, 69, 77, 152, 207–8
focus groups, 32f2.2, 152f5.6
foundations, 3–4, 10, 23–24, 26, 46–47, 69, 90–91, 96–98, 116–17, 122, 133–34, 144, 154, 158, 188f6.1, 200, 207, 214, 216, 227–28
Fredricks, Laura, 81
fund development profession, 19, 22, 28
Fund-Raising: Evaluating and Managing the Fund Development Process (Greenfield), 2
future gifts, 22–23, 61, 84, 169

gift acknowledgment. *See* acknowledgment
gift cards, 13
gift club
  affinity-based, 170–71
  benefits of, 27
  categories of, 127–28, 128f5.1
  for corporate matching gift, 154
  establishing names for, 141–42f5.4
  gifts, 139–40, 155
  guidelines for, 153–56
  at hospitals, special, 138–39
  for individual gifts, 154
  levels, 27, 132, 159
  membership benefits, 135–40, 156
  membership criteria, 131–35, 154
  name choosing, 140–43
  the other side of, 161–64
  plan for, 144–56
  pledges, 156
  program, announcing a new, 132–33
  program, creating, 129–58
  program, enhancing, 170–71, 173–75
  program, evaluating, 151–52f5.6, 156–58
  program, expanding, 170–72
  program, six steps to establish, 131f5.2
  recognition, 84–85
  special events, 155
Gilmore, James H., 35, 37
giving catalogs, 8, 213–14
gratitude. *See also* thank-you

by accountability, 181
by acknowledgment, 6f1.2, 16, 47, 54–55, 56f3.3, 79
attitude of, 6, 6f1.2
by branded gifts, 165
capital campaign and, 191–92
children and, 49
creative strategies for expressing, 37
development staff and, 44, 138, 183
donor relations and, 17
by email message, 45
expressing, 14, 16, 34
future gifts and, 22
by hand written notes, 44, 50
investments, for maximum, 22
journal, 224
love and, 145
meaning of, 7–9
by the organization, 191
for past gifts, 139
for philanthropic gifts, 46
by postcard, 62
by recognition, 79, 125
reinforced behavior and, 75
by special letters, 87
by stewardship report, 67
by thank-a-thon, 63–64
at Thanksgiving, 50–51
thoughtful, 223–24
tokens of, 166
by website posting, 210
'Gratitude unlocks the fullness of life,' 225
Greenfield, James M., 2

handwritten note, 4, 8, 15, 38, 44, 47, 52, 54–55, 63–65, 192
health-care organizations, 20, 33, 39, 56f3.3, 117, 152f5.6, 179
Heath, Dan and Chip, 37, 42n1
hospital in Texas, 41
How to Write a Nonprofit Annual Report: The E-Book, 90

Internal Revenue Service, 118, 137f5.3, 159–61
Internet, 6, 22, 191, 210, 217

Johns Hopkins Foundation Wall, 96–98

Koop, C. Everett, 38f2.5

leadership giving, 29f2.1, 124
Lifetime Giving Club, 174

long-term relationships, 24, 42, 162
loyalty of donor, 14, 20–21, 23, 116, 140
loyalty programs, 8

Made to Stick (Heath and Heath), 37, 42b1
mailing lists, 8, 16, 72, 149
major donors
  cultivation plan for, 28
major gifts, 21–24, 28, 105, 139, 163, 168, 171, 183,
    185, 206–7, 228
major giving, 28, 29f2.1, 30, 149, 167f5.7,
    168
matching-gift donor, 69–70, 77
matching gift form, 26
Mazda, 36
membership program, 28, 29f2.1
memorial or tribute donor, 59, 70–72, 77, 92,
    102–3, 208
Metropolitan Opera, 168–69
Miller, Kivi Leroux, 85, 89
misspelling donor's name, 40
multi-year giving, 168
multiple gift donor, 52, 69, 71, 77
Musical Legacy Society, 152–53

National Academies, 139–40
National Philanthropy Day, 46, 51, 160
National Public Radio, 36
newsletters, 30, 79, 86, 92, 148, 156, 192, 203, 207
Nichols, Judith, 39, 42n2
nonprofit organizations, 7, 14–15, 20, 60, 63, 72,
    75, 81, 85–86, 89–90, 115–16, 135, 141f5.4,
    149, 162, 166, 173, 179, 206
Nordstrom's, 11

outreach program, 41

personal visits, 34f2.3, 83
philanthropic gifts, 9, 46
philanthropic support, 3, 9, 20, 42, 51, 91, 105–6,
    125, 189
philanthropy
  appreciation, 200
  culture of, 9, 118
  Donor Bill of Rights and, 10, 15–16f1.3
  donor-centered approach to, 183
  donor relations, 216
  levels of, 174f5.8
  recognition of past, 111f4.3
  relationships and, 2
  report on, 87
'Philanthropy is not a purchase!', 24

phone communication, 4, 6, 14, 22, 43, 47, 49,
    51–52, 55, 61, 63–64, 66, 72, 76, 83, 132,
    138–39, 147–49, 153, 181, 192–93, 207,
    209–10
photographs, 30, 73, 75, 92, 96, 106, 183, 214
Pine II, B. Joseph, 35, 37
Pinpointing Affluence in the 21st Century (Nichols),
    39, 42n2
planned gifts, 21–24, 27–28, 97, 113f4.3, 117, 128,
    128f5.1, 133–35, 140, 206, 216
planned giving, 22, 28, 29f2.1, 30, 33f2.3, 34f2.3,
    85, 128, 142–43, 149, 153–54, 167f5.7, 173,
    175, 184, 216–17, 238
planned giving societies, 162–64
pledge, 27, 46, 60, 93–94, 97, 108, 112f4.3, 134,
    147, 156, 168–69, 191–93, 198, 201–2, 204,
    215
pooled income funds, 128
The Practice of Management (Drucker), 35
prospect
  management, 29f2.1, 30, 204
  research, 30
  tracking, 29f2.1
publications, 10, 30, 79–80, 86, 95, 125, 133, 147,
    156, 180
*Publishing the Nonprofit Annual Report: Tips, Traps,
    and Tricks of the Trade,* 90

qualitative information, 31–32f2.2, 32f2.2, 151,
    152f5.6, 156, 175, 205, 221
quantitative information, 31–32f2.2, 151, 151f5.6,
    156, 175, 205, 221

radio, 22, 60–61, 130
reactivated donor, 26, 69, 151
recognition. *See also* gift club; thank-you
  acknowledgment plan and, 59
  annual, 100, 154, 156
  of annual giving, 127
  annual reports, 85–95
  anonymous donor, 82–84, 125
  appreciation as, 5
  bequest intents and, 27
  board members and, 28
  budget for, 199
  capital campaign giving, 193–203,
    195f7.1
  category, 70
  checklist for, 237–38
  concierge programs, 138–39
  continued giving and, 21
  defined, 4

recognition (*continued*)

dinner, 162, 219f7.3

display, 10, 30, 92–93, 95–101, 106, 119, 121, 124, 167, 192, 196, 198–99

displays, vendors for, 229–32

donor acquisition and, 22

Donor Bill of Rights and, 15, 15f1.3, 221

donor first, putting the, 239

donor relations and, 2–4, 6–7, 16, 25, 163, 166, 167f5.7, 191, 204, 218, 221

Donor Relations Manual, 33f2.3

donor's preference for, 89

electronic reports on giving, 94–95

element of surprise and, 37

enduring nature of, 104

events, 34f2.3, 61, 92, 117–24, 163, 192, 208, 217, 219f7.3, 227

expectations for, 81

gift club, 27, 84–85, 102, 125, 128, 128f5.1

gift club groups, 129, 131

gifts, counting and recording, 158–59

gratitude and, 6, 6f1.2, 7, 16, 67, 79, 125

group, 87, 174

for group of donors, 61, 80

groups, 91, 157, 168, 171–74

hierarchy of human needs, Maslow's, 80f4.1

human need for, 81, 124

importance of, 79–81

Internal Revenue Service, 118, 137f5.3, 159–61

of Legacy Society, 118

levels, 87, 91, 105, 132, 146–49, 159–61, 168–69, 173, 194, 198, 202–3

of life-time giving, 27, 128, 154, 174f5.8

lists, 3, 93, 199

of matching gifts, 158–59

membership has its privileges, 135–36

for multi-year giving, 168

name tags, ribbons on, 172–73

name verification form, 150

names, listing of, 92–94

naming opportunities, 102–16, 125, 192–94, 195f7.1

naming opportunity development, 106–8

naming policies and procedure, 106–13

by newsletter, 86, 192

by photo galleries, 217

of planned gifts, 27, 128, 154

planned giving societies, 162–64

planning, 28, 82, 101, 197

plaque, 58–59f3.4, 83, 101, 106, 108, 115, 119, 124, 195f7.1

preferences, 81–84, 82f4.2

program, 52, 69–70, 119, 121, 127, 157, 168

public, 82–83, 82f4.2, 84, 125

in publications, 125

renaming opportunities, 34f2.3, 107–8, 110–11f4.3, 143

report on philanthropy, 87

reports, 162, 192–93, 196

right to withdraw, 113f4.3

societies, 33f2.3, 69, 157, 163, 202

solicitation procedures, 108

standard for, 159, 161

stewardship and, 3, 23, 182, 190–91, 227

tokens of appreciation, 165–66

tree-planting ceremony, 117

wall, 19, 83, 96–98, 125, 162, 193

on websites, 125, 193, 202, 217

written guidelines on, 27

year for, definition of, 154

RecognitionArt©, 101

RecognitionMap© Planning Tool, 101

Recreational Equipment Inc. (REI), 35–36

renaming opportunities, 34f2.3, 107–8, 110–11f4.3, 143

retention rate of donors, 32f2.2, 207–10

scripts for phone calls, 30

Secrets of Successful Fundraising (Weisman), 170

Sharing Financial Information in Your Nonprofit Annual Report, 90

Simple Unexpected Concrete Credentialed Emotional Stories (SUCCESs), 38f2.5

special events, 3, 22, 27–28, 29f2.1, 30, 34f2.3, 58f3.4, 66, 70, 92, 99, 124, 134, 149, 155, 163, 170, 199, 207

stewardship. *See also* thank-you

activities, 28

anonymous donors and, 83, 181

capital campaign and, 192, 203–4

checklist for, 237–38

components of, 180–82

consent for release of information, 179–80

consent form, 180

defined, 3–4, 34, 177–82

Director of, 227–28

donor relations and, 3, 6–7, 19, 22, 25, 28, 162–63, 166, 167f5.7, 181–82, 191, 205f7.2, 218, 221

Donor Relations Manual, 34f2.3

donor relations *vs.,* 3–4, 16

element of surprise and, 37

four components of, 181, 189–90

gift outcomes and, 184, 190
grant applications and, 183
gratitude and, 6, 6f1.2, 7
inappropriate, 40
officers, 221
plans, 28, 204, 238
president's letter, 186–88, 186f6.1
professional, 221
recognition and, 3, 23, 182, 190–91, 227
reports, 2–3, 30, 34f2.3, 67, 83, 183, 185–90, 204, 207
responsibility, Donor Bill of Rights, 15–16
return on investment, 184, 190
role of, 182–85
Silent Generation and, 219, 219f7.3
subsequent gifts and, 23, 204
for unrestricted gifts, 185
visits, 28, 34f2.3, 205
website and impact of giving, 34f2.3
subsequent gifts, 21, 23, 69, 72, 204, 209
SUCCESs. *See* Simple Unexpected Concrete Credentialed Emotional Stories (SUCCESs)

targeted marketing, 20
tax receipt letter, 23
television, 22, 60–61, 102, 170–71
thank-a-thon, 63–65
thank-you
choosing the person to say, 48f3.1
gifts, tangible, 60–61
letter, 2, 25–27, 43–47, 55, 74f3.5
notes, 13, 25, 46, 56f3.3, 70

other times to say, 46–47
saying, 67, 124
"seven times over," 44, 63–68, 77
as stewardship, 67
at Thanksgiving, 50–51
Thanksgiving card, 14, 37–38, 57–59f3.3, 68
touchpoint, 14–15

universities, 31f2.2, 33, 47, 50, 96, 103, 114–16, 122, 140, 141f5.4, 143, 143f5.5, 145, 157–58, 164, 171, 183–84, 188f6.1, 210–11, 214, 218

vendors of bookmarks, 233–34
volunteers, 13, 48f3.1, 49, 54, 63–65, 70, 86, 92, 94, 119, 124, 147, 156, 174f5.8, 184, 192, 194, 199, 207, 209, 219

Ward, William Arthur, vii
Watkins Society, 143f5.5
wealth screening, 20
website, 9–10, 14, 30, 34f2.3, 48, 60, 79–80, 85, 89–90, 92, 94–95, 101, 125, 130, 133, 136, 144, 147–48, 152, 165, 193, 202, 210
Weisman, Carol, 170
"Why Experience Marketing Pays" (Pine II and Gilmore), 35, 37
Writing the Executive Message for a Nonprofit Annual Report, 90
www.madetostick.com, 38

year-end appeal, 11, 15